The Meanings of
HÆMLET

the meanings of
HÆMLET

Modes of Literary Interpretation
Since Bradley

Paul Gottschalk

THE UNIVERSITY OF NEW MEXICO PRESS
Albuquerque

Thanks are expressed to the following for permission to quote excerpts of criticism in the present work:

Cambridge University Press for excerpts from *Art and Artifice in Shakespeare*, by E. E. Stoll; and for excerpts from *Shakespeare's Tragic Heroes*, by Lily B. Campbell.

Duke University Press for excerpts from *The Hamlet of Shakespeare's Audience*, by John W. Draper.

George Allen & Unwin Ltd. for excerpts from *The Problem of "Hamlet,"* by J. M. Robertson.

The Macmillan Company for excerpts from *Shakespeare and the Nature of Man*, by Theodore Spencer. Copyright 1942, 1949, by The Macmillan Company, renewed 1970 by Eloise B. Bender and John Spencer.

The University of Minnesota Press for excerpts from *Hamlet: An Historical and Comparative Study*, by E. E. Stoll.

Methuen & Co. Ltd. for excerpts from *Form and Meaning in Drama*, by H. D. F. Kitto; and for excerpts from *The Wheel of Fire*, by G. Wilson Knight.

Victor Gollancz Ltd. and W. W. Norton & Company, Inc. for excerpts from *Hamlet and Oedipus*, by Ernest Jones.

Xerox College Publishing for excerpts from the Kittredge Shakespeare. Reprinted by permission of the publisher from *Hamlet*, by Shakespeare, edited by George Lyman Kittredge/revised by Irving Ribner, copyright 1939 by George Lyman Kittredge, 1967 by George Lyman Kittredge, 1967 by Xerox Corporation; from *A Midsummer Night's Dream*, by Shakespeare, edited by George Lyman Kittredge, copyright 1939 by George Lyman Kittredge; and from *Troilus and Cressida*, by Shakespeare, edited by George Lyman Kittredge, copyright 1967 by Xerox Corporation through Xerox College Publishing, successor in interest to Blaisdell Publishing Company, Waltham, Mass.

This book has been published with the aid of a grant from the Hull Memorial Publication Fund of Cornell University.

Library of Congress Catalog Card Number 72-86818

International Standard Book Number 0-8263-0258-0

In memory
of
R. C. Bald

Acknowledgments

The most pleasant part of academic writing is the acknowledgment of help one has received from teachers, colleagues, and friends. I have a profound debt, both academic and personal, to my parents, as also to my wife, whose continual scholarly, editorial, secretarial, and moral assistance has been beyond measure. Doctors Helen McLean and George H. Pollock have helped me on a number of technical points concerning psychoanalytic theory, and Professors Linda Finlay and Allen Wood have advised me on some of the philosophical points of the last chapter. The original work out of which the present book grew was completed under the supervision of Professors William A. Ringler and Elder Olson, while the final version owes a very great deal to the scrupulous commentary of Professor Walter N. King. Professor David Novarr read several chapters at an early stage and offered valuable help and encouragement. Professors Anthony Caputi, Ephim G. Fogel, and Bert O. States read the entire manuscript and offered important suggestions and comments. I cannot be sure to what extent any of these would approve the final product, but I know it has benefited greatly from their frequent and generous help.

I am grateful to the staffs of the Harper Memorial Library of the University of Chicago and the Olin Library of Cornell University for their efficient and courteous help at all times. The publication has been aided by a grant from the Hull Fund of Cornell University.

My primary debt is to a former teacher, under whom I first began the work which has led to the present study, and whose influence on it has been great throughout, although he did not live to see it completed. To him the work is dedicated.

Contents

Critical Method and Critical Schools

1

*Just as a vivid sketch of a cat by a good draughtsman may
contain in a few crisp lines the entire feline experience of
everyone who looks at it, so the powerfully constructed
pattern of words that we know as* Hamlet *may contain an
amount of meaning which the vast and constantly growing
library of criticism on the play cannot begin to exhaust.*
Northrop Frye, *The Anatomy of Criticism*

1

It is axiomatic that one of the quickest roads to Pyrrhonism is to
study interpretations of *Hamlet*. Certainly the mass of volumes and
monographs that have appeared in recent years, many of them by men
genuinely learned and wise, has brought us no closer to unanimity on
the meaning of the play—if anything, quite the contrary—and since
the progress of criticism is largely the procession of new techniques
and disciplines brought to bear on the artifact, it appears that men will
not solve all the problems of Hamlet, prince or poem, until that
unlikely day when they solve all of their own and have nothing new
to offer. Thus, the outlook would seem gloomy for a work that pretends
to find a path through the maze of *Hamlet* interpretation—or, at least,
to light up a few of the dead ends. One recent scholar, surveying the
field, concludes, "There is no true, best, correct, or right explanation,

reading, interpretation, or understanding of *Hamlet,* nor can there be as long as debate and doubt are possible on the categories of explanation and on what is primary in the play. Rather, critical interpretations, understandings, statements of meaning, and readings of some or all of *Hamlet* are more or less adequate explanations of some of the describable data of the play."[1]

This conclusion, with the weariness of experience behind it, is the starting point of the present study, which aims at something perhaps more hopeful. Though it is true that man knows and cares too much about *Hamlet* now to find one answer to all its problems, it is certainly possible to find some common threads among the various answers proffered. Thus, instead of a hundred conflicting monographs, we may have, say, ten distinct schools—a simplification of the *Hamlet* problem, certainly, if not a solution. Moreover, it may be that writers of one school generally contradict writers of another but supplement those of a third. If so, we can reduce the morass of interpretation into a few multidisciplinary "overviews" of *Hamlet.* The result would still not be a single answer to a single problem: it would be a set of syndromes of mutually compatible answers proffered to mutually compatible questions and arranged around a sort of critical lowest common denominator. The present work does not aim to establish a Grand Synthesis: probably everyone who reads *Hamlet* as more than a purely scholarly exercise on the one hand or as a mere vehicle for unthinking self-projection on the other will almost inevitably establish some sort of overview for himself, tentative and, hopefully, expandable. My purpose is to suggest the major materials with which he may work and to suggest one or two of the most basic forms his construction may take.

Even such a modest proposal may seem fairly apocalyptic, for the range of modern viewpoints on *Hamlet* is immense. The play, of course, has always been a mystery, despite the recurring claims of critics with new solutions that the only mystery is why it ever was one, and this mystery has attracted the most distinguished and most varied army of interpreters ever assembled around any work of art. Scarcely a major critic—scarcely a major poet, one might almost say—has failed to add his word, and the belletrists have been joined in increasing numbers by the literary technicians: the researchers in history, in stagecraft, in comparative studies. In addition, the ranks have been swelled by significant thinkers who do not ordinarily write about Shakespeare: classicists and anthropologists, philosophers and psychologists. Everyone, sooner or later, wants to take a crack at *Hamlet*. Largely due to this proliferation of critical viewpoints, a major change has taken place in what, during the nineteenth century, was the main line of *Hamlet* interpretation: that is, the attempt to understand the play in terms of Hamlet's behavior and his behavior in terms of human nature. Perhaps the change can best be illustrated by the shift of attitudes over the last sixty years toward the critical writings of A. C. Bradley, whose work remains today the greatest expression of this main line.

Today's reader may find it hard to understand that in 1904 Bradley's *Shakespearean Tragedy* was considered revolutionary. In a paper that goes on to criticize Bradley, Professor Lily B. Campbell reminisces:

> It was a mighty book, taking Shakespearean criticism again into the realm of the universal and the significant. I well remember the enthusiasm of my teachers when they read it, for I was at an age when I wondered at their excitement. To the younger teachers of Shakespeare, willing or anxious to lay aside the analyzing of his plays according to Freytag and to cease following him "Out of the depths" and "On to the heights" with Dowden, salvation seemed to come with their new leader. . . . and they oriented all Shakespeare studies to the new sun.[2]

Perhaps it was indeed revolutionary at the time, but from a distance of sixty years, Bradley's victims scarcely seem drawn in the same scale as their vanquisher, and in the bolder reliefs of historical hindsight, his kinship with such traditional critics as Goethe and Coleridge stands out more clearly than his conflict with Dowden and Freytag. Bradley's revolution was, in fact, reactionary. True, he began his criticism of *Hamlet* by attacking the very interpretations of Goethe and Coleridge, yet only as a student correcting respected teachers. Indeed, he had to attack the two great poet-critics, because his method was the same as theirs, following the main line of psychological character-interpretation. For him to compete in their market, he had to prove their conclusions wrong.

Meanwhile, Bradley's own conclusions have in their turn been supplemented or altered and his method refined, so that today we would place his *Hamlet* lectures somewhere in the middle of a critical line beginning with the pre-Romantic Mackenzie and running through Ernest Jones. But this main line has itself branched off again and again. Critics in abundance have sprung up who deny both Bradley's conclusions and the psychological method he used to arrive at them, who prefer to investigate plot sources or imagery or theme or anthropological ritual, and who, in turn, have begun to argue among themselves, each seeking to further the cause of his own method, generally at the expense of all the rest. Meanwhile, the critical battlefield has widened to include not merely Hamlet himself but the entire play. Coleridge called the work a portrait, and Bradley, following the nineteenth-century trends, treated it as if one could understand the play by understanding its hero. One major accomplishment of twentieth-century criticism, contrariwise, is its attempt to see a work steadily and see it whole, and the title of C. S. Lewis's lecture "Hamlet, the Prince or the Poem?" would fit many studies to be treated in the following pages. While the character of Hamlet himself remains a problem, we have recognized that it is also a problem what this mysterious and fascinating man is doing in the play that bears his name but which obviously has to do with far more than him alone. At the same time we have come to question how a popular stage play can embody a profound mystery in the first place. Critics have turned from character to plot to imagery to stage effects to theme and back again, and to the relation of all these to each other, and it is now almost impossible to deal at length with *Hamlet* without discussing the very nature and function of drama itself.

These changes in the interpretation of *Hamlet* since Bradley are the subject of the present work. By *interpretation,* I mean criticism whose primary goal is a statement of the meaning of a work as opposed to an examination of its literary genesis or its structure. The scope of the present study, then, excludes a considerable body of recent *Hamlet* scholarship except insofar as it bears on interpretation proper. I will deal little with critical processes that precede interpretation, such as the establishment of a text, except when these lead to a new interpretation or reflect upon an old one, as with the textual geneticists C. M. Lewis and J. M. Robertson. Likewise, I shall not deal much with what might be called organic critics, whose concern is with the artifact as a consistent, unified whole and with the teleological relationship between its parts, a relation analogous to that between the parts of a biological organism. An organic critic will examine the way individual components of the work—an image, a character, a scene—relate to other components or to the entire work that subsumes them. I can treat such writers here only insofar as their writings are predicated upon interesting interpretations. Therefore, critics such as L. L. Schücking, Francis Fergusson, and Harry Levin will receive less attention than the scope and excellence of their writings on *Hamlet* might suggest. Finally, I shall avoid discussing evaluations of the play—judgments of its greatness or its weaknesses—except insofar as they derive from specific interpretations. After three centuries and more, to attack *Hamlet* is in vain, as T. S. Eliot's efforts have shown, and to praise it is presumptuous. The present work, then, is an analysis of several recent and predominant schools of thought on what *Hamlet* means—an examination of their scopes, their strengths, and their relationships to one another.

2

In arriving at a definition of an interpretative school, some remarks by Northrop Frye may be useful. Observing that a poet's labors are "centripetally directed" towards putting words together rather than "aligning words with meaning," he continues:

> It is not often realized that all commentary is allegorical interpretation, an attaching of ideas to the structure of poetic imagery. The instant that any critic permits himself to make a genuine comment about a poem (e.g., "In *Hamlet* Shakespeare appears to be portraying the tragedy of irresolution") he has begun to allegorize. Commentary thus looks at literature as, in its formal phase, a potential allegory of events and ideas.[3]

Interpretative allegory, then, is the critic's process of making explicit the tissue of meaning that he feels is implicit in a work. By allegory we usually mean that a literal symbol (the word "knight," for example) is used consistently not only to represent its ordinary denotation (that is, such and such a knight) but also, and indeed primarily, an ulterior meaning of some sort (holiness, the Church of England, and the like). An interpretative allegory, then, is one that attaches an ulterior meaning to the literal construct of the play, as in Professor Frye's example above, where the idea of "irresolution" extends far beyond the specific limits of Shakespeare's text. *Hamlet* (or Hamlet) would stand in relation to irresolution in much the same way that Guyon stands in relation to temperance in *The Faerie Queene*. And if for "irresolution" we substitute "revenge-tragedy hero," "oedipal conflict," "Elizabethan theodicy," and the rest of a list almost unimaginably long, we see that most of the works recently written on *Hamlet* are, in this sense, allegorical. The difference—and it is a crucial one—is that we usually call something an allegory when we sense that a universal meaning is primary in the author's mind and that the embodiment of it in specific characters and actions is secondary. In *Hamlet,* on the other hand, the existence of Hamlet and Ophelia, Claudius and Gertrude clearly precedes any historical, moral, or metaphysical essences that we may attach to them. Sir Guyon was created to elucidate the nature of temperance; irresolution has been put forward to elucidate the nature of Hamlet. In *The Faerie Queene* the allegorical is implicit in the literal story; in *Hamlet* it is extrinsic. In *The Faerie Queene* the poet makes the poem allegorical; in *Hamlet* the critic.

Now, if *Hamlet* interpretation generally involves fitting an extrinsic idea to the specific text, it is important to know where that idea comes from. The examples I have given above derive, respectively, from the study of Elizabethan stage conventions, psychoanalysis, and Elizabethan popular theology—all general studies that exist quite independently of *Hamlet;* and in this respect, the examples are typical of recent *Hamlet* criticism in general. Therefore, when we say that *Hamlet* interpretation is allegorical, we mean that the critic hypothesizes a priori that some area of experience or of academic inquiry can be applied to *Hamlet*. To E. E. Stoll's insistence, then, that "what Wordsworth said of poets is obviously still truer of playwrights—'that if their works be good, they contain within themselves all that is necessary to their being comprehended,' "[4] we must add that if the spectator be good, he too must contain within himself all that is necessary to comprehending.

Interpretation is not to be confused with the sorts of commentary alternately called hermeneutics, description, or explication, and which avoid any general ideas not explicit in or immediately inferable from specific details in the text.[5] Such commentary deals with the most immediately representational aspects of literature, with literature as pure mimesis. At its simplest this mimetic commentary tends toward paraphrase, like the Recorder who retails Buckingham's speech to the populace in *Richard III*: "Thus saith the Duke, thus hath the Duke inferr'd" (III.vii.32). Technically, its realm is the conventional in literature: all representative art imitates nature through specific conventions, and the mimetic commentator operates by applying a given set of mimetic conventions to the text. It is true that most people within a given culture respond to the mimetic conventions of that culture's literature so automatically that the conventions become transparent and the spectator looks at the literary work as a direct representation of reality. Thus, mimetic commentary is often treated in loose terms as a direct expression of the "text itself," though it is the application of convention to text and not the text alone that generates the commentary: that we agree on the convention even to the point of ignoring it as such altogether makes this confusion acceptable.

Yet it is possible to conceive of a spectator to whom the mimetic conventions of the Elizabethan drama are so foreign that to him *Hamlet* would be no more than a rhapsody of words: suppose that he did not know that standing on a platform in an amphitheater represents spatial and temporal dislocation, that wearing certain dress represents a complete change of identity, that blank verse represents prose, and so forth. If such a person seems inconceivable, we should remember how absurd *King Lear* seemed to Tolstoy simply because he refused to understand one or two of its conventions. And no mimesis has an unmediated correspondence to reality: the representation of nature in art always occurs, in every detail, through convention.

The essence of both mimetic and interpretative commentary is the drawing of correspondences between the objects represented in the literary work and objects in nature, between the world of Ilium, Lilliput, or Elsinore and the actual world. Mimetic commentary, on the one hand, deals with the relationship of the artifactual world to the world of naked fact and experience shared by all spectators: it describes the world shaped by the literary work through the mimetic conventions appropriate to the work, and once we agree on the appropriate conventions, we can generally reach considerable unanimity about the basic world that the work represents—that is, we can *identify* the objects in this world and many of their attributes and qualities. But that is because mimetic description is limited to experience common to all men. If a man could be found who had never experienced dejection, anger, or anxiety, our most obvious commentaries on *Hamlet* would escape him; they might even puzzle Miranda.

Once, on the other hand, we move beyond the obvious and conventional forms of representation and begin to ask questions about the relevance of the literary work to aspects of our own world that are not an ineluctable part of every man's experience—once, that is, we seek to explain what we have already identified—then we are in the realm of literary interpretation proper. Interpretation relates the world of the literary work not to the common experience of all men but to systems of thought that man has erected to order, explain, or qualify what would otherwise be shapeless or mystifying in the world—including the world of the past, about which we theorize in precisely the same manner in which we theorize about the present. In the simplest terms, mimetic description discusses the relation of literature to experience, interpretation the relation of literature to theories about experience; mimetic description identifies objects represented in art, interpretation seeks their meaning.

Let us take three critical statements about *Hamlet* as examples, the first two being mimetic and the third interpretative. (1) "Hamlet meets the players shortly after encountering Rosencrantz and Guildenstern." This is information obvious to anyone reading or seeing the play and aware of the convention that on the stage (unlike the movies, where "flashbacks" are common) events are almost universally understood to take place in the order depicted. (2) "Hamlet greets the players with enthusiasm." This is inference rather than information supplied directly by the text: we cannot peer into Hamlet's mind to see if he is really enthusiastic, but his greetings to the players can be explained by enthusiasm and by nothing else (we would automatically dismiss the notions, for instance, that he is being cold or hypocritical). Such ineluctable inference is a part of mimetic commentary and is based on the degree of realism in character portrayal that Elizabethan mimetics permit. (3) "The enthusiasm of Hamlet's greeting of the players reveals his eagerness to take his mind off his duty of vengeance." This is interpretative. It is not pure inference in that it involves a *bringing to* the specific text a certain prior view of Hamlet's personality (for example, Hamlet as irresolute, or melancholy, or neurotic). And it is not ineluctable: the contrary point could just as well be argued, that Hamlet welcomes the players with enthusiasm because he already foresees that they can help him prove Claudius's guilt and thus further his revenge. The text clearly implies the enthusiasm, but only the critic or the reader himself can explain it, and thus explanations may vary.

In theory, mimetic commentary aims at a single, definitive commentary on the play, while the number of possible interpretations is limited only by the number of allegorical hypotheses that critics may invent. On the other hand, mimetic commentary will vary radically from genre to genre in ways that interpretation does not. A thorough mimetic commentary on a novel will be utterly inapplicable to a film based on that novel, while an interpretation (a historical interpretation, say, of *Gone With the Wind*) may apply to both quite well.

Of course, almost any extended commentary on *Hamlet* will contain both mimetic commentary and allegorical interpretation: both description of what is given or implied in the text and explanation of these data in terms of some wider range of knowledge. In the course of the present study we shall have to separate the critic's description from his interpretation, his data from his abstract conclusions. Such a process is important. Historians know how easy it is to choose one's facts to suit one's case, and even in *Hamlet,* where the facts at hand are far more limited than in history, the opportunities for such distortion are manifold.

Because it involves an a priori application of an extrinsic idea to the play, interpretation has a potential range of inaccuracy that is immense. In theory, mimetic commentary ought to provide a check on the more obvious interpretative vagaries—and, indeed, it often can. Since interpretation works *from* an external body of thought *to* the text, from the outside in, so to speak, and mimetic commentary works from the inside out, they ought to meet somewhere in the middle. If they do not, it is most likely the interpretation that is at fault.

However, mimetics cannot always provide an outside check on an interpretation or on a conflict between two interpretations. Often a critic's allegorical hypothesis itself will limit the data he considers relevant to his conclusions. One critic may censure Hamlet for delaying his revenge two months, the evidence for the delay being Ophelia's statement during the play scene that " 'tis twice two months" since his father's death, coupled with Hamlet's statement in his first soliloquy that the marriage of Claudius and Gertrude took place not so much as two months after the death of the elder Hamlet. But another critic, who insists that Shakespeare wrote for the stage and that *Hamlet* is to be interpreted in terms of stage conventions and theatrical technique, may argue that the careful calculation necessary to derive the long delay from the fleeting details of the text could not possibly be performed by any member of Shakespeare's audience and that therefore the two months' delay is not strictly part of the text at all. Here, an explicatory hypothesis about dramaturgical technique limits the data available for interpretation. Our first critic, however, assumes that the play, down to its minutest details, is true to nature, and thus, as in nature, that there is no part, however small, that cannot be used to interpret the whole. Here, in effect, an allegorical assumption determines the nature of the mimetic data themselves.

Even if two critics accept the same datum, such as Hamlet's assumption of the "antic disposition," they may not agree on its significance. Thus one critic may think that Hamlet is preparing a disguise through which he will be able to bare his inmost thoughts, while another may see the lines as having been forced upon Shakespeare by an audience that expected to be entertained by the melancholic rantings of the hero. Both accept the assumption of the antic disposition, but one will derive Hamlet's character largely from his mad talk, while the other will not. Reference to the text will obviously not resolve such disputes; the disputants may not even agree as to what precisely the text is, and the controversy is likely to boil down to an unprofitable argument about the author's intentions. (I have dealt with two major problems of this sort—Hamlet's doubt of the Ghost, and the significance of his slaying Polonius—in separate appendices.)

3

It is, in fact, at this point that inquiry into interpretative method begins. Since we cannot, of course, know for sure what Shakespeare's intention was, an allegorical hypothesis is in essence a suggestion about what Shakespeare intended to say in *Hamlet*—or, more precisely, of what *Hamlet* may say to its audience. Therefore, any questions about the correspondence of an interpretation to the mimetic data of the text or to the author's putative intentions must await the isolation of the allegorical hypothesis, upon which the rest of the critical structure stands.

For the purpose of organization I shall define an interpretative school as a group of critics all adhering to the same basic allegorical hypothesis. The following chapters are arranged accordingly. The definition is arbitrary, but it should avoid some confusion that has built up in the past. Using allegorical hypotheses as criteria, for instance, one speaks of the historical school, the psychoanalytical school, and so forth. But such usage can be vague, as with the term "historical," which can include critics with highly contradictory views of the play: history is too vast to be univocal. To make matters worse, some schools have been defined by the part of the play that they examine, such as imagery—and even then, not all students of Shakespeare's imagery are concerned with interpretation. Lest we be forced to place *Hamlet* interpretations on a Cartesian graph, with allegory as the ordinate and subject examined as the abscissa, I have allowed myself the liberty of simplifying. Helpfully, in any case, certain allegories tend to deal particularly with certain subjects within the play. Psychoanalysis, obviously, deals largely with character, while critics who seek for meanings that character alone cannot explain are likely to focus on elements of the play that may reflect its meaning as a whole, such as structure or metaphor.

The next five chapters, then, do not follow abstract categories. Rather, they seek to analyze five highly influential schools of interpretation that have evolved in the last several decades. No one school has a record of perfect unanimity among its members, but the tendency toward agreement has seemed to me more impressive than the tendency toward fragmentation.

A final word of caution. The Hamlet of the Romantics has been pretty much exploded, but something that he stood for remains important to us. He is still, like it or not, the Hamlet that many cherish: the Hamlet too fine or too meditative or too melancholy for the harsh action that Denmark requires. He is the Hamlet that emerges as soon as the question of the delay is broached in freshman classes. He even appears, lean and moody, on the cover of a recent paperback edition of E. E. Stoll, who did his level best to destroy him. If Hamlet did not exist, it would be necessary to invent him. And he has endeared himself to me: while writing I have found that I am most sympathetic toward those critics who show some means of retaining his mystery and his melancholy, though without the sentimentality and gross inaccuracy that so often accompanied these in the last century. I mention this preference now so that the reader may be on his guard against it. I have tried to avoid open editorializing, but a polemic tendency repressed can become all the more insidious for being less recognizable.

The Evolutionist School

2

1

The traditional view of Shakespeare, ratified by the great poets of the early nineteenth century, used to be that the dramatist was a sort of god: that his mind, mirroring nature, brought forth an artistic universe as consistent as nature's own, and scarcely less complex. And, as with a mystery in nature, a mystery in Shakespeare was alternately an object of philosophical exploration or of not-so-mute adoration. If it could have been proven that Shakespeare wrote *Hamlet* in six days and rested on the seventh, no one would have been surprised.

But later in the nineteenth century the Book of Genesis, and with it the alleged completeness of God's creation, were sorely tried by the new biology; and fifty years after that, *Hamlet* was to undergo a similar trial. Darwin could find no divine purpose underlying the vermiform appendix, and the critics we shall study in this chapter confessed themselves equally baffled by much of *Hamlet* that had hitherto been held sacred. Like the evolutionists, they hypothesized that what could not be assigned to a unifying intelligence must be the result of external influence. Thus, they shifted the critical emphasis from the form of the play to the process of its creation, and the way was paved for statements such as E. E. Stoll's that Hamlet's vindictiveness "is owing to the Senecan *atrocitas* as well as to the Ghost's command and the part he must play in the well-known and popular stage story."[1] This remark fuses Shakespeare's motives with Hamlet's. Only the Ghost's command would influence Prince Hamlet; the Senecan literary convention and the commercial motives would concern Hamlet's creator.

This chapter will examine what I will call the evolutionary school of *Hamlet* criticism, which seeks to explain Shakespeare's play in terms of the various external pressures to which the poet had to adapt, and which includes among its proponents Charlton M. Lewis, J. M. Robertson, Levin L. Schücking, E. E. Stoll, and T. S. Eliot. Four of their major works appeared in the same year, and so the order in which I treat them must be logical, not chronological. If several critics in several countries begin independently and at about the same time to broach the same ideas, it is likely enough that these ideas react to some widely recognized critical problem or impasse, that they fulfill some general critical need.

The evolutionist school sprang up in the first and second decades of the twentieth century largely in response to difficulties in the leading explanations of Hamlet's feigned madness and delay. Of these, the most influential was the Romantic-psychological criticism that had just culminated in the work of Bradley and that explained Hamlet's delay in terms of some sort of spiritual or intellectual malady—propensity to thought, skepticism, over-delicate sensibilities, or metaphysically induced melancholia—that rendered the Prince incapable of deliberate action. Yet another interpretation, one that had gained considerable attention by the end of the nineteenth century, posited an objective barrier to revenge, so that Hamlet's delay stemmed not from spiritual inhibition but from the inherent difficulty of the task, either because the King was too well guarded, because the evidence of the Ghost was doubtful, or, as the German Karl Werder insisted, because Hamlet had not merely to kill the King—an easy enough matter—but also to establish public justice.[2]

None of these interpretations, however, reconciles contradictions that the evolutionists find in the text. Charlton M. Lewis, for example, is bothered by Hamlet's decision, almost immediately after first speaking with the Ghost, to assume his "antic disposition." The "subjective" interpretation can explain this decision only awkwardly, if at all, since the antic disposition is Hamlet's tacit acknowledgment that his task is supremely difficult, a fact that, if his inhibitions are purely internal,

Hamlet could not have known until he had tried to act and failed. The immediate assumption of the antic disposition, then, suggests some immediately recognizable objective barrier to revenge. Yet no such barrier is apparent.[3] And indeed, the evolutionists see the *Hamlet* criticism of the nineteenth century as an unsuccessful attempt to foist order onto a play shot through from beginning to end with structural anomalies: phrases, passages, even entire scenes that not only fail to contribute to the main action as a whole but that render worthless the very attempt to define the action as a whole. Among these are the dispatch of Voltimand and Cornelius to Norway and their reception on their return; the return of Laertes to Paris; Polonius's dispatch of Reynaldo to spy on Laertes; Fortinbras's Polish campaign; Hamlet's interrupted voyage to England; Laertes' parting scene, with Polonius's counsel to Ophelia; and the dumb show.[4]

The nineteenth-century "subjective" and "objective" interpretations of *Hamlet,* conflicting as they seem, are alike in one important respect: they both explain the Prince's delay through the *form* of the play—they both assume that the delay is part of the mimetic structure that Shakespeare carefully created. Such interpretation assumes that the artist is looking at nature through the lenses of some system of facts; all the critic does is present the system and show how the facts portrayed in the piece fit it. But such interpretation becomes impossible to a critic who assumes that the artist's process of imitation has broken down, that, in fact, no consistent system regulates the ordering of the events that unfold and the words that are spoken on stage. Such a breakdown is precisely what the evolutionists find in *Hamlet,* and to solve Hamlet's mystery they turn from the play's form to Shakespeare's own process of creation: "The light from within invariably resolving itself into a multiplicity of shifting lights, we are compelled to seek light from without."[5] If *Hamlet* is not a consistent whole, the reason may be that Shakespeare was not a consistent worker:

> If Shakespeare elaborated a character not in one heat, but at intervals extending over one or two years, he might easily lose hold of the conception with which he started. . . . Or, if, instead of rearing a drama out of his own invention, Shakespeare merely

rewrote or repolished a tale already told, perhaps already dramatized, he might easily alter part of the significance of his plot or
his characters, and yet retain passages and traits that harmonized
only with the older meaning.[6]

This explanation of *Hamlet* in terms of the external circumstances
of its creation underlies all evolutionist interpretations. And underlying
this explanation, in turn, is the theory that Shakespeare's text is a
palimpsest: that the *Hamlet* we have today, though primarily by
Shakespeare, shows the influence of Thomas Kyd, who was the apparent author of the lost *Hamlet* mentioned in Henslowe's diary, June
9, 1594, and who, first dramatizing the old Hamlet saga written
down by Saxo Grammaticus and revised by Belleforest, provided
Shakespeare's direct source. Shakespeare's play, according to the evolutionists, is a revision of this so-called *Ur-Hamlet,* and the First Quarto
edition of *Hamlet* (1603) is a garbled version of Shakespeare's first and
very incomplete attempt at revision, while the Second Quarto (1604–
05) and First Folio (1623) derive from Shakespeare's final version. A
contemporaneous, highly corrupt German play, *Der Bestrafte Brudermord,* is presumed to derive from the *Ur-Hamlet* and provides some
evidence as to the nature of that play, as does Kyd's extant *Spanish
Tragedy.*[7] Thus, the picture the evolutionists draw is not of a *Hamlet*
sprung full-grown from Shakespeare's brow, but of a slowly evolving
organism with Shakespeare as the last influence on it of many.

It is typical of the main line of *Hamlet* criticism to find the meaning
of the play in Hamlet's delay (as with Goethe's metaphor of Hamlet
as a delicate vase in which the oak tree of duty has been planted, or
Schlegel's hypothesis of action-inhibiting skepticism). The evolutionist
critics, however, find that the delay, like the various structural anomalies they have observed, stems from Shakespeare's failure to digest his
source material thoroughly, his failure to recognize (or care) that with
Kyd's introduction of a secretive ghost (who did not appear in Saxo or
Belleforest) the objective need for feigned madness and delay ceased
to exist. It is not Hamlet, Robertson asserts, but "the process of trans-
mutation which creates the mystery of the play,"[8] and so begins a grand
dismissal of the various hearts of Hamlet's mystery that the nineteenth
century had plucked out.

2

The palimpsest theory, of course, is not itself an interpretation; it simply attempts to establish the genesis of the text that lies at the critic's hand. Turning now to Lewis and Robertson, we see that their interpretations are fairly conservative. They are original only in that they apply to a disintegrated text. Having weighed formal interpretation in the balance and found it wanting, Lewis and Robertson attempt to glean from the historical hodgepodge of the text Shakespeare's original contributions and to examine these by themselves. The result is the almost total divorce of character from plot, of Hamlet from *Hamlet,* and, indeed, of Hamlet at one moment from Hamlet at another.

The Hamlet that Lewis portrays is drawn half from Kyd and half from Goethe. Superimposed on the brutal, vengeful hero of the early play is a far different man of Shakespeare's own creation, "sensitive, affectionate, impulsive," who achieves his revenge "in spite of almost infinite reluctance."[9] Shakespeare inherits Hamlet's actions themselves from Belleforest and Kyd, where, Lewis postulates, the antic disposition was no more than a practical response to an objectively difficult task. Hamlet's spiritual paralysis is thus merely an invention of the critics meant to bridge the discrepancy between the Kydian and Shakespearean texts—an unnecessary invention once we realize that Shakespeare was a willing victim of Kydian circumstances: "Shakespeare has projected some of these circumstances into the fourth dimension, but by what right may we treat them as non-existent?"[10] The answer to that question, of course, is that no spectator and few readers are equipped to sift through the layers of textual development as the play unfolds in the theater or in the closet. Lewis insists, to be sure, that Shakespeare "has portrayed his hero so vividly that the glaring inconsistencies of the plot pass unnoticed"[11]—though why a "glaring inconsistency" is not itself vivid I cannot tell. Lewis is not much concerned with the theater, however. To him, as to earlier critics, Shakespeare is primarily a poet and psychologist, not a practical playwright, and if the text of *Hamlet* is not of a piece, the reason is no more than artistic indolence on Shakespeare's part. To carry our metaphor of evolutionism a step further, a text, like an organic species, is shaped by its environment, and Lewis views this environment in the traditional light of the nineteenth century: the isolated, profound soul of the sublime artist, whose "genius was creative, not critical,"[12] an artist such as Goethe had envisaged eighty years earlier:

> Shakespeare . . . wrote these plays out of his nature, and then, his time and the organization of the stage at that time placed no restrictions on him. . . . Nevertheless, this is by no means to be regretted, for what Shakespeare has lost for us as a dramatist he has won as a poet in general. Shakespeare is a great psychologist, and one learns from his plays the feelings of men.[13]

With Robertson, we see the environment widen, and as it widens it becomes the exact opposite of what Goethe described. Shakespeare, Robertson posits, had "the gift or penchant for compliance with his economic and social conditions."[14] And first among these conditions were the people who paid to see *Hamlet* at the Globe, many of whom demanded the bloodiness, the antic disposition—all the old, stagey situations of the *Ur-Hamlet*.[15] Remnants of the old play remain, then, because they will sell: Shakespeare would rather have been inconsistent than displease his patrons. The practical playwright cannot be the perfect artist.

Like Lewis, Robertson interprets separately each historical layer of the text, and, again like Lewis, he finds Shakespeare's final contribution to the character of Hamlet himself the most interesting—and the most problematic. Shakespeare himself could not explain the delay that Kyd's addition of the secretive ghost rendered unnecessary: he simply accepted it. The mystery of the play, then, is simply a matter of camouflage, "a masterly effort to hint a psychological solution of the acted mystery, while actually heightening it by the self-accusing soliloquies."[16] More specifically, ". . . Shakespeare did very subtly and strikingly indicate again and again a possible line of explanation for the delay, to wit, that for Hamlet, so deeply wounded by his mother's action before he had any notion of the murder, mere revenge on his uncle was no remedy."[17]

Robertson's interpretation, then, simply emphasizes the paradox that Schlegel had observed long before about *Hamlet*: "What naturally most astonishes us, is the fact that with such hidden purposes, with a foundation laid in such unfathomable depth, the whole should, at a first view, exhibit an extremely popular appearance."[18] We have a play written in poetry that rises in quality far above the primitive plot. We have a hero who is princely and supersubtle, to please Shakespeare's more cultured patrons, and yet whose actions are barbaric and bloodthirsty enough to attract those who preferred their Kyd unadulterated with genius. Finally, we have an effective piece of entertainment that does far more than entertain.[19] Like Lewis, Robertson superimposes his allegory of Hamlet onto the textual history that he proffers, and the psychological allegory he proposes, like Lewis's, is nothing new. What is new is Robertson's special attempt to relate this psychological interpretation closely to the play's theatrical environment. Robertson's *Hamlet* is a play without a center; it is all things to all people, a chameleon of literature. Aesthetically, it is a failure.[20] Robertson's Shakespeare is not concerned with aesthetics, however, but with success, success as measured in the coffers of the Globe, and there the play did not fail, there all faults of composition, all lack of consistent meaning, all contradictions of action and character were made good.

T. S. Eliot's famous critique, "Hamlet and His Problems,"[21] is the ultimate step in disintegrationist thinking. We have seen that Lewis, conservatively unwilling to admit any serious chinks in Shakespeare's armor of genius, gets into serious critical difficulties by insisting that Shakespeare's contributions to the final artifact of *Hamlet* constitute an independent work in themselves and can be treated as such. Robertson, more concerned with the effect of the play as a whole, observes that the whole is faulty but that it works. Eliot even denies that it works.

Eliot's preliminary conclusions are based primarily on Robertson. He considers "irrefragable" Robertson's conclusions that the text is a palimpsest, and he accepts Robertson's reading of the text—particularly, that Hamlet's emotions toward Gertrude are hints inserted by Shakespeare to make sense of the old Kydian plot. But he goes further: the disintegration of *Hamlet* stems not only from commercial pressure from without but also from artistic disintegration from within. Even Shakespeare's contribution to the multilayered text is not of a piece: "*Hamlet*, like the sonnets, is full of some stuff that the writer could not drag to light, contemplate, or manipulate into art."[22] The evidence for this inability, Eliot says in a famous passage, is the lack of an "objective correlative" to Hamlet's emotions: "Hamlet (the man) is dominated by an emotion which is inexpressible, because it is in *excess* of the facts as they appear. And the supposed identity of Hamlet with his author is genuine to this point: that Hamlet's bafflement at the absence of objective equivalent to his feelings is a prolongation of the bafflement of his creator in the face of his artistic problem."[23] Gertrude is the cause of Hamlet's feelings, yet, as Eliot acutely observes, her character is too insipid to explain the feelings that she arouses: "it is just *because* her character is so negative and insignificant that she arouses in Hamlet the feeling which she is incapable of representing."[24] An objectless emotion is irreducible to art because it cannot be expressed, and art is expression.

Eliot's critique has itself been criticized, often more strenuously and harshly than it deserves: it is, after all, essentially a review, not a closely reasoned scholarly argument, and it is based not so much on facts and logic as on an appeal to difficulties that, Eliot implies, the intelligent reader has long perceived in the play and has never been able to formulate: what oft is thought, but is inexpressible. And indeed, Eliot is perhaps the first to perceive in *Hamlet* a problem that subsequent critics have dealt with, tacitly or explicitly, over and over again: the problem of the absolutely mysterious in art.

This problem, I think, scarcely occurred to the nineteenth-century critics, who usually came to the perplexities of *Hamlet* along one of two paths, both of which skirted the problem of objective correlatives. The first of these, seen in Herder or Schlegel, was to deal with the play on such a high level of abstraction that Hamlet's emotions could not be in excess of the facts as they appeared simply because these facts scarcely appeared at all in the critics' work. The other approach was to admit freely that Hamlet's behavior was mysterious and to account this mystery all to Shakespeare's credit: *Hamlet* thus lay close to the insoluble riddle of existence, in some area remote from the critic's own poor powers of perception. "We are deeply convinced that Shakespeare knew his men," Lewis himself says, "and that if they seem unintelligible or impossible the blame should be ours, not his."[25] Lewis himself makes an exception of Hamlet, but his nineteenth-century forebears did not.[26]

Now both of these critical approaches tacitly assume, with Goethe, that Shakespeare was primarily a great psychologist, not a playwright. Their Hamlet moves in a spiritual world of his own, untrammeled by the exigencies of the stage whenever these prove inconvenient. To Coleridge, Hamlet was a portrait; to Goethe, a clock with the movements partially exposed; to Schlegel, an irrational equation. Eliot's accomplishment—and it is an important one—is to have taken the Romantic Hamlet of Robertson's version and tacitly placed him in the theater, where the audience, who can neither delve below the script nor single out Hamlet for exclusive attention, must apprehend the play as a whole. In the theater, objective correlatives are of the utmost importance, and a character's tone must correspond to "the facts as they appear" if the play is to be made clear to an audience that perceives both equally. Perhaps, of course, the audience itself will consider its own mystification a great artistic achievement, but Eliot thinks not: "probably more people have thought *Hamlet* a work of art because they found it interesting, than have found it interesting because it is a work of art."[27] Eliot's chief service, I think, is thus to have accepted the exigencies both of the Romantic psychological portrayal of Hamlet and of theatrical clarity and to have shown their incompatibility. E. E. Stoll, we shall see, escapes the dilemma by denying the Romantic Hamlet, and in so doing Stoll has had many followers. Others, however, have met Eliot head on, and the results have been fruitful.

Finally, then, we see that Lewis and Robertson have accepted, within a special historical framework, the two leading views of their day that they began by attacking. The Romantic, spiritually upset Hamlet is Shakespeare's contribution to the text, while Werder seems to have perceived Kyd's original plan lurking below the surface and to have taken it for the whole. Both interpretations are seen as partially right, but each becomes hopelessly confused in trying to absorb the inconsistencies between itself and its rival. Lewis and Robertson relegate these inconsistencies to the fourth dimension, where Lewis is willing to study them as part of the artifact, and where Robertson says that at least they make no difference on the Elizabethan stage. Eliot, unable either to accept or to reject this fourth dimension—enlarged in his essay to include Shakespeare's own personal perplexity—writes the most serious and important attack on *Hamlet* ever penned.

3

The three critics we have examined so far deal with a fairly traditional *Hamlet* seen through the refracting medium of the palimpsest theory. It remains to establish a new interpretation that grows out of this theory rather than being superimposed on it, to abandon traditional allegories altogether and see Shakespeare's most famous creation as the necessary and sufficient product of Shakespeare's newly postulated method of creation. Such is the contribution of L. L. Schücking.[28]

In his pioneering study of the conventions in Shakespearean character portrayal Schücking starts from much the same position as Lewis and Robertson. He sees Shakespeare as an often careless adapter of other men's plots, as one who "*lacked the conscience of the artist who is determined to do everything as well as he can*" (italics Schücking's).[29] But now this careless workmanship is largely justified by a genuine dramaturgic principle that Schücking sees in Shakespeare: the dramatic baroque. Like its architectural counterpart, the dramatic baroque aims at striking effects through detail and contrast—in *Hamlet*, for instance, contrast in imagery, as with Hamlet's changes from the loftiest to the homeliest of speech; contrast in the swift turns of the action from comic to serious and back again; contrasts in scene, from the cold midnight battlement to the color and pageantry of the assembled court; and, of course, the manifold contrasts in Hamlet's own characterization. Contrast, brilliancy, and vividness of the individual parts are the striking features of the work. "There is a ground plan, certainly," Schücking says, "but it is almost obscured by an abundance of individual detail."[30] Of course, to explain *Hamlet* by calling it baroque is no better than to explain it by calling it confusing. We must ask what caused the dramatic baroque and what its functions were. Schücking's answers to these questions provide his major contribution to *Hamlet* interpretation.

Central to Schücking's theory of the baroque is the doctrine of "episodic intensification," the stressing of the individual episode for its own sake, the tendency "to arrange the circumstances [of a scene] in such a manner as to produce the greatest effect for the moment," even at the expense of losing "the sense of a connected whole."[31] Episodic intensification stems from the audience's taste for the "old popular form of the epic drama,"[32] with its loose, episodic construction. Shakespeare was always alert to public tastes, and the episodic construction provided opportunity for the easy excitement demanded by the unsubtle, easily bored audience that Schücking envisions.[33] Once again, Shakespeare becomes a product of his environment, of the requirements of his audience.

With the doctrine of episodic intensification, Schücking can fit the apparent structural anomalies of *Hamlet*, so bothersome to Robertson and Lewis, into a genuine (if inferior) artistic form in which "the situations change with kaleidoscopic rapidity and the interest of the audience is continually stimulated anew."[34] At its best, as with the Ophelia subplot, this intensification can be "a beautiful dramatic luxury."[35] At its worst, it merely indulges the audience's bad taste; it is a sort of artistic hedonism, sacrificing ultimate coherence for immediate pleasure. Finally, Schücking excuses all the digressions en masse since, by suspending the action, they heighten dramatic tension.[36] In short, then, the problem of the apparent structural anomalies is not to be solved through any complex allegorical formula, for Shakespeare has sacrificed mimetic consistency to immediate theatrical appeal. Once more, the problem of *Hamlet* is relegated from form to process.

Into this pattern of the baroque Schücking fits the character of Hamlet, applying an allegorical formula under which all the complexity of his action and utterance can be subsumed.[37] This formula is that of the Elizabethan melancholiac. Schücking derives the formula from three separate sources, each of which drew a picture that the Elizabethan audience would recognize as highly conventionalized: the Theophrastian portrait of the melancholiac by Sir Thomas Overbury; the stage portrayals of melancholiacs, in both tragedy and comedy; and the social affectations of the time—Childe Harold had his predecessors even among the Elizabethans.[38] The convention of melancholy, as thus established, is fairly vague, and there is virtually no out-of-the-way behavior that it cannot account for. Thus, Hamlet's erotic imagination and his misogyny are typical of the melancholy character, as are his intolerance of Polonius, his tendency to lose himself in thought, his pessimism and disgust with the world, his self-lacerating introspection, and even the originality and ingenuity of his ideas.[39] But most important, he is sleepless and therefore languid and exhausted, weak and irritable, capable of letting the most solemn duties elapse unless spurred by momentary excitement; Hamlet's delay is accounted for.[40] Thus, more than any of the other evolutionists, Schücking approaches the recondite character analyses of the nineteenth century. His Hamlet is complicated, revealed as much by his frenzy as his meditation; yet at bottom he is consistent. The difference is that for Schücking this consistency rests entirely on a stageworthy convention.

Like the other evolutionists, Schücking writes in reaction to Romantic criticism, with its major premise of Shakespeare's unfathomable profundity, and seeks to replace what he feels are its psychological vagaries with a sound knowledge of the dramatic conventions to which Shakespeare acquiesced. So wholehearted is his turning away from modern prejudice that he treats Shakespearian dramaturgy as far more primitive than subsequent critics have come to see it. (At one point, indeed, he is forced into a rather sad antithesis between modern/beautiful and historical/true.[41])

Nevertheless, Schücking has presented a coherent solution to the problems that the disintegrationists pose. Hamlet and *Hamlet* are once again rejoined as the Prince becomes, not a true though fragmentary psychological portrait, but a highly popular character type evolved from a popular play to meet the demands of a popular audience. Schücking's convention of melancholy, moreover, by allowing for a broad range of behavior, permits the playwright to indulge continually in the striking and the unexpected, to play with surprise and suspense without worrying about uniformity of character. With the erratic, melancholy protagonist, the opportunities for episodic intensification are enormous, and if Schücking's *Hamlet* is not great tragedy, it is nevertheless exciting popular entertainment.

4

Lewis and Robertson contributed to the criticism of *Hamlet* by insisting on Shakespeare's debt to Kyd; their criticism is primarily preinterpretative. By examining the text as a palimpsest, as the result of literary forces from without, both critics stress parts of the play that a more naturalistic school of criticism would not: in effect, they change the contents of the text. Such allegory as they subsequently attach to the text is derived primarily from the main line of *Hamlet* criticism. Lewis allows for the coexistence of both Kyd's revenge allegory and a modified Coleridgean interpretation, while Robertson invokes a Bradleian view of melancholy, though he seems ambivalent about the importance to be attached to it; its major function is to indicate a way out of the self-contradiction of the plot, whose handmaiden it is.

It has remained for Schücking to derive allegorical hypotheses from the theatrical conditions out of which *Hamlet* presumably evolved. In this he is joined by E. E. Stoll, one of the most eloquent and influential of recent Shakespearean scholars. Yet the interpretations of the two writers are profoundly different. Schücking's is like the Romantic critics' in that both see the drama as a conflict between protagonist and plot. Behind their writings lies the question: What is such a person as Hamlet doing in such a story as *Hamlet?* Almost invariably the romanticists answer that the delicate or meditative Prince was not meant to partake in the bloody revenge business at hand. And the conflict that Schücking draws between the duty of revenge and the weakness of the melancholiac is not far different. Stoll, then, is unique in seeking to reunite the revenge hero and the revenge action, in insisting that Hamlet is indeed well suited to the burden that the Ghost lays on his shoulders. Shakespeare's concern, Stoll insists, was not with the characterization of Hamlet, but with the play as a whole, and so Stoll's critical effort is to find a Hamlet "in keeping with the whole play, of which he is only an inseparable component. . . ."[42] To do so, he too enters the realm of the audience and of the conventions that the audience fosters.

Once more, confusion stems from Kyd. If, like the Greek revenge tragedians, Kyd had concentrated on depicting the consummation of the revenge, all might yet have been well, but he and his audience were interested in the beginning of the action as well as its culmination. So he introduced the Ghost, and with it all our critical woe, for if Hamlet had indeed swept immediately to his revenge, where would the play be? " 'But why in the world,' " asks Bradley's ingenuous interlocutor, " 'did not Hamlet obey the Ghost at once, and so save seven of those eight lives lost in the play?' "[43] To which Stoll replies that "had the hero . . . gone promptly or most naturally to work—*plus de pièce possible!*"[44] Bradley is concerned with saving lives, while Stoll is concerned with saving the play: once more, our attention is called away from form to process.

Since we are to see revenge instigated and then fulfilled, and since five acts are to elapse in between, Shakespeare must find some way of marking time. The traditional solution is to make the hero unequal to the task, but Stoll is out to prove the contrary: "A revenger, who for four acts has little or nothing to do, must be a dubious and sorry figure; and yet this revenger was certainly meant for an heroic one. How, then, could Shakespeare as he took up the story, save his hero?" Ultimately the form of the play supplies no answer. Shakespeare had recourse "not to psychology, but to hedging and finesse."[45]

According to Stoll, Shakespeare's hedging and finesse are to meet the demands of an audience that forced *Hamlet* into the mold built by Kyd and revenge tragedy in general:

> . . . the Kydian revenge play had recently come back into favor. Ben Jonson had just penned "additions" to the *Spanish Tragedy* . . . and the Lord Chamberlain's company at the Globe must needs have something like it to keep even. And who so fit for this as Shakespeare, their chief poet, who, in *Titus Andronicus,* years before, had beaten Kyd at his own game? Neither Shakespeare nor Jonson, we may presume, was expected to make the story over. Kyd's two plays had been universally popular; and what the company—what the public—wanted was *Hamlet* or the *Spanish Tragedy,* nothing less. . . . The story, the telling situations, the essential conception of the characters,— these they could not easily surrender. Indeed, the great popular artist, such as was Shakespeare, in sympathy with his public and their likings and cravings, would himself not desire that they should surrender them. He was not the one to risk disappointing an audience assembled to witness a familiar and favorite performance on the stage and applaud a popular hero. Rather, he would run to meet their prepossessions and predilections. He always followed the tradition of the stage, he never ignored it or defied it.[46]

Once again, but more emphatically than before, we are asked to interpret Hamlet by external commercial standards—indeed, by the standards of survival of the fittest, for Shakespeare and the Globe are seen in the light of business competition, of "keeping even" with a rival product. Thus, Stoll is assuming that Shakespeare was a "popular artist" whose first concern was to please his audience—an audience which, unlike Robertson's with its uneasy mixture of lords and groundlings, is unanimous in its demands.

What are these demands? To Stoll, they are that above all the play be simple to understand and exciting to watch. Ease of comprehension, we have seen, was of great importance to Schücking, too; but where he treated it as an unfortunate primitive requirement, Stoll insists that it is a requisite of all great popular art, the appeal of which is more to the senses and imagination than to the intellect.[47] *Hamlet,* always Shakespeare's most popular play, has no recondite meaning, and mental passivity yields fruit where careful closet-study merely perplexes and retards: "The reader should, like the true Elizabethan spectator, surrender to the story, following the main trend, heeding the plain, bold outlines; he should not impede the current of interest by looking backward to construct more of a figure than is there."[48] The story line of the play, handed down from Belleforest and Saxo Grammaticus before him, is central to Stoll's interpretation. And the interest in *Hamlet* is not psychological or philosophical any more than it was in Saxo. It comes simply from the old and ever-popular excitement and suspense of watching the hero surmount all-but-insurmountable odds to achieve his goal; it is "the struggle," as Stoll puts it, "of the noble nature in the toils, the magnificent effect."[49] In Shakespeare's hands it is a tale told better than ever before, but a twice-told tale nonetheless. Its function is to arouse emotion, its contents are "contrasts and parallels, developments and climaxes, tempo and rhythm."[50] In short, it is melodramatic, for melodrama was what the audience liked in its tragedies.[51] And melodrama requires an active hero: "An irresolute and vacillating hero would in this case have been unacceptable; and if Shakespeare had solved the problem insofar as it was one in psychology, he would have left it unsolved insofar as it was one in art"[52]—"art" being defined, apparently, as what the audience requires.

To turn away from the audience's point of view, according to Stoll, was the sin of the sentimentalist Mackenzie, the professorial William Richardson, author of *Essays on Some of Shakespeare's Dramatic Char-*

acters (1797), and the following generations of Romantic critics, who, from the end of the eighteenth century onward, proclaimed the doctrine of Hamlet's weakness. But these men were merely *readers* of the play, and

> At bottom . . . the trouble with the [Romantic-psychological] method is simply this: the critics are not witnessing the play but reading it. Nay, they are rereading it, are poring and puzzling over it; and in the light of what they find or think they find in the soliloquy at the end of Act II they turn against the Prince what he incidentally says about the Danish national fault in Act I, scene iv, when as yet there has been no trace of a hint of any fault in him. That is not the way to read a play, still less to see it.[53]

Indeed, before the Romantics retired *Hamlet* from the stage to the closet, Stoll maintains, we find no indication that Hamlet was ever considered unequal to his task. The people, the theatergoers of the seventeenth and eighteenth centuries, speak of no weakness in Hamlet, and "was it not for the people that the play was penned?"[54]

Clearly, Stoll's argument for a heroic Hamlet is in part a priori: only a heroic Hamlet would have been acceptable; Hamlet was accepted; therefore, he was heroic. The task of reconciling the syllogism to the text remains, and it is to this attempt that we must now turn. Stoll's argument is very circumstantial, and to discuss it in its entirety would be rather more lengthy than interesting. I must therefore pick only a few of his major points that, I think, faithfully reflect his method at large.

Central to Stoll's hermeneutics, as we have seen, is his stress on the plot. Everything else is subordinate to the story line, including Hamlet's self-reproaches, erstwhile grist to the Romantic mill: "To save the story, [Shakespeare] lets the hero heap upon himself reproaches for his inaction; to save the character, he contradicts the effect of these by his own words, those of others, and the whole impression of his conduct."[55] There is no formal consistency, Stoll claims, for Shakespeare was out to create drama of situation, not to reproduce nature. Any inconsistency of character is to be excused if it serves the story. The bothersome delay is, alas, part of Shakespeare's *donné*, and the self-reproaches simply "serve to motive it. They motive it, that is, not in the psychological sense of grounding it in character, but of explaining it and bridging it over. They motive it by reminding the audience that the main business in hand, though retarded, is not lost to view."[56] They further the plot, they answer the all-important question, "What is going to happen next?" for an audience that looks, not before and after, but only before.

Nor is there any evidence of vacillation on Hamlet's part so striking as to turn the spectators away from their preconceived notion of the heroic avenger and their enthrallment with the mounting excitement on the stage. The two-month delay is not noticeable on the stage. Hamlet's doubt of the Ghost and his sparing of the King at prayer are motivated respectively by traditional demonology and literary convention, and the audience would accept his reasons at face value. The pretended madness, derived from Kyd, was ever-popular and gave Hamlet a means to entertain the audience by at least outwitting the King he could not kill until the last act, while his own lack of a definite plan is all to his credit, since the audience would admire less a hero with "a deliberate and definite, crafty and insidious, homicidal plan."[57] Finally, Hamlet enters the final and fatal duel with no plan—a carelessness that drew sharp criticism from the motive-seeking Bradley but elicits only praise from Stoll, who is concerned less with Hamlet's motives than with his creator's: "For Shakespeare the real and only question is how the tragedy shall remain a tragedy, and at the same time the hero act like the gallant gentleman he is and yet be not a fool."[58]

As we might expect, Stoll's emphasis on the plot and on melodrama makes Hamlet into a less ambivalent, simpler personage than most critics have considered him. His personality resides essentially in the manner of his speech: "by the rhythm, the phrasing and the accents, the role holds together."[59] After all, Hamlet is not a man but a role; he is the words of a poet, not a psychological entity, and though these words are full of sound and fury, apparently to Stoll they signify, if not nothing, at least less than we are used to.

Indeed, with an allegory stemming from the conventions of melodrama, the play loses high seriousness; and if Stoll has nothing to say about Hamlet the neurotic, he has little more to say about Hamlet the philosopher. The "To be or not to be" soliloquy becomes a mere theatrical device; it gives Hamlet "something to do while these arrangements [for the play] are making, and until his eyes shall light on the girl." It is "only" a philosophic discourse—and fortunately so, since the walls have ears. We may, Stoll observes, be thankful that Hamlet did not choose to ponder his mousetrap here.[60] Again, Hamlet's words, "The time is out of joint," concern neither the time nor the character, but the plot: again, they prepare us for the delay.[61] Here, Stoll's allegorical hypothesis influences his hermeneutics, for if these words "be meant also to indicate a real antipathy to the task of revenge, they contradict the spirit of Hamlet's words and deeds elsewhere. But not every word or act of the hero, as we have seen, means character. . . ."[62] Now the text gives no indication of which lines (if not all) in Hamlet's role are relevant to his character or, if his character is contradictory, which aspects of the character represent Shakespeare's final intention. Lewis, we have seen, stresses exactly those parts of Hamlet's speech that Stoll relegates to the story line: the doubts, the reluctance to revenge. But then, Lewis's allegory is psychological, and Stoll's is melodramatic. In either case, a presupposition about the author's intentions (Shakespeare as psychologist versus Shakespeare as entertainer) shapes the interpretation.

Stoll has opted for Shakespeare as entertainer, and to him, ultimately, *Hamlet* is a game well played whose chief attraction is the enjoyable tension of the contest. It is a *Hamlet* largely stripped of the melancholy and introspection that has endeared it to the Romantics and to many people today, but it is an artistic whole. Stoll's Hamlet is not a compromise with the plot, as is Robertson's, or with heroism itself, as is Schücking's. Of all the evolutionist Hamlets, he alone is comfortable in the role imposed upon him by Shakespeare's artistic environment.

5

The major works of the evolutionists were written fifty years ago. Reacting against what they considered the projection of the Romantic critics' own psychology onto the play (and writing, after all, only a generation after Pater), the evolutionists gave battle against literary impressionism on behalf of objectivity. Robertson laments that "fallacious 'subjective' solutions" have so long held the critical field, while Schücking attacks the dictum that "the impression is the play" and proposes "new methods for an historically correct conception of [Shakespeare's] characters."[63] In this quest, the evolutionists place their faith in historical research. After examining to what extent the history they portray is clearly factual and also to what extent more recent research has borne out their conclusions, we will be in a better position to assess their contribution to the evolving picture of *Hamlet* in this century.

To begin with, the palimpsest theory of *Hamlet* is no longer generally accepted. The First Quarto, far from a preliminary effort, is now thought to be derived from Shakespeare's final version, while *Der Bestrafte Brudermord* is simply a literary mongrel, representing Kyd no more than Shakespeare.[64] Thus we can be less sure than ever what was in the *Ur-Hamlet* and, accordingly, less sure than ever that Shakespeare was forced to incorporate certain episodes simply because they were in Kyd. Moreover, *Hamlet* no longer appears to be a gradual rewriting of Kyd, and, indeed, Peter Alexander has shown that even in his earliest plays Shakespeare was not as prone to revision of earlier works as had been previously thought.[65] Thus, recent textual theory no longer forbids us to regard *Hamlet* as an artistic whole.

Of course, the evolutionists also find evidence of the play's lack of artistic unity in the apparently extraneous episodes that Robertson and Schücking, in particular, listed. By unity, however, the evolutionists mean unity of action, for it is in the unfolding of the action, with its climaxes and contrasts, that the play's value as popular entertainment lies. As we shall see, however, more recent studies of Elizabethan dramaturgy stress unity of conception over unity of action and in so doing find greater order in the play than the evolutionists have. Here, in any case, is a problem that has been stated with great clarity and detail, a challenge for later critics.

Despite their hopes for historic objectivity, furthermore, the evolutionists have not agreed on Hamlet's character. Lewis and Robertson, of course, go back largely to the main line for their explanations. Stoll and Schücking derive their allegories directly from Shakespeare's theatrical milieu and the pressures that this brought to bear on the playwright, yet one arrives at a strong Hamlet and the other at a weak Hamlet. Where does the inconsistency lie?

Essentially, it lies in the audience that each writer envisages. For a public that demands episodic intensification, for whom the individual scene is most important, Shücking provides a melancholy Hamlet, weak and subject to the most violent and unpredictable emotions, a character who excites through erratic and unexpected action or utterance. To Stoll, such a hero is inconceivable, because his audience is not the same: "By morbid, realistic figures, weak or vacillating characters, the popular imagination cannot be touched. The imagination of the people—and of the English people in particular—is simple and healthy, is romantic."[66]

Raising the specter of the audience probably creates more problems than it solves, for the critic must then determine what these men and women were like, and the cynical reader may think he perceives the critic shaping them to fit his criticism. Shücking's Elizabethan is entertained by the melancholy and weakness that Stoll's Elizabethan finds disgusting, while Robertson's spectator seems able to enjoy what appeals to his own taste and ignore the rest in a play that is as motley as the crowd around him. Yet what little we know of Shakespeare's actual patrons indicates that they were more literate and sophisticated than Shücking, at least, suggests,[67] while Stoll's simple and healthy spectators seem to derive from the Natural Man of the Romantics whom, as critics, he impugns with so much energy. Stoll does back up his claim of a healthy Hamlet for a healthy audience, as we have seen, by arguing that in the stage tradition of the late-seventeenth and eighteenth centuries the delay and melancholy went largely unnoticed, but even this evidence is illusory. To begin with, the post-Restoration stage *Hamlets* were cut to emphasize the active Prince at the expense of the hesitant[68] or even, as with Garrick, completely rewritten to provide a heroic, melodramatic ending.[69] What the audience saw was not all of what Shakespeare wrote—was, at times, not all Shakespeare. And even then, Hamlet's delay and melancholy were not totally ignored. Boswell's recently discovered London Journal describes an account of *Hamlet* by another man of the stage, Thomas Sheridan, that adumbrates the view of the delicate and irresolute Prince of the Romantics more than a generation before Goethe.[70] England before the Romantic age, then, was by no means univocal in its view of *Hamlet,* and, furthermore, it is questionable whether either the dashing Prince of Garrick or the indecisive one of Sheridan reflect Elizabethan views.

Stress on the audience has borne fruit in other regards, however. For one thing, it calls attention to *Hamlet* as popular drama. "Why," Nietzsche asked with aristocratic contempt, "should the artist be bound to accommodate himself to a power whose strength lies merely in numbers?"[71] Yet Shakespeare was popular in his own time, and the public's pleasure ultimately made him a wealthy man. To suggest that the evolutionists have gone too far in making *Hamlet* a stage entertainment and a stage entertainment alone is not to exculpate the Romantics from going too far in the opposite direction. Goethe's denial of Shakespeare's dramaturgical ability is not easily pardoned, nor are we likely, with Coleridge, to consider the Hamlet story merely "in the same light as a painter regards his canvas, before he begins to paint—a mere vehicle for thoughts—as the ground upon which he has to work"—in the case of *Hamlet* as a mere vehicle for character portrayal.[72] The evolutionists, and particularly Stoll, shift the critical balance in a direction it badly needed in pointing out the close relation of *Hamlet* to the melodramatic revenge literature of its time and in observing that the play is richer in murder and counter-murder, sound and excitement, than any other play Shakespeare wrote and that its hero is accorded a soldier's funeral amid the firing of cannon—the same cannon that counterpoint the duel in which he meets his death.[73] Again, where the nineteenth-century critics tended to treat Hamlet as if he were a real person (sometimes with an independent existence quite irrelevant to the text), the evolutionists have stressed Hamlet as the result of an artistic process, the product of dramatic convention and structural necessity, a functioning part of a larger, governing whole. Thus, both thematically and structurally, Hamlet has been rewedded to *Hamlet*, and subsequent critics have largely abandoned the attempt to untie this knot. If, then, the evolutionists have lost a number of specific battles, they have nevertheless won a major critical war, for most critics have since agreed that to interpret Shakespeare, nature unadorned is not enough.

Finally, the evolutionists' stress on *Hamlet* as popular drama challenges all recondite Romantic interpretation. If, after all, *Hamlet* is difficult and mysterious, how did it manage to become so popular from the very outset? Perhaps, however, the issue appears so divisive only because the evolutionists have the notion—itself rather Romantic—of the poetic genius as isolated, alienated from his audience. They lose sight of the fact that what is profound is not necessarily recondite, and even that what sounds recondite when stated explicitly is nevertheless implicit in the fundamental experiences of all thoughtful men, for the most arcane language may be necessary to analyze the most common facts of human existence. Over and over again, critics have rejected Eliot's claim that *Hamlet* is an artistic failure because it does not bring to light the basic problem that lies at its heart. More remarkable, however, is that many critics who reject Eliot's conclusion cheerfully accept his initial premise that the play will not yield easily to rational analysis. Not all of them, of course, are deliberately refuting Eliot; whether or not they are, however—and perhaps even more significantly if not—they recognize the problem of clear, conscious theatrical communication that he was among the first to raise, and they incorporate this problem into interpretations that posit the artistic success of the play.

In short, though time has greatly altered our acceptance of the evolutionists' interpretations, nevertheless, many newer views have arisen from the ground that they first broke. In this study, they stand as the first major reaction to Bradley and the main line of nineteenth-century criticism, and as a point of departure for critics of the next decades.

Elizabethan Psychology

3

1

In general, interpretation seeks the "meaning" of a literary work, a central idea that informs the parts and gives unity to the whole. In *Hamlet*, however, critics have often been content to study the apparent mystery of the Prince's behavior without looking further. The critics whom we shall examine in the present chapter apply to *Hamlet* the complex doctrines of Elizabethan faculty psychology—or moral philosophy, to use a nobler term—and in so doing they sometimes deal exclusively with the Prince himself. With *Hamlet*, as with few other works, psychological interpretation can arrive at extremely important conclusions and yet say nothing at all about the work as a whole: this may be bad aesthetics, but the history of *Hamlet* criticism gives it proof.

To some extent the present chapter is a prologue to the next, which will deal with other interpretations based on Elizabethan intellectual history. For the moment, however, we shall be examining critics who deal primarily with Elizabethan psychology and only by extension with wider metaphysical themes of the Renaissance. The following chapter will deal with critics who reverse this process and read character in the light of more general themes of the Elizabethan ethos.

2

With the rise in the 1920s and 1930s of studies in Elizabethan faculty psychology,[1] *Hamlet* criticism once more reacted to Bradley and his Romantic forebears. The evolutionists, as we have seen, turned away from the form of the play to the process of its creation. Like the evolutionists, the students of Elizabethan psychology sought to view *Hamlet* through Elizabethan eyes; unlike the evolutionists, however, they assumed with the main-line critics that the reason for the Prince's delay rested purely in his own character and thus was a part of the play's form.[2] But the Elizabethans, the psychologists argued, could hardly have understood (nor Shakespeare himself have anticipated) the modern and sometimes recondite psychology of the Romantic critics and their psychoanalytic successors. Instead, both poet and audience would have conceived Hamlet in terms of their own faculty psychology, and it is in these terms, therefore, that the modern critic would have to describe him. Once again, Shakespeare's environment was called into play—not the theatrical environment, this time, but the intellectual.

A summary of sixteenth-century faculty psychology is far beyond the scope of the present work. Throughout, I shall state Hamlet's alleged problems in their simplest terms, without, I hope, greatly oversimplifying. We have already had a glimpse of this psychology in Schücking, but he treats it in the form in which it passed into a simplified literary and social convention. We are now concerned with the elaborate physiological and moral structure that had been building through the Middle Ages and reached Renaissance man in the writings of physicians and philosophers such as La Primaudaye, Timothy Bright, and Robert Burton.

Most important, for us, is the psychology of action and inaction. Theodore Spencer summarizes it:

> Ideally speaking, before a man performs an act of any kind, an elaborate process takes place. Through the working of the animal spirits, the outward senses perceive an object, an impression of it is conveyed to the imagination, the imagination refers this impression to the affections as pleasing or displeasing, reason debates the matter and presents its verdict to the will, the Queen of the soul, who finally dictates back to the sensitive appetite (the function which desires), telling it to act or to refrain from action, according as the object is seen as good or evil.[3]

In short, action ultimately involves the cooperation of reason and the senses, through the mediation of their respective agents, will and appetite (or passion). "The object of Appetite," observed Richard Hooker, "is whatsoever sensible good may be wished for; the object of Will is that good which Reason doth lead us to seek. . . . Appetite is the Will's solicitor, and the Will is Appetite's controller. . . ."[4] But if will governs action, it is appetite that provides the motive force to act.

Had Hamlet indeed swept to his revenge, his thought processes must then have been as follows: the sense-impression made by the Ghost would have aroused in Hamlet a passion for revenge; reason, acknowledging Hamlet's filial duty and loath to let Denmark remain under the hand of a regicide, would prescribe revenge; the will, possessed of reason's mandate and the energy of passion, would lead Hamlet to kill Claudius. Hamlet's inability to act must thus stem from a disharmony of reason and passion. He must either have some rational objection to the act (in which case his difficulty is not psychological) or he must be lapsed in passion, as he himself admits to the Ghost (III.iv.107). The simplest explanation of Hamlet's delay in Elizabethan psychological terms is that he no longer has the passion, the emotional fuel, necessary for action.[5]

Critics have carried the use of faculty psychology even further, however, in the attempt to find out what caused Hamlet's loss of passion. Following them, we enter the realm of Elizabethan abnormal psychology. To Shakespeare's audience, mental disease was passion uncontrolled by reason. Reason itself, as Timothy Bright observed, "in the meane time of these stormes and tempests of passion, these delusions, feares, false terrours, and poeticall fictions of the braine, sitteth quiet and still, nothing altered in facultie, or any part of that diuine and impatible disposition, which it obtaineth by the excellencie of creation."[6] In the sixteenth century one did not lose one's reason, though one could sorely neglect it. Hamlet would thus have appeared to Shakespeare's audience as a slave of an unregulated passion disrupting his powers of action. Somewhere in the multitudinous "stormes and tempests of passion" catalogued by Elizabethan philosophers we must seek Hamlet's problem.

For some critics Hamlet's passionate character is enough to explain the delay: the courses of men who failed to balance head and heart were not expected to run smooth.[7] Other critics have tried to trace Hamlet's behavior even deeper into the diagnostics of Renaissance psychology, into the physiological changes worked by emotion on the four humors of the body: blood, choler, phlegm, and melancholy. Their conclusion is that Hamlet, like legions of his contemporaries, suffers from melancholy. This diagnosis by itself is not very enlightening, however, for melancholy was pretty much the factotum of Elizabethan abnormal psychology, causing men to err in almost any direction. No other state, avers Burton in his introductory poem to *The Anatomy of Melancholy*, is so sour, so sweet, so harsh, so fierce, so damned, and yet so divine as melancholy.

Part of the confusion over the term is due to ambiguity. There are two types of melancholy: natural and adust. Natural melancholy is simply the predominance in the bloodstream of the melancholy humor. Such melancholy, generally chronic, is not usually severe; Jaques suffers from it enjoyably in the Forest of Arden. Melancholy adust, meanwhile, is actually three different diseases, occurring when the sanguine, choleric, or melancholy humors burn through an "excessiue distēper of heate," Bright says, and turn "into a sharp lye."[8]

Three features of melancholy adust are important to students of *Hamlet*. First, its symptoms are like those caused by the original humor in its natural state, only more severe. Second, adustion may be brought about by immoderate passion, such as grief or unrequited love.[9] Finally, melancholy could have caused Hamlet's inaction. It is unclear whether such melancholy was necessarily adust; in any case, more than one writer of Shakespeare's time claims for melancholy—in its severer forms, at least—the ability to breed in its victims "a negligence in their affaires, and dissolutenesse, where should be diligence."[10]

A precise description of Hamlet's psychological state would have to identify Hamlet's dominant humor, to determine whether or not the humor was adust, and to determine the cause of the excess or adustion. We must consider, then, whether *Hamlet* lends itself to such physiological precision.

The most celebrated and detailed analysis in Elizabethan terms of Hamlet's mental state is Lily B. Campbell's study in *Shakespeare's Tragic Heroes: Slaves of Passion*.[11] Here she argues that Hamlet suffers from adustion of a predominant sanguine humor. How well does the text bear the diagnosis out? To begin with, the initial premise that Hamlet is predominantly sanguine rests on shaky ground: first, that Hamlet is from a northern nation, where "the cold and moist humours must prevail, either phlegm or blood," abetted by the characteristic drunkenness of the Danes, which Hamlet himself mentions; second, that Hamlet is corpulent—his flesh is "too, too solid," and in the duel scene he is "fat and scant of breath."[12] But "fat" is probably to be taken in the Elizabethan sense of "sweaty,"[13] and (assuming that the reading "solid" is correct, and not "sullied," which many recent editors prefer) Hamlet's profound pessimism must hinge on corporeality, not corpulency. As to national characteristics, the evidence that Campbell gives might apply to every character in the play—except, on one point, Hamlet, who does not drink. The facetious and congenial characteristics of the sanguine type which Campbell cites from Thomas Walkington[14] may be apt enough, though "quipping without bitter taunting" is not typical of the Hamlet we have seen, nor does the wariness "to lay himself open to any daunger, if the final end of his endeavor and toile bee not plausible in his demurring judgement" describe the rashness of the man who rushes on board the pirate ship or, against his friends' advice, after the Ghost. More important, even granted that Hamlet had been originally sanguine, Campbell does not prove that it is the predominant humor that must necessarily suffer adustion. (Bright, moreover, is of the opinion that a man may suffer from a variety of humors, natural or adust, in fairly rapid succession).[15] And, though another humor may have been dominant, it is likely enough that the adust humor would gain dominance through adustion itself.

Most important, the symptoms of sanguine adust simply do not correspond to Hamlet's behavior. Adustion merely exaggerates the genial characteristics of the sanguine personality. It causes the heart to rejoice, it supplies the defects of his mistress in a lover's eyes, and, even in its extremest form, "euery serious thing for a time, is turned into a iest, & tragedies into comedies, and lamentation into gigges and daunces."[16] Campbell, evidently with this last passage in mind, cites Hamlet's jests in the graveyard, "for the sanguine adust turn tragedies into comedies as does Hamlet here while he jests with horror."[17] But it is hard to see in Hamlet's bitter irony even a trace of the genial humor that Bright describes. "Imperious Caesar, dead and turn'd to clay,/ Might stop a hole to keep the wind away" (V.i.236–37)—that may be witty, but it is not a jig or a dance.

A second, more cautious diagnosis of Hamlet's mental physiology is that of Professor Lawrence Babb in *The Elizabethan Malady*. To Babb, it appears that Hamlet is suffering, not from sanguine adust, but from melancholy—whether natural or adust, Babb does not make clear; the point might depend on the authority cited. La Primaudaye, whom Babb quotes, appears to be thinking of a heavy preponderance of natural melancholy:

> this blacke melancholy humour . . . will make the spirit & mind darkish, whereby it groweth to be blockish, & the heart loseth al his cheerefulnes. And because the braine is cooled therby, it waxeth very heauy & drowsie. Now when griefe is in great measure, it bringeth withall a kinde of loathing & tediousnes, which causeth a man to hate & to be weary of all things, euen of the light & of a mans selfe so that he shal take pleasure in nothing but in his melancholy . . . refusing all ioy & consolation. To conclude, some grow so far as to hate themselues, & so fall to despaire, yea many kil & destroy themselues.[18]

Such is the plight of Hamlet, to whom all the uses of this world seem weary, stale, flat, and unprofitable. Since in this melancholy the mind grows blockish and the heart loses all its cheerfulness, Hamlet's two chief attributes are accounted for: inaction and misanthropy.[19]

The only difficulty with this interpretation is that it links misanthropy and inaction with a brain "heauy & drowsie," as if the victim's behavior were the result of sheer lassitude. Nowhere in Shakespeare do we see a character of more intense mental activity than Hamlet— and rarely a character of more intense physical activity.[20] Even his first soliloquy, where his melancholy is at a peak, is quick, energetic, and abrupt in its rhythm, as if Hamlet were suffering, not from dullness, but from some pain. It might be argued that it is this very pain that gives rise to his subsequent melancholy, and, indeed, his words later to Rosencrantz and Guildenstern are more amenable to Babb's interpretation: it goes heavily with his disposition; man delights not him.[21] And yet nowhere does it appear that his feelings are the result of a depressant humor rendering "the spirit & mind darkish." Surely

Hamlet greets his friends cordially enough, before he begins to suspect them:

My excellent good friends! How dost thou, Guildenstern?
Ah, Rosencrantz! Good lads, how do ye both? (II.ii.228–30)

And he later complains of being "most dreadfully attended" (l. 276). Moreover, if man delights not him, the actors do, and he eagerly insists straightway on a speech. La Primaudaye's melancholiac, meanwhile, "takes pleasure in nothing but in his melancholy."

True, melancholy is subject to cycles of hot and cold (although Babb does not mention these in connection with Hamlet). Thus, melancholiacs are capable of the most extravagant fury, and yet when the humor has burnt itself out, "they . . . condemne and deteste yesterdayes deedes, and are much ashamed."[22] Such may be the explanation of Hamlet's behavior during and after the slaying of Polonius (especially if we credit Gertrude's remark that "He weeps for what is done" [IV.i.27]). Such would also be the explanation for his "tow'ring passion" at Ophelia's grave, and for his regrets about it later. Melancholy's hot phase, in short, can account for Hamlet's manic behavior. And yet there is no passage in the play in which we see Hamlet at a really low point in this cycle of hot and cold: he is never dull, never heavy, but almost always active, mentally and physically. We may presume that he spends the interval between Acts I and II in a state of lethargy, but this is presumption only, and nothing that we see in his behavior before or after gives a sign of such lethargy.[23] Elizabethan psychology teaches us that depression is a dullness of the spirits. Hamlet is depressed, but his spirits are never dulled. He has many of the secondary symptoms of severe melancholy, but not the main one.

Certainly the greatest issue in the psychological criticism of Hamlet is the question of what psychological facts or conventions Shakespeare must have had in mind when he created his most famous character. It is this issue that so sharply divides the reader of Freud and the reader of Bright, who otherwise may approach the Prince in similar fashion. In creating Hamlet, did Shakespeare imitate life, or did he imitate those conventions concerning life that the moral philosophers had written down and that so many of their contemporaries held to be true? To answer, we must distinguish between a disease and a syndrome. The effects of melancholy were well known and were probably derived largely from empirical observation,[24] but their cause remained unclear. Melancholy is nothing if not various. According to the hour of the day, the season of the year, or the changes of the weather, the melancholiac may be sad, mirthful, or outrageous—or all three in rapid succession. "It looks somewhat," Babb concludes, "as if melancholy embraces all irrationality, for there is hardly a mental disease which is not associated with melancholic humors by one author or another."[25] This is clearly true, for while the syndromes may sometimes be a matter of observed fact, the disease itself, the melancholic humor, is a fiction. The psychology based on the four humors developed as part of a cosmology that required all things to be fashioned from four elements, yet the resultant disease of melancholy had somehow to accommodate itself to all the complexities of human behavior. Like the epicyclical system of Ptolemaic astronomy in confrontation with the increasingly complex data of planetary motion, Renaissance psychology grew ever more cumbersome, and the physiological concept of melancholy, having to contort itself into the intricate pattern of fact, became all but meaningless. I would suggest that Shakespeare evoked the syndrome, not the disease.

Lily B. Campbell insists that "every character in a Shakespearean play is engaged in saying exactly what Shakespeare wanted the audience to know and in saying it over and over again. . . . It is quite safe to trust the characters to tell the truth about themselves."[26] But what does Hamlet say about himself? He says that he is melancholy, but wherefore he knows not. He says that he cannot act, and professes not to know why. In his tirade at Gertrude in the closet scene, as elsewhere, he exhibits a detailed knowledge of Elizabethan psychology, and yet he never says that his delay springs from melancholy (or melancholy adust, or sanguine adust). The reason, I would suggest, is that it does not. For had it been Shakespeare's intention to imitate the conventions of one of these humors, he would have made the symptoms clear, whereas Hamlet's symptoms are as vague, from the point of view of Elizabethan physiology, as the term "melancholy" itself. Surely, if Shakespeare had had a physiological type in mind, it would have been evident to experts such as Campbell and Babb, who probably know far more about Elizabethan psychology than most Elizabethans did. Instead, their analyses contradict not only each other but much of the text as well. If Shakespeare was attempting to portray such a type, then *Hamlet* is a failure in communication.

If the disease seems uncertain, what about the cause? Campbell and Babb agree that Hamlet's melancholia is brought on by excessive grief, and Campbell goes so far as to view the entire play as a study in grief: Hamlet, Laertes, and Fortinbras each provide variations on the central theme of loss of fathers.[27] It is to this theme that we must now turn.

We have already seen that melancholy may spring from violent grief, but the issue goes deeper still. Elizabethan England inherited from the Middle Ages the belief that man was equidistant from the angels and the beasts in the hierarchy of creation. His reason was angelic, his appetites bestial. Neoplatonic doctrine and the Christian desire ultimately to join the ranks of the angels combined to make the prime moral rule of psychology the domination of the reason over the passions. The student of Elizabethan psychology, following this doctrine, will treat *Hamlet* as a tragedy in which the catastrophe is brought about by the hero's surrender to passion: this, in the time-honored phrase, is Hamlet's tragic flaw.

Is Hamlet dominated by grief? Claudius and Gertrude seem to think so in the second scene, and Campbell agrees with them,[28] but is grief what Shakespeare is stressing? Hamlet's outburst to Gertrude before the assembled court indicates something else:

> Seems, madam? Nay, it is. I know not 'seems.'
> 'Tis not alone my inky cloak, good mother,
> Nor customary suits of solemn black,
> Nor windy suspiration of forc'd breath,
> No, nor the fruitful river in the eye,
> Nor the dejected haviour of the visage,
> Together with all forms, moods, shapes of grief,
> That can denote me truly. These indeed seem,
> For they are actions that a man might play;
> But I have that within which passeth show—
> These but the trappings and the suits of woe. (I.ii.76–86)

This speech Campbell calls "a cry of passion, of grief that will not be consoled."[29] Hamlet, however, is stressing not the depth of his grief but its genuineness. He appears not so much disconsolate as angry—angry, as his first soliloquy will make abundantly clear, at the Queen, who has shown all too much willingness to console herself for her first husband's death.[30] This soliloquy, in fact, is the lengthiest statement of Hamlet's misery, yet it contains not a word of sorrow at the loss of his father but only praise for him, contempt for Claudius, and bitterness at the Queen. And throughout the play, Hamlet's most violent emotions are unleashed by thoughts of perfidy, not of his father's death. I think, then, that we must reject the interpretation of *Hamlet* as a tragedy of grief, as a study of three men each reacting differently to his father's death. Surely such a theme is there, but, equally surely, Hamlet's case is not so simple. (Laertes and Fortinbras, we may remember, have no mothers.)

All of which is not to say that studies of Elizabethan psychology are useless to our understanding of *Hamlet*. Certainly, throughout *Hamlet* Shakespeare uses the psychological terminology of his day, a terminology that beautifully evokes the image of a humanity mentally or spiritually disturbed and that, though failing to pluck out the heart of Hamlet's mystery, yet indicates that the mystery is there. In short, Shakespeare's evocation of the melancholic figure is perhaps best understood in terms of what it would lead the audience to expect and accept, not what it would enable them to understand and explain. Suffice it that Hamlet was recognized as a melancholiac: the audience would then accept as probable the cynicism, the sadness, even the delay. Such evocation would have been a useful dramatic device; its use does not indicate that Shakespeare's character portrayal went no further.

3

So far, we have been dealing only with physiological and moral diagnostics. In Campbell's hands, however, Elizabethan psychology opens into a systematic study of tragic theme and structure in *Hamlet*.

Although the idea of involuntary psychological behavior was already far advanced in Shakespeare's lifetime, the modern corollary that a man was not totally responsible for his actions had not arisen. However much a man might be swayed by his passions, it was his duty to control them with reason and patience:

As it is . . . a poynt of treason, that suche lewed perturbations
. . . shoulde rage rebell & take vpon them the rule of the hole
man, contemptuously despysynge the auctorytie of the mynde,
so it is extreme foly for the mynde, to be slaue vnto fonde affec-
tions, and to serue at a becke, the vyle carkeys, neyther the
dignitie of nature, neyther the expresse lawe of god, any thyng
regarded.[31]

The evocation of treason in this passage is no idle metaphor. For
passion to rebel against reason, the Elizabethan knew, was analogous to
a subject's rebellion against his anointed sovereign or, on a larger
scale yet, of Creation's rebellion against God. Adam's fall had in
essence involved all three. One law of order governed macrocosmos,
cosmos, and microcosmos alike; mental illness, in Shakespeare's lifetime, was not far removed from original sin.

This doctrine of moral responsibility, according to Campbell, is
central to the Renaissance conception of tragedy:

Tragedy [in the Middle Ages] started to picture the fall of
princes. It came to seek an explanation that could justify the
ways of God to men. It came to seek the justice which must inhere
in such falls if there was a God of justice in his heaven. And it
found that justice in the error or the folly which caused men to
bring down evil on themselves. And gradually it came to find in
men's passions the cause of their errors and their folly, and therefore the cause of the evil which they bring upon themselves.[32]

Tragedy was didactic, and the lessons to be learned from it were con-
veyed most pleasingly and convincingly from the stage. It is not in our
stars but in ourselves that we suffer adversity. Accordingly, the characters in tragedies were drawn so as to reinforce the moral significance
of the play; nature took a back seat. "In fact," Campbell states, "the
inductive method for artists had not yet been discovered. The artist
took his characters from moral philosophy."[33]

The degree of the poet's dependence on critical theory is one of the
most perplexing of aesthetic problems. It is especially perplexing when
one deals with the Elizabethan stage, which practiced a rapidly evolv-

ing eclecticism and yet paid service to a traditional and prescriptive body of critical theory. It has been convincingly argued that the Elizabethan playwright was influenced by literary tradition and theory but by no means enslaved to them: they provided a starting point, not a goal.[34] We must now consider how that conclusion applies to Campbell's treatment of *Hamlet*.

A major danger in reducing any work of art to a tradition is, of course, in oversimplifying the work of art, but there is also the danger of oversimplifying the tradition. Thus, Campbell relates *Hamlet* exclusively to the didactic species of *de casibus* tragedy, whose roots lie in the fertile soil of Boccaccio and Chaucer and whose Renaissance fruits were such prose "tragedies" as Lydgate's *Fall of Princes* and the influential *Mirrour for Magistrates*, whose 1559 title page proclaims: *Wherein may be seen by example of other, with howe greuous plages vices are punished: and howe frayle and vnstable worldly prosperitie is founde, even of those, whom Fortune seemeth most highly to fauour.* In placing Hamlet in the *de casibus* tradition, Campbell either ignores or distorts other competing modes of tragedy, especially the tragedy of revenge, which owed less to Renaissance theodicy and more to Seneca and his transfiguration in the fertile mind of Thomas Kyd. She sees revenge tragedy as teaching the philosophical lesson that "an unquiet mind is the inevitable reward of evil doing," and that "the man sins who would undertake to execute privately the justice of God."[35] Yet plays such as *The Spanish Tragedy, Titus Andronicus,* and a host of others in later generations culminated in exceedingly brutal revenges over thoroughly unrepentant villains—sometimes before indifferent gods. It is impossible to gauge the precise reaction of the Elizabethans to such deeds. Certainly, orthodox opinion frowned on blood revenge,[36] but it is easy to imagine a scholar several centuries hence concluding that James Bond was a villain because he was violent and unchaste. Campbell's statement on revenge tragedy may not be literally wrong, but its mildness belies the frank appeal of intrigue and atrocity found in Marston, Webster, and others.

Even *de casibus* tragedy was not always exclusively or even primarily didactic and devout. In *Cambises* the wicked king is killed by a morally vindictive *deus ex machina* (the title page proclaims that we shall see "His Odious Death by God's Justice Appointed"), but his demise, however edifying, is no more than a brief, structurally isolated episode at the end of a play that, if it does not make vice attractive, does make it good entertainment. Shakespeare's *Richard III,* far more sophisticated, has something of the same appeal.

In *Hamlet,* though, where villainy is decidedly unattractive, the ending is unhappy, and some critics find that Shakespeare is raising serious questions about the goodness of the universe, straining the limits of the orthodox theodicy of simpler tragedies. According to Campbell, Renaissance tragedy required Fortune to be the servant of God: in a moral universe, a man's fate had to correspond to his deserts.[37] And, indeed, a play like Dekker's *Old Fortunatus* could follow such teaching quite closely. But Rosencrantz and Guildenstern admit ambiguously that they are Fortune's "privates." "O most true," Hamlet replies, "she is a strumpet"; and "Out, out, thou strumpet Fortune!" exclaims the First Player a few minutes later in a passage that depicts an unmitigated and unjustified evil.[38] The lessons of Elizabethan tragedy are not univocal.

The didactic tradition was undoubtedly influential, yet it appears most clearly outside of the drama itself—in tragic fiction such as the *Mirrour for Magistrates,* or in the preachings of critics. Campbell derives the principle of dramatic tragedies as *exempla* from the writings of such men as Ascham, Lodge, Sidney, Thomas Newton, Puttenham, Nashe, Harington, Heywood, Bacon, and Overbury. Obviously the tradition was widespread, yet most of these did not write for the stage. And even when a professional tragedian like Heywood stresses the moral effects of tragedy, he may do so at least in part because people had been complaining about the immorality of the theater. Who is to say whether Lodge's defense of the theater provides a more accurate picture than Stephen Gosson's *Schoole of Abuse,* to which Lodge was replying? The Elizabethan critics are not so much describing actual practice as laying down a traditional defense against current attacks. Their theories are derived no more from the drama itself than from classical writers such as Aristotle and Horace, often as altered and trans-mitted by the critics of the Italian Renaissance. A playwright such as Jonson might work happily within the classical tradition, adding to it and shaping it to his own ends, but it does not follow that what Heywood preached, Shakespeare practiced.[39]

On both these counts—the variety of tragic experience and the largely extradramatic nature of the didactic tradition—the tragedian was left with a freer hand than Campbell allows for. Perhaps even more important, however, are the demands that drama by its very nature may make on its creator. By Shakespeare's time, the dramatist, writing a comparatively realistic story for real actors, was more apt to call upon his memory of living deeds and voices than was his nondramatic colleague the fabulist. The less edifying facts of life have more room to intrude on the stage, where, as Hamlet knew, the clown may have a mind to speak more than is written down for him. The inductive method of characterization, as Campbell observes, may indeed not yet have been discovered by critics such as Dryden, Rymer, Brumoy, and Dr. Johnson, but it may still have been used by Shakespeare and his contemporaries.

All of which is not to argue that Shakespeare's plays, and *Hamlet* in particular, are amoral. That Shakespeare was familiar with the moral philosophy of his time there can be no question. That he used the issues and terminology of this philosophy in *Hamlet* is equally certain, and we are grateful to the writers we have seen for making the philosophy clear to us. But we can by no means conclude that the play was made to promote it. Rather, we must ask whether the orthodox morality is the end of the play or simply part of the subject, whether *Hamlet* may be understood through orthodox beliefs or whether its mystery calls orthodoxy itself into doubt. In any case, Campbell has reduced *Hamlet* to one theory of tragedy out of several that were at work in an age that was eclectic and in which artistic creation commonly outstripped theory. In doing so, she has given us one of the most thoroughgoing, systematic attempts to relate Shakespeare to specific moral and aesthetic traditions of his time, and even for the reader who does not accept her conclusions, she provides an invaluable index by which to gauge Shakespeare's originality.

4

Any school of criticism, if followed too exclusively, may distort our perception of the artifact. Having examined the validity of Elizabethan psychology as a critical tool, we must now consider its completeness, for any critical assertion may be true so far as it goes and yet not state the complete truth.

To begin with, Elizabethan psychology can be rather hard on its subjects. In essence, it says that Hamlet delays because he was not his "true self" and that the meaning of the play is the necessity of heeding our higher natures. Hamlet is a morbid case, and most of the psychological critics are inclined to treat him rather severely.

But too strong an insistence on the control of passion and on orthodox moral values can lead us to ignore compassion, the compassion that we feel for many a character in Shakespeare who, in the hands of a lesser dramatist, might have become a simple villain—Shylock, Falstaff, Hotspur, even Claudius himself. Hardin Craig presents such a charitable view in his essay "Hamlet's Book."[40] Like the students of Elizabethan psychology, Craig approaches the play through the inner nature of the hero and describes this nature in terms of ideas prevalent in the Elizabethan era. Once more, we have a Hamlet who hesitates because his lower nature momentarily triumphs. Yet, where Campbell condemns, Craig sympathizes. The difference lies in their allegorical hypotheses.

To Craig, *Hamlet* is an allegory of Jerome Cardan's famous work *De Consolatione,* first translated into English as *Cardanus Comforte* in 1573, and of the important segment of Elizabethan thought that this book represents. One of the most popular of the widespread books of consolation current in the sixteenth century, Cardan's *Comforte* had its roots in the stoic literature of the classics and in the related literature that grew out of Pope Innocent III's *De Contemptu Mundi.* Hamlet's remedy for his own problem is the same as Cardan's cure for the evils that beset mankind: "He must exercise fortitude," Craig summarizes, "control his own mind, and above all he must act."[41]

This sounds similar to the pronouncements of Elizabethan psychology, but whereas psychology lends itself to the study of individual characters, to specific diagnoses for specific persons, Cardan discusses the general plight of mankind. Craig's interpretation makes Hamlet into a sort of Renaissance Everyman:

> Hamlet's situation as a grief-stricken hero caught in the toils of innumerable difficulties and dangers is typical, and is the one

presented by Cardan, who says that all men are in like case and
that the remedy lies in curing the mind so that it will rise above
the trials of life. . . . Hamlet is not weak as an individual;
he is merely the representative of weak humanity. He rebukes
himself, not for his own faults, but for those of humankind.[42]

What Craig gives us, then, is not a normative view of *a* human condition, but a sympathetic view of *the* human condition. His basic assumptions about Hamlet's character remain the same as Campbell's, but his
allegory is derived, not from professionally rigid moralists nor from
defensively didactic critics, but from a compassionate humanist. "Be
thou therefore perfect" might be the motto of the interpretation based
on Elizabethan psychology. In reply Craig asks, "Who are the absolutely brave?"[43] In seeking the Elizabethan attitude toward *Hamlet,*
we must remember that there is more than one Elizabethan attitude.[44]

But the major limitation of Elizabethan psychology is, in fact, a
corollary of its chief virtue. It is a tool for the study of character, and
most students of Elizabethan psychology are content to isolate and
examine a given personage alone: to diagnose his frailties and draw the
moral conclusion that is always the corollary of any Elizabethan psychological diagnosis. A greater critical unity may be achieved only by
drawing analogies between the psychological problems of several
characters. This Campbell alone does, viewing the play first as a study
in different types of grief and second as a morality play in which most
of the characters meet their doom as a result of their overruling
passions, and where the survivors are those who temper passion with
reason.[45]

Nevertheless, psychological interpretation does not allow for criticism where character is not paramount. Where Stoll, for instance, examines the commercial aspects of the play and thus envisages an
audience eager to be entertained and a playwright eager to please,
Campbell examines a widespread moral and literary tradition and
consequently envisages an audience eager to be edified and a playwright glad to teach. Moral philosophy cannot deal with *Hamlet* as
dynastic tragedy, cannot deal with the tragedy not only of Hamlet and
Claudius but of Denmark as well. Again, moral philosophy cannot
treat *Hamlet* as an expression of late Elizabethan skepticism, or as one
of the first plays to express the perplexities of the modern world.

In fact, a major issue in criticism as in life is the relationship of mental pathology to moral thought. It is easy, and sometimes justifiable, to attribute eccentric philosophies to mental aberration; the psychological argument *ad hominem* is nothing new. Elizabethan abnormal psychology, stressing the attack of passion and humor on reason, had a concept of intellectual delusion as thoroughgoing as the modern notion of psychosis. Hamlet, few have denied, is a profound pessimist. The question that Elizabethan psychology raises is whether this pessimism, if seen as a symptom of melancholy, is not invalidated as a philosophical doctrine. As Ruth Leila Anderson observes:

> Any violent passion blinds rationality. The organs of the external and the internal senses undergo alteration and thus the latter senses evolve distorted ideas. One sees everything according to the color of the passion. . . . The temperate see the world as an organized universe in which divine and human law operate. They may know that "Something is rotten in the state of Denmark," but they know also that the evil may be cured: "Heaven will direct it." Only the distempered regard the earth as a "sterile promontory," the firmament as a "pestilent congregation of vapours". . . .[46]

But such is the position of medieval cosmology, and by the seventeenth century, as the Church splintered and empirical science arose, medieval cosmology was beginning to lose its hold on the minds of men. What shall we make of the Marstonian malcontent when his creator is himself a melancholiac? The issue is not simply one of ambiguity in *Hamlet,* but of ambiguity in the ethos of Shakespeare's own era. It is an issue that cannot be solved by recourse to the Elizabethan audience because the audience itself would have been sorely divided. It is an ambiguity inherent, possibly in human nature, certainly in the nature of Shakespeare's time, for *Hamlet* is the product of an era that may be called both the end of the Middle Ages and the beginning of the modern period.

The Elizabethan Ethos

4

1

By stressing the inherited revenge plot, the evolutionists have tended to look on *Hamlet* as entertainment. Stressing the moral philosophy of Shakespeare's time, the school of Elizabethan psychology has tended to regard the play as a means of edification and self-improvement. In the present chapter we shall examine a third group of historical critics. Their interpretative allegory is drawn from the complex of religious, political, and moral beliefs prevalent at the end of the sixteenth century: the various systems of thought that reveal to us the Elizabethans' ideals and the relation of these ideals to the potentially intractable world of fact. These critics hypothesize that *Hamlet* is organized to illustrate some aspect of Elizabethan cosmological or ethical thought. To them, Shakespeare neither helped the spectator escape from his world nor incited him to improve it, but, for better or for worse, involved him in it.

The Christian cosmology of the Middle Ages, as is generally observed, was still prevalent in Elizabethan England.[1] God, it had always been granted in this view, revealed His purpose through His word and through His creation, through Revelation and through Nature. It was assumed a priori that these would reveal a universe created to serve man and instruct him during his sojourn on earth. Since the rise of humanism, it is true, man had regarded his own earthly existence more favorably than before; nevertheless, he continued to look at the world under the aspect of eternity. The universe was a sacrament, not a collection of phenomena. Man looked closely at nature's meaning, as revealed by God and the authorities of antiquity, but not at nature itself. Reason examined articles of faith and applied them to the world; observation was at a minimum, for it was assumed that facts would comply with reason. Bacon was being revolutionary indeed when he defended his new science by refusing, as he said, to justify God with a lie. Richard Hooker, his roots in the Middle Ages, could confidently assert:

> Notwithstanding whatsoever such principle [of knowledge] there is, it was at the first found out by discourse, and drawn from out of the very bowels of heaven and earth. . . . The knowledge of every the least thing in the whole world . . . serveth to minister rules, canons, and laws, for men to direct those actions by, which we properly term human.[2]

As Carl Becker observes of medieval philosophy, "the function of intelligence was . . . to demonstrate the truth of revealed knowledge, to reconcile diverse and pragmatic experience with the rational pattern of the world as given in faith."[3] It is even questionable to what degree the philosophers of Saint Thomas's day, or of Shakespeare's, allowed themselves to be bothered by experience at all. Lawrence Babb's description of Elizabethan psychological research indicates no particular concern with induction:

> Elizabethan psychology . . . was essentially deductive and static. It sought an explanation of human nature, not through observation, but in the works of Plato, Aristotle, Galen, Avicenna, Aquinas, and other great writers of elder times. In other words, Elizabethan psychologists shared the general and profound respect for authority. . . .
>
> . . . If [the psychologist] found Galen and Averrhoes in disagreement, he was likely to assume that both were right and attempt a reconciliation.[4]

It is this neglect of fact that caused Bacon to complain that "the entire fabric of human reason which we employ in the inquisition of nature, is badly put together and built up, like some magnificent structure without any foundation."[5]

The change from medieval toward modern, then, consisted largely in the rising interest in facts themselves—indeed, in the very concept that facts in themselves could be important. Emblematic of the change that was occurring was Kepler's refusal to compromise Tycho Brahe's astronomical data by trimming them to meet the mathematical requirements of the Ptolemaic epicyclical system of planetary motion, while the divorce of the state from metaphysics yielded the practical, cynical power politics of Machiavelli.

Perhaps the most important aspect of the conservative Elizabethan cosmology—or of any cosmology—was its function as a filter of knowledge: only those facts were recognized that fit the system. Men refused to look through Galileo's telescope at the moons of Jupiter or, looking, protested that they saw nothing. To the conservative man of the Renaissance, all facts presumably conformed to the concept of an ordered universe created by a benign God for a rational man. It is true that this universe had lapsed from perfection because of man's original sin, yet this lapse was itself a manifestation of God's justice and would in time be redeemed through God's providence. Man, however prodigal, was still God's darling, the center of His universe.

Thus, the orthodox Elizabethan subscribed to a Christian-platonic ideal and to a cosmology that explained the relationship of facts to this ideal. In the sixteenth century, however, with the rise of empirical and pragmatic observation, and with the consequent proliferation of new facts about man and the universe, this old system underwent the first wave of attacks that have resulted in the modern age. The foregoing, to be sure, describes only one aspect of a highly complex era, but the interpretations we shall be examining in this chapter tend to reflect this particular polarity in the age. Ethical-historical approaches to *Hamlet,* then, move in two distinct directions: one that posits the integrity of the old cosmology and one that posits the conflict of this cosmology with empirical fact.

2

If the critic assumes that *Hamlet* implicitly accepts the conservative orthodoxy of its time, the resulting interpretation will picture Shakespeare grappling with ethical problems but not with the conservative code of ethics itself. If *Hamlet* is a puzzle, a good grasp of the orthodoxy will solve it for us. Thus, for example, the critic may see *Hamlet* as a problem in casuistry: the Prince may be unsure what moral code applies to his problem, and the critic proposes a search into the morass of Elizabethan revenge ethics to reveal the dilemma. Or again, Hamlet may be seen as having insufficient evidence to plot his course, and the critic begins to investigate the reliability of sixteenth-century ghosts. In such a view, something in the ethical or metaphysical nature of his task makes Hamlet pause in his revenge. Such interpretations are the cultural historian's equivalent of the Werderian "objective barrier" school. It is to these reexaminations of Hamlet's objective task that we must now turn.

Contemplating the freshly slain body of Polonius, Hamlet observes to his mother:

> For this same lord,
> I do repent; but heaven hath pleas'd it so,
> To punish me with this, and this with me,
> That I must be their scourge and minister.
> I will bestow him, and will answer well
> The death I gave him. (III.iv.172–77)

By the allegory of scourge and minister Fredson Bowers explains Hamlet's delay and death.[6]

The difference between a scourge and a minister to the Elizabethan mind, Bowers points out, is twofold. First, though both are agents of God's vengeance, the minister is righteous and in overthrowing evil directly establishes good in its place, while the scourge is evil: though he may destroy the sinful, he is already irretrievably caught up in sin himself and damned in the very act of vengeance. Second, while heaven will provide the minister with an opportunity to act in fulfillment of public justice, the vengeance of the scourge takes the form of a common crime, in which he makes his own opportunities. Thus, concludes Bowers,

> we may see with full force the anomalous position Hamlet conceives for himself: is he to be the private-revenger scourge *or* the public-avenger minister? If scourge, he will make his own

opportunities, will revenge murder with murder, and by this means visit God's wrath on corruption. If minister, God will see to it that a proper opportunity is offered in some way that will keep him clear from crime, one that will preserve him to initiate a good rule over Denmark.[7]

Hamlet delays, awaiting the God-given opportunity to act with justice, but impatience rankles: "In moments of the deepest depression, it could be natural for doubts to arise as to his role, and whether because of his 'too too sullied flesh' he may not in fact have been appointed as a scourge, in which case his delay is indeed cowardly."[8] At last, in fury, he kills Polonius and thus destroys his own innocence. He regains equilibrium only at the end of the play and, in the providence speech, places himself in God's hands once more. He enters the duel scene without a plan, and God guides him to a public vengeance; but his own hands have been stained, and he must die in the general slaughter. Bowers's interpretation takes fully into account Hamlet's delay, his self-laceration, and his apparent change at the end of the play. True, the delay is never explicitly motivated (the minister and scourge speech occurs fairly late in the play),[9] but "this crux for Hamlet has not really been pointed up, in part because Shakespeare had no need to make it explicit for his audience."[10] We shall hear other historical critics ring the changes on this theme.

Bowers's theory is carried even further by Eleanor Prosser in her recent book *Hamlet and Revenge*,[11] who argues that the revenge that Hamlet undertakes is completely unjustifiable and who draws her detailed argument from both Elizabethan beliefs and literary conventions. Studying documents that reflect Elizabethan attitudes toward revenge, she concludes that it is almost universally condemned, in homily, in story, and in poem.[12] In the drama itself, moreover, revenge is generally the prerogative of the villain, and the man who is willing to wade through blood to his wild justice is damning himself in the process. From 1562 to 1607, the stage revenger was clearly villainous[13]—only Kyd's Hieronimo, Shakespeare's Titus Andronicus, and Marston's Antonio are even ambiguous exceptions to the rule. An artist, of course, can create a moral universe of his own, into which his audience will enter readily enough, and with *Hamlet* the time-approved argument has been that the Ghost imposes on the Prince a sacred duty to revenge, thus giving the play an *ad hoc* moral standard that frees it from the trammels of orthodoxy. Prosser's most startling point is the denial of that argument: the Ghost, she says, is a devil and does indeed abuse Hamlet to damn him.

With Marcellus's comment on the Ghost's final disappearance in Act I, Prosser argues, Shakespeare sets the Ghost in a specifically Christian context:

> It faded on the crowing of the cock.
> Some say that ever, 'gainst that season comes
> Wherein our Saviour's birth is celebrated,
> The bird of dawning singeth all night long;
> And then, they say, no spirit dare stir abroad,
> The nights are wholesome, then no planets strike,
> No fairy takes, nor witch hath power to charm,
> So hallow'd and so gracious is the time. (I.i.157–64)

Accordingly, Prosser sets out to judge the Ghost by the standards of Renaissance pneumatologists: Lewes Lavater, James I, Pierre Le Loyer, and others.[14] By these standards, it appears evil. It stalks away "offended" when Horatio first charges it "by heaven" to speak, and again when the cock crows (though benign spirits were supposed to be able to appear at any hour of the day); in the cellarage scene, it moves with ease through the earth, as only a devil can. Above all, its words to Hamlet reveal diabolic intent: it dwells on the horrors of purgatory rather than the justice, skirting specific detail and relying on "the ghastly inference, the harrowing hint"; it relies on sensual imagery of lust and incest to arose Hamlet's emotions. "If thou hast nature in thee, bear it not": the appeal is to what is violent in Hamlet's nature, not to what is reasonable. Finally, its command is not one of "health and consolation" as would befit a heavenly spirit, but one that violates Christian teaching: revenge. In view of all this, the warning "Taint not thy mind" becomes a mere piece of hypocritical trickery: the Ghost has been doing nothing else.[15]

Thus, Hamlet's dilemma is staggering. On the one hand, he knows that Christians must often suffer the slings and arrows of outrageous fortune. On the other, the Ghost has skillfully touched a sensitive nerve: hatred and outrage and filial love call Hamlet to sweep to his revenge. Small wonder, then, that he delays: his avowed doubt of the Ghost in the soliloquy "O what a rogue and peasant slave am I" is both real and reasonable; his inaction is due to "a thoroughly warranted concern over a real moral issue."[16] As soldier, son, and Renaissance courtier, he is called upon to act, and who would not sympathize? Yet the command to action comes in such a questionable shape that both he and the audience must remember Christian exhortation to charity and patience: this is the burthen of the great "To be or not to be" soliloquy, and "the resolution of the soliloquy on the word 'action,' Hamlet's rejection of coward conscience, and his actions following the Play Scene all indicate that he has accepted the [Ghost's] challenge. He has decided to act."[17]

So deciding, Hamlet veers ever closer to utter villainy. He is murderously angry after the play scene, and his motives for sparing the King at prayer are those of the arch-criminal. (Indeed, the closest parallel to Hamlet's intentions in the prayer scene is the hideous vendetta of Nashe's arch-villain Cutwolf.[18]) It is thus of crucial importance that before his death Hamlet turn to a simple faith in providence, that he relinquish his diabolically inspired task and place himself in the hand of God.

Prosser's general interpretation makes several important contributions to our view of *Hamlet*. Not only does it make excellent sense of the "To be or not to be" soliloquy as a debate between patience and revenge and lend special significance to Hamlet's final conversion, but it also allows a careful, unsentimental view of what many critics have skirted: the wide villainous streak in Hamlet's actions. If Hamlet himself is "about some act that has no relish of salvation in't," his needless lashing out at Ophelia in the nunnery scene or at Gertrude in the closet scene—where he continues to harp on her depravity long after she has confessed and yielded—become clear indices of the precarious state of his own soul. The prayer scene, which critics have sought to explain away by arguing that Hamlet's attitude is perfectly respectable or, equally unconvincingly, that Hamlet does not mean what he says, now can be accepted at its horrible but ineluctable face value, along with the cheerful savagery with which Hamlet engineers the deaths of Rosencrantz and Guildenstern.

Most readers, however, will boggle at the notion of the Ghost as devil. Many hints are thrown out, as we have seen, but a number of these, perhaps, would be lost on those who had not come fresh from a reading of Lavater. If doubt of the Ghost is to be a chief element in the plot, it must be dramatized directly; otherwise, it is easy for the spell of the dramatist to outdo the teaching of the theologian. And, in fact, Hamlet's expressed doubt of the Ghost in his second soliloquy has failed to convince many sensitive readers of the play—it is certainly an awkward bit of staging, perhaps deliberately so (see Appendix A). If we doubt Hamlet's doubt, the Ghost becomes ambiguous at worst. To distrust the sincerity of what Hamlet says and yet feel certain that the Ghost is evil is to put ourselves into the unlikely position of seeing more deeply into things pneumatological than Hamlet himself. If Hamlet does not really doubt the Ghost, has he then been fooled? Has he failed to recognize what, according to Prosser, any apprentice in the audience should have grasped immediately? And is he still fooled after the play scene when he says, "O good Horatio, I'll take the ghost's word for a thousand pound"? For the Ghost can tell the truth about Claudius and still be leading Hamlet on to take revenge and damn himself. Would Hamlet have failed to perceive this? And would Horatio as well? The man who doubted foul play in his father's death, the man who almost immediately smelled out the motives of Rosencrantz and Guildenstern, whom he had no reason to mistrust, would still have doubted the Ghost here, whom he had distrusted at the very first. The difficulty is that we seem to be confronted with two contradictory sets of facts. The first is pneumatological: Elizabethan writings on ghosts indicate that the Ghost in *Hamlet* is indeed diabolic. The second is dramatic: Shakespeare has contrived the play, and particularly the character of Hamlet himself, in such a way that the Ghost's diabolism simply has not been clearly dramatized. The man seeing *Hamlet* believes in Hamlet. While he is in the theater, he will believe in Hamlet to the exclusion of all else. And if Hamlet, for whatever reasons, says he will test the Ghost, and afterwards is convinced that the Ghost has passed the test, then so is the audience.[19] Even the doubt that Prosser sees in the "To be or not to be" soliloquy reflects more than misgivings about the Ghost, for until the play scene is over, Hamlet cannot know whether the injunction to take arms against a sea of troubles is in fact diabolic: he would seem to have embarked on a crucial moral debate without even having investigated the metaphysical provenance of one whole side of the argument. Far from crystallizing Hamlet's doubt of the Ghost, therefore, the soliloquy seems to transcend it, to make it more ambiguous than ever.

Moreover, though the Ghost's speech seems evil from the point of view of the orthodox pneumatologist, it would seem mild indeed to anyone who had recently seen the ghosts of Kyd's Andrea or Marston's Andrugio in the theater: these are bitterly vindictive, and yet their authenticity is unquestioned, nor do their respective plays indicate clearly that they are evil. If they are evil it is because of their extreme bloodthirstiness, and if we look at the Ghost in *Hamlet* from the point of view of a literary tradition rather than of pneumatology, we get the impression that Shakespeare is deliberately toning him down, making him less threatening than the audience might have expected.[20] To be sure, Prosser argues, the ghost of Hamlet is set in a specifically Christian context by Marcellus's speech on the crowing of the cock—but even that is not quite so, for earlier Horatio evokes a completely non-Christian view of ghosts:

> A little ere the mightiest Julius fell,
> The graves stood tenantless, and the sheeted dead
> Did squeak and gibber in the Roman streets. (I.i.114–16)

Christian pneumatology denied such *ad hoc* resurrections of the flesh; these are the ghosts of literature and folklore that always coexist, however inconsistently, with our theologies. We do not know much about ghosts, and neither do the people in the play. "So I have heard," Horatio replies to Marcellus's speech on the crowing of the cock, "and do in part believe it." In *Hamlet* we are in that strange realm where theology, folklore, and poetry come together, and it is scarcely surprising that under such circumstances Shakespeare should create something new and hard to define, something that "shakes our disposition with thoughts beyond the reaches of our souls."

Whether or not the Ghost is "honest," however, does not affect Prosser's argument that in following its dictates Hamlet becomes villainous—though we would have to add: in following its dictates *as he does*.[21] Devil or purgatorial spirit, it bears true witness, and the real issue is how Hamlet will react to the information. To Prosser, there are but two ways: he can take revenge, thus yielding to the devil, or he can wait with Christian patience—God's will be done. There is, however, a third possibility: the impersonal, political revenge. Indeed, Hardin Craig has argued, Hamlet's regal authority distinguishes him from other avengers: "It is no doubt true that revenge for personal injury is regarded as a criminal passion, but is Hamlet's revenge a personal revenge? . . . Hamlet nowhere stresses his position and his responsibility as a prince and a divinely chosen heir to the throne, and yet the play is permeated with that idea."[22] Hamlet himself seems clearly to grasp this notion in Act V:

> Does it not, think'st thee, stand me now upon—
> He that hath kill'd my king, and whor'd my mother;
> Popp'd in between the election and my hopes;
> Thrown out his angle for my proper life,
> And with such cozenage—is't not perfect conscience
> To quit him with this arm? And is't not to be damn'd
> To let this canker of our nature come
> In further evil? (V.ii.63–70)

Prosser finds this speech embarrassing and can only suggest that it is a bit of undigested material that got stuck into the play at that point through the vagaries of textual evolution.[23] But if revenge is sometimes a political act and not merely a personal one, if Hamlet has more in common with Malcolm than with Tourneur's Vendice, then the speech is an integral part of the play's resolution, for here Hamlet's concern with his own problems and antagonisms is merged perfectly with concern for the state. Claudius has killed his "king," not his "father." Hamlet sees himself as the rightful heir to the throne; the present king is a canker to "our" nature—the nature of the state as a whole. To kill him is an act of conscience, which need no longer make cowards of us all.

Prosser's achievement is twofold. First, more than almost any other critic, she calls attention to and attempts to define Hamlet's near approach to villainy; thus, she makes dramatic sense of the perplexing polarity of the prayer scene and the providence speeches, and in her we reach the utmost limit of the reaction to the sentimental Hamlet of the last century. Second, her work itself presents an important problem in the nature of the historical allegory. With great care she posits a clear doctrine of Christian patience underlying the action of the play and concludes that for the audience that bears this doctrine in mind the play is freed from the mystery, the perplexity with which seven generations have endowed it. The play's horizons become clearer, if narrower. But, as we shall see, there is no better proof of the extrinsic nature of interpretation than the ease with which this argument can be reversed. Hamlet lives in perplexity; we can resolve his perplexity with our doctrines or we can find that his perplexity makes our doctrines dubious. At the end of the play Hamlet seems to have reached a solution to his problems: have we reached it with him or, like Horatio, have we been waiting for him to catch up?

Modern historical critics have not limited themselves merely to reassessing the ethics of revenge, for *Hamlet* does not present an ordinary revenge but, rather, the plot of a prince upon the life of a king: it is a political tragedy with a vengeance. Hamlet must find his way in an ethical maze of vengeance and divine right, of civic corruption and royal prerogative. Thus, with John W. Draper's book *The Hamlet of Shakespeare's Audience*,[24] the critical horizons expand to embrace, in the guise of Elsinore and Denmark, the bustling society of Shakespeare's own age. To Draper, *Hamlet* is an imitation of men "in the widest possible social relationships, and in the act of doing and thinking the very deeds and thoughts proper to the occasion and to their social rank,"[25] and, in particular, of thoughts and deeds "in relation to the predominant social institution of the age, the court."[26]

In his treatment of Hamlet's personality, accordingly, Draper stresses those features that correspond to his allegory:

> Shakespeare especially develops Hamlet as the courtier, the ideal gentleman of the Renaissance. . . . Hamlet is master of every note in the gamut of courtly behavior: he can be gracious and winning with Horatio, elaborate and affected with Osric, merry and intimate with Rosencrantz and Guildenstern; he can show mock ceremony to Polonius, and to his mother, a mixture of affection and disgust. He can move among the social

classes graciously giving to each one just a trifle more than its due of courtesy: the normal Hamlet is truly the "mould of form."[27]

As his father's son and the admirer of Fortinbras, as an expert fencer, and as the daring man of action who unhesitatingly accosts Ghost and pirates, Hamlet is "a soldier in training, in ideals, and in execution."[28] That Hamlet is a courtier is true; that he is "especially" a courtier is true, of course, only in an interpretation that looks at the play from the point of view of the court.

Having envisaged such a hero, Draper naturally rejects the Romantic interpretation of a subjective barrier to revenge. The overcontemplative Hamlet of Coleridge or Schlegel would be alien to the Elizabethan rejection of the *vita contemplativa*, alien, indeed, to the creator of Prospero, who renounces his studies to return to his dukedom.[29] That Hamlet is melancholy, Draper does not deny. He argues, however, that the melancholy is caused by his chafing at his own inaction and that this inaction stems from his concern over the proper course for him to take.[30] The delay of Hamlet the courtier-soldier in no way tarnishes the image of the noble man of action. Rather, his hesitation is perfectly reasonable. At first, he refuses to commit regicide on the dubious evidence of the Ghost, and once he has tested the Ghost with the play-within-the-play, he no longer has an opportunity to act.[31] Thus, we see a Hamlet unwillingly caught up in palace intrigue,[32] a Hamlet "in revolt against the deviousness of his task; the man of action whom events have forced to pause and weigh and wait."[33] Once more, the barriers to revenge have been erected in the external world of ethics.

Ultimately, to Draper, the theme of *Hamlet* is regicide, the most primal court antagonism:

> This matter of regicide is the politico-moral question that lies behind Claudius' assassination of the Elder Hamlet; this is the question of "conscience" that gives Hamlet pause, and makes him unwilling to damn his soul by killing God's Anointed, unless he is doubly sure that the Ghost spoke truth; Divine Right wins Laertes to the side of Claudius; and the horror of his treacherous

murder of his Prince makes Laertes confess as he dies, and at once brings on the killing of Claudius. A play of regicide was a play on the political theory of the Divine Right of Kings. Shakespeare's *Hamlet* is such a play; and its repeated acceptance of the Divine Right theory is quite what one would expect of a tragedy written about the time of the accession of James I. Indeed, a court-dramatist could hardly have written otherwise of government.[34]

Passing over the enormous probability that *Hamlet* was written well before the accession of James I, we should observe that the text of the play permits this far-reaching interpretation of regicide but does not require it. It is true that Claudius is a regicide; yet regicide is not the sole moral issue that underlies the murder of the former king. Indeed, when Claudius himself refers to his offense, his first thought is that "It hath the primal eldest curse upon't,/ A brother's murther!" (III.iii.37–38). Again, there is nothing in Laertes' dying words that requires us to assume that his remorse is increased by Hamlet's rank; nor, indeed, is there any textual ground for believing that Divine Right dulls his wrath against Claudius:

> To hell, allegiance! vows to the blackest devil!
> Conscience and grace, to the profoundest pit!
> I dare damnation. To this point I stand,
> That both the worlds I give to negligence,
> Let come what comes; only I'll be reveng'd
> Most throughly for my father. (IV.v.131–36)

And he is argued into peace only when he decides that to revenge is to cooperate with Claudius, not to defy him.

Most important, of course, is Draper's assertion that unwillingness to commit regicide is what stays Hamlet's hand until the Ghost's word is verified in the play scene. Again, there is no direct evidence in the play that such is Hamlet's concern. In the soliloquy "O, what a rogue and peasant slave am I," Hamlet does wonder if the Ghost does not abuse him to damn him (see Appendix A), and toward the end of the play he enumerates Claudius's offenses to Horatio and then asks, "is't not perfect conscience/ To quit him with this arm?" (V.ii.67–68). But were Claudius innocent, Hamlet would be damned whether his victim were king or not, and although Hamlet may show some regicidal scruples at the end of the play, there is no direct evidence that he has had them all along.

It is true that regicide is a recurrent theme in the play. Events are set in motion by Claudius's initial act of regicide. Laertes, in the speech just quoted, knows the consequences of killing a king, though he is determined to ignore them, and in the face of his threats Claudius says to Gertrude,

> Do not fear our person.
> There's such divinity doth hedge a king
> That treason can but peep to what it would,
> Acts little of his will. (IV.v.122–25)

After the play scene, Guildenstern talks to Claudius of the

> holy and religious fear it is
> To keep those many many bodies safe
> That live and feed upon your majesty, (III.iii.8–10)

and Rosencrantz echoes him with the famous "cesse of majesty" speech. It does not follow, of course, that such speeches constitute the author's message: each character says what under the circumstances comes naturally to him, as avenger, as King, or as toady. In any case, such speeches are absent from Hamlet's role, perhaps conspicuously absent. It can well be argued that they are absent because Hamlet's motive is so obvious that it may safely remain tacit, but it could just as well be argued that the widespread concern with regicide is conspicuous in its failure to explain Hamlet's motives, which lie elsewhere, and thus that his mystery is deepened. Indeed, in his book *Conscience and the King* Bertram Joseph provides an interpretation paralleling Draper's in most points but ignoring the theme of regicide:

> Here are the bare bones of the tragedy: we are given a simple clear-cut issue—indeed, it might be taken as a classic instance of the tragic dilemma. On one side everything noble in the Prince impels him to strike and avenge his father; on the other looms the terrifying possibility that the Ghost may be false, in which case to kill Claudius means eternal punishment in Hell. If, as I

believe, the Elizabethans realized this, they also understood that until the problem was disposed of, Hamlet must delay.[35]

The argument for the allegory of regicide, like so much historical allegory, must assume that what is obscure today would be clear to an Elizabethan audience. Thus, a hypothesis about the play is verified by a related hypothesis about the audience. Here, the assumption is that the Elizabethan (or Jacobean) audience would have been quick to detect the theme of regicide.[36] But we have also been told that they would have been quick to perceive Hamlet's melancholia, or the primacy of the plot, or moral scruples concerning the nature of revenge. Many reasons for delay may be supplied by a putative audience; the point is that none is explicitly supplied by the play. In emphasizing the court allegory Draper must go beyond the text; perhaps, in his neglect of the self-laceration of the soliloquies, he even goes counter to the text.

Draper's interpretation of *Hamlet,* however, is a useful corrective to many of the excesses of Romantic criticism. Prince Hamlet may dominate the play, yet it is not the monologue that the Romantics would sometimes seem to make it. Draper calls attention to the society in which the characters move. He has given us one of the most thoroughgoing interpretations of *Hamlet* as a dynastic tragedy, and if the issues of dynasty are not the major concern of the hero, there can be no doubt that they are one of the chief concerns of the play, which reaches beyond the hero to depict "a perennial social struggle, the *one* against the *many,* the individual in revolt against a society that has, unwittingly or not, compromised with evil until it cannot, or should not, stand."[37] Draper is certainly not wrong in ascribing political issues to *Hamlet;* if he errs, it is in ascribing purely political motives to the play's hero and thereby in making a part of the play into the whole. Thus, however, is raised the important question of how a philosophically inclined melancholiac is to be artistically fused with a play containing strong political themes. To Robertson, Hamlet's melancholy serves to motivate the delay and thus lend probability to the action; Draper, looking beyond action, indirectly asks whether the theme of the neurasthenic is compatible with the theme of regicide.

3

The critics we have studied so far in this chapter and the last show us a Hamlet grappling with problems presented by orthodox morality or struggling with facts (such as his own weakness) adequately accounted for in Elizabethan cosmology. In neither case does he question this morality or doubt this cosmology. If these critics were inclined to heed T. S. Eliot's claim that Hamlet's emotion is in excess of the facts as they appear, they would answer the problem with an historical elucidation of these facts: Hamlet's emotion is not in excess of the facts as they would appear to an Elizabethan. The sixteenth century, however, was in a sufficient state of intellectual flux to make possible an entirely different interpretation, one that finds the facts as they appear quite equal to Hamlet's emotion, not because they are horrible in themselves but because orthodox systems of belief cannot explain them.

As Elizabeth's reign drew to a close, Geoffrey Bush notes in *Shakespeare and the Natural Condition,* men increasingly perceived the difference between *natura naturata* and *natura naturans,* between things in nature and the natural laws supposed to govern them.[38] To a poet such as Spenser, the two natures were unified: the natural changes in the world were part of the world's design. Such was the orthodox doctrine, which stemmed from the Middle Ages. The more modern Bacon, however, planned to "isolate and explore natural events by themselves, to perfect . . . 'a natural philosophy pure and unmixed.' "[39] Both writers were optimistic because they both ignored the possibility of a conflict between *natura naturata* and *natura naturans*— Spenser by blinding himself to much of the world of phenomena, Bacon by choosing to ignore totally the old natural order. We have now to examine those critics who suggest that Hamlet is denied the optimism of either system and that in *Hamlet* "we are made to see the fatal collision between fact and idea, and we witness the effort of human character to reach a settlement, without aid, between these two aspects of the natural situation."[40]

If the critic assumes such a conflict between fact and idea, then his interpretation is quite different from the criticism we have just examined. The solution to Hamlet's problem now lies neither in orthodox schemes of moral self-improvement nor in casuistry. Rather, Hamlet is shaken with thoughts beyond the reach of his soul, is torn between his allegiance to his old system of thinking and the new facts that he perceives. The conflict in his mind cannot be resolved until the importance of either the system or the facts is rejected. This conflict is the subject of the play, and the mental tension that the conflict causes results in Hamlet's melancholy and delay.

In his essay "The Philosophy of Hamlet," Joseph E. Baker observes that *Hamlet* portrays "what actually happens in the mind of a man when he suddenly finds that the world does not live up to his ideals."[41] The worlds of natural events and natural law are torn asunder: "What we find in *Hamlet* is, to put it in five words, an opposition between spirit and phenomena. . . . *Hamlet* is not a tragedy of shattered idealism. It is rather a tragedy of awakened idealism, of shattering idealism."[42] Hamlet, Baker continues, is the spiritual heir of Plato and of medieval Catholic realism.[43] This is not to say that Hamlet is a man of ideals alone, a spiritualistic monist. Rather, he is a dualist for whom, nevertheless, "physical and biological Nature is by no means the key to human life; indeed, he definitely takes higher ground and rejects, morally if not metaphysically, all that we can see around us, all that we recognize as reaching us through the senses, all those portions of experience that come within the range of science."[44] But by stressing Hamlet's idealism in order to prove that Hamlet "is at the farthest pole removed from the modern scepticism which denies the validity of moral laws,"[45] Baker is inclined to neglect Hamlet's deep concern with matters of physical fact. If Hamlet exhibits platonic contempt for the uses of this world and the glory of mortal things, he nevertheless lacks the serenity of a Plato. He is not only upset at Gertrude's behavior, his imagination is obsessed with all its physical details:

> Nay, but to live
> In the rank sweat of an enseamed bed,
> Stew'd in corruption, honeying and making love
> Over the nasty sty! (III.iv.91–94)

Hamlet seems unable to extricate himself from the more sordid facts of the physical reality that he scorns.[46] He perceives evil that the old cosmology cannot explain. He retains the ideals of this cosmology; what is gone is the relationship between ideals and the facts of earthly existence. Earth seems cut off from heaven; the evil that exists is not, nor it cannot come to good (I.ii.158). Amid this apparently irreconcilable conflict Hamlet must act, involved with the things of this earth, yet without confidence in them. *Hamlet* thus becomes not a tragedy of idealism but something far more frightening: a tragedy of cosmic absurdity.

Probably the most celebrated exposition of this view is Theodore Spencer's *Shakespeare and the Nature of Man.* In *Hamlet,* Spencer argues, the orthodox beliefs in the liaison between natural order and natural fact "are an essential part of the hero's consciousness, and his discovery that they are not true, his awareness of the conflict between what theory taught and what experience proves, wrecks him."[47] The specific experiences in question, for Spencer, are Hamlet's own inaction and Gertrude's o'erhasty marriage, both proving that "the traditional order in which reason should be in control of passion is only an appearance."[48]

Surely there is much that is ideal-shattering in Hamlet's new experience: that the crown of Denmark should be in the hands of an unworthy man, that this "smiling" king should be a regicide and fratricide, that Gertrude should have married him, and that Hamlet himself seems unable to do anything to remedy the situation. Hamlet's problem is that of a man suddenly come face-to-face with evil. But a realization of evil might or might not take an orthodox form. As Spencer observes: "In the immediate intellectual background of the late sixteenth century, two main attacks were being made on the idealistic picture of the nobility and dignity of man. There was the traditional attack, which described man's wretchedness since the fall, but which was still based on a firm belief in man's crucial place in the center of things; and there was the newer attack [of empiricism], which . . . threatened to destroy that belief itself."[49] The crucial question, therefore, is whether Hamlet's new view of evil transcends orthodox explanation. Spencer himself is not perfectly clear on this point. Commenting on Hamlet's praise of reason in the soliloquy "How all occasions do inform against me," he observes:

The standard which Hamlet's soliloquy describes is not only the standard which his own lack of action so agonizingly seems to violate, it is also the standard which was violated by Gertrude in mourning so briefly for her first husband, and in unnaturally yielding to her lust. . . . And it is because he has this high standard that he is so torn apart by discovering that the traditional order in which reason should be in control of passion is only an appearance, and that the reality of his mother's action proves human beings to be only beasts, their specific function gone.[50]

This passage is somewhat ambiguous. On the one hand, Hamlet's problem seems no more than an awareness that man is bestial when ungoverned by reason—an awareness which is at the heart of orthodox Christian belief. Or, on the other hand, is the very cosmic structure that admits this bestiality no more than an "appearance"? Gertrude yields "unnaturally" to her lust; yet we cannot tell whether Spencer is using the word in its normative or descriptive sense. Are Hamlet's standards "violated"—or do they suddenly cease to exist?

The text itself, I think, resolves the ambiguity in the allegory of "man as tradition said he should be and what experience proved he was."[51] The two facts that seem most to torture Hamlet are, as Spencer has observed, his mother's remarriage and his own inaction. These provide the content of three soliloquies plus the long tirade (barring interruptions, his longest single speech) in Gertrude's chamber.[52] E. M. W. Tillyard has likened Hamlet's shock at Gertrude's remarriage to the anguish of the abandoned Troilus when he sees Cressida with Diomedes:[53]

> This she? No, this is Diomed's Cressida!
> If beauty have a soul, this is not she;
> If souls guide vows, if vows be sanctimonies,
> If sanctimony be the gods' delight,
> If there be rule in unity itself—
> This is not she. . . .
> Instance, O instance! strong as Pluto's gates:
> Cressid is mine, tied with the bonds of heaven.
> Instance, O instance! strong as heaven itself:

The bonds of heaven are slipp'd, dissolv'd, and loos'd;
And with another knot, five-finger-tied,
The fractions of her faith, orts of her love,
The fragments, scraps, the bits, and greasy relics
Of her o'ereaten faith, are given to Diomed. (V.ii.137–60)

Here is outrage so great that Troilus's words give it cosmic proportion.
Yet Cressida's sin upsets nothing in the orthodox order of the universe.
The explanation of her action lies on her own lips:

Ah, poor our sex! this fault in us I find,
The error of our eye directs our mind.
What error leads must err. O, then conclude
Minds sway'd by eyes are full of turpitude. (V.ii.109–12)

In short, she is letting her senses sway her reason; her sin is great, but
for all that, it is perfectly conventional. For one critical moment,
indeed, Troilus's world does seem shattered: he stands on the verge of
general misogyny such as Hamlet exhibits in the nunnery scene, and
in the passage above he momentarily challenges the "rule in unity
itself." But Troilus ultimately does not go as far as Hamlet: the
Cressid before his eyes is, indeed, not the Cressid whom he loved,
and his misogyny dissolves into bitter personal hatred:

O Cressid! O false Cressid! false, false, false!
Let all untruths stand by thy stained name
And they'll seem glorious. (V.ii.178–80)

According to Tillyard, such a shock, showing human beings to be
"capable of all baseness," is what Hamlet feels at Gertrude's choice
of Claudius: she, too, indulges in the error of her eyes. But Gertrude's
choice appears worse to Hamlet than Cressida's to Troilus, and
Hamlet's shock is deeper. Hamlet hints early at the problem, giving
expression to the standard moral comparison of man and beast—but
with a difference:

O God! a beast that wants discourse of reason
Would have mourn'd longer. (I.ii.150–51)

Gertrude is not bestial, as Cressida is, but somehow worse than bestial

—guilty of a sin that the standard formula fails to account for. This was sometime a paradox, but now the time gives it proof. What is a hint in the first act becomes explicit in the third, when Hamlet confronts his mother with the portraits of her two husbands:

> Have you eyes?
> Could you on this fair mountain leave to feed
> And batten on this moor? Ha! have you eyes?
> You cannot call it love; for at your age
> The heyday in the blood is tame, it's humble,
> And waits upon the judgment; and what judgment
> Would step from this to this? Sense sure you have,
> Else could you not have motion; but sure that sense
> Is apoplex'd; for madness would not err,
> Nor sense to ecstacy was ne'er so thrall'd
> But it reserved some quantity of choice
> To serve in such a difference. What devil was't
> That thus has cozen'd you at hoodman-blind?
> Eyes without feeling, feeling without sight,
> Ears without hands or eyes, smelling sans all,
> Or but a sickly part of one true sense
> Could not so mope. (III.iv.65–81)

Gertrude's action is inexplicable to Hamlet, for her choice is so bad that even man's potentially bestial nature fails to explain it. Theologians such as Richard Hooker could take such choices in their stride:

> The object of Appetite is whatever sensible good may be wished for; the object of Will is that good which Reason doth lead us to seek. . . .
>
> In doing evil, we prefer a less good before a greater, the greatness whereof is by reason investigable and may be known.[54]

Such was Cressida's choice. The "sensible good" of Diomedes' love conquered her heavenly vows to Troilus, which reason should have led her to keep. But Gertrude does not even choose the lesser of two goods: in Hamlet's eyes the choice of Claudius is purely bad, justified by neither sense nor reason, and expressable only by the exasperated, irresolvable paradox that frost doth burn.[55]

Hamlet's mind is quick to generalize, as Spencer points out,[56] and the Elizabethan cosmology, in which all facts were related by analogy, was quick to encourage such generalization, so it is not surprising that one evil fact should be sufficient to blacken Hamlet's view of the entire universe. Gertrude's act is

> such a deed
> As from the body of contraction plucks
> The very soul, and sweet religion makes
> A rhapsody of words! Heaven's face doth glow;
> Yea, this solidity and compound mass,
> With tristful visage, as against the doom,
> Is thought-sick at the act. (III.iv.45–51)

If Hamlet cannot comprehend Gertrude's action, he can no better understand his own inaction. He praises reason, we have seen, then goes on to admit that reason is insufficient:

> I do not know
> Why yet I live to say 'This thing's to do,'
> Sith I have cause, and will, and strength, and means
> To do't. (IV.iv.43–46)

Cause and will are the motive and motion of reason; Hamlet has "excitements of his reason and his blood" (l. 58), yet lets all sleep—another paradox from the point of view of orthodox psychology. It is as if, in Bush's words, "there is doubt whether it is sufficient to be our natural selves."[57]

Granted such an interpretation, Hamlet's final allusions to providence assume prime importance. The notion that "there's a divinity that shapes our ends, rough-hew them how we will," expresses a faith that heaven is somehow working upon earth after all, that the facts of human existence are somehow justified, though no longer by the intricate superstructure of explanation built up in the Middle Ages. Hamlet's new serenity approaches that of Montaigne, who turned sceptically from reason and philosophy to a humble faith in God:

Ce n'est pas par discours ou par nostre entendement que nous

avons receu nostre religion, c'est par authorité et par commande-
ment estranger. La foiblesse de nostre jugement nous y ayde
plus que la force, et nostre aveuglement plus que nostre
clervoyance.[58]

And at the end of the play the uses of this world no longer seem to
Hamlet weary, stale, flat, and unprofitable: his dying concerns are his
earthly reputation and the settlement of the kingdom. The obvious
implication is that he once more realizes the possibility of a link
between ideal and fact, between heaven and earth.[59] Spencer observes
the significance of his calmness:

> He is no longer *in* the tumult, but above it; he is no longer
> "passion's slave," but a man who sees himself as a part of the
> order of things, even though his final view of that order, ex-
> hausted, resigned, and in a way exalted, is very different from
> the youthful rosy picture his Renaissance theoretical education
> had given him. . . . To be resigned, as Hamlet is resigned,
> is to be made, by experience instead of by theory, once more
> aware of the world's order.[60]

Again, Spencer is not clear as to whether Hamlet has transcended the
Elizabethan cosmology or has simply felt it reinforced by experience. I
have suggested that Hamlet's final state is not an awareness of the
world's order but rather a faith that somehow this order, though
different from what he had thought, nevertheless exists. As Bush
maintains,

> His rashness is rewarded: his life reaches a point of perfect
> quiet and complete possibility, and in this moment of sudden
> comfort it is made known that to share knowingly in time is to
> arrive at an extremity of natural existence where the readiness
> is all, and where time and what is beyond time come together.[61]

4

Early in his book, Draper provides what may be taken as a classic
manifesto of much historical criticism:

Only by making himself over into an Elizabethan, if that be possible, and seeing the play given complete, on an Elizabethan stage and in Elizabethan fashion, could the subjective critic achieve a result that would approximate Shakespeare's meaning; and Shakespeare's meaning, in so far as it can be learned, is the only true or important meaning.[62]

One danger of this position is that it may sometimes lead the critic to confuse the typically Elizabethan with those aspects of Elizabethan life that differ from our own and thus to ignore the possibility of a wide range of beliefs and attitudes that the two ages have held in common. Historical criticism at its worst can sink into the purely esoteric. The chief difficulty with a position like Draper's, however, is that it assumes that the attribute "Elizabethan" is unambiguous, and that the Elizabethan reaction itself to Hamlet must have been univocal. Granted this assumption, the critic can stress a priori those features in the play that reflect what he has found to be typically Elizabethan. But we have now studied a number of interpretations of Hamlet, each of them based on a careful research into Elizabethan ethical thought, and these interpretations are not all compatible. Which of them is to be accepted cannot, of course, be determined by an examination of the Elizabethan ethos; the very possibility of such different views of Hamlet indicate that this ethos is too vast and too variegated to provide an unambiguous approach to such a complex work. If melancholia might—but need not—paralyze the will, then the reaction of the Elizabethan audience to Hamlet's delay could rest in part on each spectator's own idea of melancholy. The allusion to providence at the end of the play might stress the control of the action by God and be derived from orthodox Elizabethan sermons,[63] or it might stress Hamlet's own conversion of soul as he abandons this orthodoxy to seek peace in a devoutness refined by Montaignesque skepticism. In either case, historical criticism can correct the anachronistic view of the modern reader, who may be inclined to dismiss the validity of providence altogether, but the further question of how providence functions in the play remains unsettled; as with all other schools of interpretation, the historical can suggest solutions but not compel acceptance.

What each critic considers central to the play depends, once more, on the hypothesis that he brings to bear on the text. Spencer stresses the aspects of Hamlet's behavior that Draper ignores or denies:

> Hamlet's disillusionment is a partial expression of a general predicament. . . . His discovery of the difference between appearance and reality, which produced in his mind an effect so disillusioning that it paralyzed the sources of deliberate action, was a symptom that the Renaissance in general had brought with it a new set of problems, had opened new psychological vistas, which the earlier views of man had not so completely explored.[64]

Once more, the play *Hamlet* reflects a general idea, and Hamlet himself becomes a sort of Everyman. Not only Hamlet's character but the crucial fact of the plot, the delay, becomes simply a corollary of Hamlet's new and painful awareness.[65] The conflict between ideal and factual gives shape to everything else in the play: "The difference between appearance and reality is continually referred to throughout the play by other people besides Hamlet himself; Polonius, the ghost, the king, all mention it in one way or another; the frequency with which images of painting, of covering up hidden diseases, are used is another illustration of its prevalence; and it is the central idea of Hamlet's meditations in the graveyard."[66] For the ethical-historical critic in general, it is not the action that is the soul of the play, as in Aristotle or Stoll; nor character, as in Campbell. Rather, the essence of the play is historically formulable thought.

The play's purpose, meanwhile, depends on the allegory. Bertram Joseph expresses the conservative view that "the audience finds itself responding to a story which reaffirms what has been said countless times, but which now comes with the force of a fresh assertion in its new imaginative form."[67] If the conservative world view is challenged simply in its overoptimistic form and is ultimately vindicated, then, as Paul N. Siegel suggests, the play challenges the complacency of the audience, "only to renew their basic faith and render it richer and deeper by having been forced to assimilate what Hamlet and Lear saw."[68] Finally, for the critic who posits the breakdown of the orthodox order, the play serves neither as a reassurance nor as a reinforcement of orthodox beliefs but as a "stretching into hitherto inarticulate reaches of experience."[69]

The intellectual history of Shakespeare's time presents many faces to the student: we must know how to use an interpretation of *Hamlet* that begins, overtly or otherwise, with an interpretation of *Hamlet*'s original audience and Shakespeare's commitment to it. It is difficult under any circumstances to draw a priori conclusions about a playwright's intellectual commitments; it is more difficult when he lived in an age substantially different from our own; and it becomes especially difficult if he lived in an age of intellectual flux, in which it is sometimes hard, looking back, to distinguish between orthodoxy and reaction, and in which the same opinion may have been uttered with complacency one day and militancy the next. Hooker's *Ecclesiastical Polity*, we need to remind ourselves, was not a scholastic treatise but a polemic against the rising new orthodoxy of the Puritans. King James's doctrine of Divine Right, political orthodoxy in its own day, nevertheless becomes revolutionary when seen against the background of the Middle Ages, whose political theorists grant authority to government through the intermediary of the people; while the radical *Vindiciae contra Tyrannos* shares fundamental points with John of Salisbury's venerable *Polycraticus*.[70] Certain views, to be sure, were held more widely than others, and a playwright may well have shared and expressed them. But though we may find such advocacy in his works, we cannot assume it beforehand. On the contrary, the variety of approaches dealt with in this chapter suggests that each major facet of Elizabethan intellectual life may have the potential to suggest a new facet of *Hamlet* and that a broad historical view of the play must therefore share the complexity of the age from which the play emerged. This is not to suggest complete historical relativism or the futility of historical interpretation. It is to suggest that both play and age are rich.

Psychological Interpretation:
Main-Line Criticism Since Bradley

5

1

Even in the twentieth century, the criticism of Coleridge has not ceased to bear fruit. Bradley attacked the conception of an over-intellectual Hamlet, of a Hamlet possessing "great, enormous, intellectual activity, and a consequent proportionate aversion to real action,"[1] yet not long after Bradley delivered his lectures on Shakespeare, E. K. Chambers could write: "[*Hamlet*] is the tragedy of the *intellectuel*, of the impotence of the over-cultivated imagination and the over-subtilized reasoning powers to meet the call of everyday life for practical efficiency."[2] And later still, W. F. Trench seems to have taken up Bradley's suggestion of Hamlet as a "tragedy of moral idealism"[3] only to further an interpretation hearkening back to Goethe himself:

> The situation, then, is this: an idealist has been brought of a sudden face to face with actuality, and finds himself called upon to play a man's part in a simple and primitive form of life's conflict. And in Denmark in the days of Hamlet idealism will surely fail as signally as it did in Egypt in the days of King Akhnaton. For Hamlet, characterized by a scrupulous morality, and possessed of the highly nervous temperament often associated with great refinement, is peculiarly unfit for primitive conditions. . . . Made for something immeasurably better than

Danish politics and regicide, he finds those to be his uncongenial sphere and this [revenge] his burdensome duty.[4]

In the first decades of this century, then, the main line of *Hamlet* criticism exhibited its inheritance from the great Romantic critics of a century earlier, sometimes to the point of mere repetition.

An important innovation of Bradley's was his claim that the hyperintellectuality of Coleridge's Hamlet and the skepticism of Schlegel's were no more than symptoms of melancholy—a melancholy "adverse to *any* kind of decided action."[5] In the light of the interpretations that were to come, perhaps Bradley's most pregnant statement was: "I have no doubt that many readers of the play would understand it better if they read an account of melancholia in a work on mental diseases."[6] So saying, Bradley paved the way for allegories made possible by modern psychology at a time when modern psychology was first coming into its own.[7] Later, the psychoanalyst Ernest Jones could follow Bradley's lead by asserting: "The play is mainly concerned with a hero's unavailing fight against a disordered mind. Hence it is surely appropriate for a medical psychologist to offer a contribution based on his special knowledge of the deeper layers of the mind where such disorders arise."[8] The allegorical hypothesis is clear. As F. L. Lucas puts it: "One cannot talk rationally about human behaviour if one realizes so little how fantastically irrational it often is. . . . I believe it the critic's business to learn more of men as well as books—of men in their perpetual unreason."[9] According to this allegory, literature is an imitation of man's soul, and thus knowledge of the one must go hand in hand with knowledge of the other. The critic and the psychologist become one.

The critic who seems most to have followed this suggestion of Bradley's is Joseph Quincy Adams. Hamlet is an idealist, and the events of the play destroy his idealism. "A series of blows, coming one fast on the heels of another, is to shatter his very being, and make him reel upon the verge of madness."[10] Most interesting for our purposes is the fact that Adams cites the psychiatrists Krafft-Ebing, Macpherson, and Régis in his diagnosis of Hamlet's behavior. From them Adams concludes that Hamlet is suffering from "sub-acute" melancholia, characterized by *tedium vitae,* suicidal impulses, desire for solitude, irritability, and gloomy brooding.[11] Most important of all, the melancholiac suffers from loss of will. Adams quotes Régis:

> The whole [sub-acute melancholia] is comprised in or limited to a general condition of depression, inaction, and impotence. The patients avoid all labor, all occupation, and all society; . . . [they are] incapable of wishing, or deciding on, or of making an effort.[12]

Hence, of course, the delay. We may note that Hamlet's melancholia as described by Adams is similar to that described by Renaissance moral philosophers, though the more modern psychiatrists have dispensed, of course, with the cumbersome and fictitious Elizabethan physiology—as well as with the moral attitudes implicit in Elizabethan psychology. Adams does mention the likelihood of Shakespeare's familiarity with such writers as Timothy Bright but saves the day for modern psychology by asserting that Shakespeare's knowledge of melancholia "doubtless was derived from actual observation of its working on some one close to him, or what is more likely, from his own personal experience with a serious and prolonged attack."[13]

Three objections to Adams's interpretation offer themselves. First, of course, the psychiatrists he cites wrote near the turn of the century and do not represent the latest thinking on melancholia. More important, the aboulia, or loss of will, that these psychiatrists describe is total: "a general condition," as Régis says, "of depression, inaction, and impotence." But as we have seen in the case of Elizabethan psychology, and as Bradley had been at great pains to point out, "depression," "impotence," and "inaction" are hardly the words we would use to describe the Hamlet who discourses wittily to the players, leaps on board the pirate ship, rigs the elaborate mousetrap, or breaks away from his friends to follow the Ghost to the farther reaches of the battlements. Hamlet cannot be suffering from the melancholia that Krafft-Ebing describes when he says that "the solidarity of the psychic activities causes the depression to be total."[14] In this respect, Bradley is more accurate than his disciple. Bradley has some conception of Hamlet suffering from a specific aboulia: Hamlet is indeed active as he plans the play or foils the King's plot to have him killed in England, but "these were not *the* action on which his morbid self-feeling had centered."[15]

But the most important objection to Adams's interpretation is that it divorces Hamlet's melancholia from anything that can give the play human significance. The psychiatry that Adams uses is essentially diagnostic. It has none of the moral overtones of Elizabethan psychology, and, unlike psychoanalysis, it has no bearing on universal spiritual conflicts. As Freud observes:

> It is true that the psychiatric branch of medicine occupies itself with describing the different forms of recognizable mental disturbances and grouping them in clinical pictures, but in their best moments psychiatrists themselves are doubtful whether their purely descriptive formulations deserve to be called science. The origin, mechanism, and interrelations of the symptoms which make up these clinical pictures are undiscovered.[16]

The early psychiatrists that Adams cites deal only in symptoms, and symptoms of mental illness are not particularly interesting when considered apart from a cause that links them to universal experience. In their own ways, faculty psychology and psychoanalysis each supply such a cause, but to call Hamlet a melancholiac, in Adams's sense of that word, can evoke no more feeling in the spectator than to announce that the Prince has a common cold. Adams himself recognizes this problem: "It would be a grave error to assume that Shakespeare's main interest lies in revealing the symptoms of this emotional illness. His prime interest lies in a study of the *disillusionment* of an idealist; melancholia is thus merely incidental. Yet," Adams adds, "so important is it for an understanding of Hamlet's behavior that we must know its general features."[17] In this manner the chief point of interest in the play is rather awkwardly separated from the chief motivating agent of the plot, the tragic from the psychological. Moreover, if for an understanding of Hamlet's behavior we must indeed be familiar with the workings of melancholia, then we are caught in what must be an uncomfortable dilemma for a Bradleian writing after the evolutionist critics. Either we must admit that a certain amount of esoteric information is necessary to the enjoyment of the play, in which case the play cannot be popular entertainment, or we must have recourse to historical criticism ("To the Elizabethan audience, Hamlet's melancholy would have been clear," and so forth). In either case the play becomes unclear to the average modern theatergoer. To all of these problems psychoanalysis provides a solution, though in the process it raises a number of highly interesting difficulties of its own.

2

Psychoanalytic criticism is often thought of as an attempt to probe beneath the surface of an object that consists only of surface. It is frequently seen as a gratuitous foisting of a complex human soul on a body of words, with no apparent concern for the author's initial concept or the audience's response. And indeed, a fairly large proportion of psycholanalytic criticism does seem arbitrary and ultimately—to the layman, at least—worthless. "If Hamlet has an Oedipus complex," more than one critic has asked, "what business is it of ours?" The question is not rhetorical. If the analyst aims at more than simply illustrating his latest theory or case history with a reference to *Hamlet,* he must answer it. In the remainder of this chapter, thus, we will examine not only what psychoanalysis has to say about *Hamlet,* but also why what it says may be our business.

The first psychoanalytic interpretation of *Hamlet* appeared in a footnote to Freud's *The Interpretation of Dreams* (1900).[18] This footnote is appended to Freud's first explanation of the Oedipus myth and thus occupies a central position in psychoanalytic thought. The complex that bears the name of Oedipus might well have been named after Hamlet instead—with what effects on Shakespearean criticism it is interesting to speculate. Since 1900, the initial oedipal view of Hamlet has been modified by analysts who describe the play in terms of pre-oedipal states, myth, Jungian archetype, and the like.[19] Some of these later views, notably the mythological study of Otto Rank, have been incorporated into Ernest Jones's *Hamlet and Oedipus,* the last and most detailed of his several Freudian treatments of the play; in any case, very few analysts attack the Freudian interpretation of *Hamlet,* though many seek to expand its scope, and those who attack it outright are not generally convincing.[20] Freud's note and the successive expansions of it by Jones have been widely enough accepted among psychoanalysts to constitute the "classic" psychoanalytic interpretation, and it is with this interpretation that we shall deal primarily, the more so as it raises problems common to all psychoanalytic interpretation. Besides, Jones has taken pains to inform himself about Shakespearean criticism and has thus not lost sight of the play as a work of art in a conventional sense. In this regard his colleagues have not always been so scrupulous.

The Freudian interpretation has not been so widely accepted among literary critics. Some have objected to psychoanalysis as a critical tool, and these we shall examine in due time. Other objections, however, have been to psychoanalysis itself. These range from the outright hostility of Stoll (who calls Freud "the Mephistophelian searcher and sifter of motives on the Danube")[21] to the somewhat politer irony of G. K. Chesterton:

> I have seen too many unfortunate sceptics . . . committing suicide by self-contradiction. Haeckel and his Determinists, in my youth, bullied us all about the urgent necessity of choosing a philosophy which would prove the impossibility of choosing anything. No doubt the new psychology will somehow enable us to know what we are doing, about all that we do without knowing it. These things come and go, and pass through their phases in order, from the time when they are as experimental as Freudism to the time when they are as exploded as Darwinism.[22]

Darwin is still with us, however, though now freed from the distortions of the journalistic popularizers who have also plagued psychoanalysis. So, for better or for worse, is Freud. To examine the validity of psychoanalysis is well beyond the scope of this book and my own abilities; I must simply assume that anyone who utterly denies this validity must either be very far ahead of the times or very far behind.

Like Bradley and others, Ernest Jones examines and attacks previous interpretations. His objections to the interpretations of Coleridge and Werder are similar to those of other authors we have examined. More interesting are his objections to the evolutionist school's assertion of *Hamlet's* formal inconsistency: "Where the traits and reactions of a character prove to be harmonious, consistent, and intelligible when examined in the different layers of the mind, the surface ones tallying with those of the depths, this consideration may well be added to others in determining what is a 'perfect work of art'. 'Hamlet' in my opinion passes this test however stringently it be applied."[23] Indeed, we shall see that it is this hypothetical descent into the depths of the mind that permits Jones to reconcile the superficial inconsistencies of Hamlet's behavior that the evolutionists stress so much. It is not merely with the depth of Hamlet's character that Jones is concerned, however: "No disconnected and intrinsically meaningless drama could have produced the effect on its audiences that 'Hamlet' has continuously done for the past three centuries. The underlying meaning of its main theme may be obscure, but that there is one, and one which touches matters of vital interest to the human heart, is empirically demonstrated by the uniform success with which the drama appeals to the most diverse audiences."[24] Whereas Stoll might have been inclined to dispute whether *Hamlet's* effect on its audience over three hundred years has indeed been uniform, we shall see that an important part of the psychoanalytical interpretation is the assumed universality of the audience's reaction to the play, however obscure the roots of this reaction may be, however hidden from the audience's conscious mind.

The Freudian interpretation of *Hamlet* is like Bradley's in assigning to the hero a specific aboulia. Unlike Bradley, however, Freud makes the cause of this aboulia quite clear:

> The plot of the drama shows us . . . that Hamlet is far from being represented as a person incapable of taking any action. . . . What is it, then, that inhibits him in fulfilling the task set him by his father's ghost? The answer . . . is that it is the peculiar nature of the task. Hamlet is able to do anything—except take vengeance on the man who did away with his father and took that father's place with his mother, the man who shows him the repressed wishes of his own childhood realized. Thus the loathing which should drive him on to revenge is replaced in him by self-reproaches, by scruples of conscience, which remind him that he himself is literally no better than the sinner whom he is to punish. Here I have translated into conscious terms what was bound to remain unconscious in Hamlet's mind.[25]

The Freudian interpretation, then, derives directly from the Oedipus complex, with its insistence on the small boy's attachment to the mother and consequent antagonism to the father, who, in the case of an only child like Hamlet, is his only rival for the mother's affection. This juvenile antagonism is necessarily repressed and, in the thoroughly mature person, outgrown. Gertrude's remarriage to an unworthy man, whom Hamlet obliquely associates with himself ("no more like my father/ Than I to Hercules"—I.ii.152–53) excites once more those old feelings; so, Jones notes, does the subsequent duty to destroy his present father: "The call of duty to kill his stepfather cannot be obeyed because it links itself with the unconscious call of his nature to kill his mother's husband, whether this is the first or the second; the absolute 'repression' of the former impulse involves the inner prohibition of the latter also. It is no chance that Hamlet says of himself that he is prompted to his revenge 'by heaven and hell'."[26] Such, very briefly, is the basic psychoanalytic interpretation of *Hamlet*. To Jones and Freud, Shakespeare's play is an allegory of "the mechanism that is actually found in the real Hamlets who are investigated psychologically."[27]

There is little in the character or actions of Hamlet that will not fit the psychoanalytic allegory. His delay, his depression and self-contempt, his activity, and the lightening of his depression when he need not be concerned with the Claudius-Gertrude nexus all fit into the malady that Freud and Jones have described. The Freudian interpretation offers an explanation for what Lily B. Campbell had to gloss over: the fact that Hamlet feels less sorrow at his father's death than at his mother's remarriage. The neurotic's tendency to react to adult situations as if they were identical to the painful oedipal experience of childhood also explains Hamlet's hostility to Polonius and Ophelia, who certainly receive harsher treatment at Hamlet's hands than they deserve, but no more than the child would wish to dole out to the interfering father and neglecting mother.[28]

Psychoanalysis also offers an explanation of the various reasons that Hamlet gives at one time or another for his inaction. It is instructive to compare this explanation with that of the evolutionist Stoll. To Jones, Hamlet's professed reasons for delay—cowardice, doubt of the Ghost, the wish to insure Claudius's damnation, and the rest—are all pretexts for postponing the action that he so much dreads: "When a man gives at different times a different reason for his conduct it is safe to infer that, whether consciously or not, he is concealing the true reason. . . . The alleged motives excellently illustrate the psychological mechanisms of evasion and rationalization."[29] To Jones, then, Hamlet's behavior is to be understood in terms of human nature—and human nature at its most subtle, at that. Stoll, however, judges Hamlet's behavior otherwise: "It has been demonstrated that his doubt of the Ghost is an honest doubt, that the sparing of the King at prayer is for the reason given; and there is no indication that anything else Hamlet does is more of an evasion than these. On the stage, even more than in life, pretences and excuses should appear to be lugged in or snatched at, and evasions should look like evasions."[30] Jones willingly admits that Hamlet's reasons are plausible—"but surely no pretext would be of any use if it were not plausible."[31] Here, then, is another instance where inference from the text is determined by the critic's method. To Stoll, a pretence must be clearly implausible to be clearly a pretence: such are the requirements of theatrical clarity. To Jones, a pretence must be plausible to be genuine: such are the requirements of psychological realism.

Finally, the Freudian allegory offers an explanation of Hamlet's ultimate triumph in death, for, Jones asserts, it is only in death that Hamlet *can* triumph:

> In reality his uncle incorporates the deepest and most buried part of his own personality, so that he cannot kill him without also killing himself. . . . The course of alternate action and inaction that he embarks on, and the provocations he gives to his suspicious uncle, can lead to no other end than to his own ruin and, incidentally, to that of his uncle. Only when he has made the final sacrifice and brought himself to the door of death is he free to fulfill his duty, to avenge his father, and to slay his other self—his uncle.[32]

Gertrude is dead, Hamlet is dying; the family knot has been cut. In his last moments Hamlet is freed from the bonds that had earlier held him back.

3

Psychoanalysis is based largely on the principle that "mental trends hidden from the subject himself may come to external expression in ways that reveal their nature to a trained observer."[33] Accordingly, Jones's interpretation assigns to Hamlet feelings and motives that are never directly expressed in the play. Thus, there is no mimetic evidence that to Hamlet Polonius is a modified father figure or Ophelia a mother figure, no immediate evidence of Hamlet's incestuous attraction to his mother or of hidden antagonism toward his father; even his identification with Claudius, though perhaps inferable from the text, is not indisputably oedipal.[34] Indeed, Hamlet expresses nothing but love for his father and nothing but contempt and hate for Claudius. These facts do not in themselves contradict the psychoanalytic interpretation, for presumably Hamlet's conscience would not only demand that his guilty emotions be utterly repressed, but that his conscious mind avow only their direct opposites. The text, of course, contains only these avowals of his conscious mind. Yet all of Hamlet's hidden emotions, particularly those involving his mother, his father, and Claudius, are central to any Freudian interpretation of the play, and their absence from the text provides the critics of Freud their chief weapon and his friends their main stumbling block. F. L. Lucas, who accepts psychoanalytic interpretation in principle, nevertheless boggles at the assumption of Hamlet's hostility to his father: "If we are to speak in terms of the Oedipus-complex, we can only say that its mother-love is conspicuously present in the play, but its father-hatred concentrated wholly upon the new step-father, Claudius."[35] But if we are to speak in terms of the Oedipus complex, then we must accept that complex in its entirety, and that entirety includes antagonism toward the father. That Hamlet should conceive, *ex nihilo,* an oedipal dislike of Claudius may seem more true to the text, but it makes nonsense of Freud.

Morris Weitz, indeed, makes Hamlet's hostility to his father the issue on which the Freudian interpretation must stand or fall:

> In *Hamlet* there is no textual evidence that Hamlet is lying or even deceiving himself, consciously or unconsciously, about his

love for his father. . . . In real-life situations, I suppose, we are prepared to accept explanations of emotions that convert them into something else, even into their very opposites. . . . But in Shakespeare's *Hamlet* we must accept what may in real life appear strange and implausible. We have no alternative except to open up the possibility of reading any datum of any text in any way that we like. And, clearly, that way lies chaos, not criticism.[36]

This is a very serious charge, and we should examine what psychoanalysis can bring to its defense—especially since the defense may clarify the principles of this unusual mode of interpretation.

Even if, as I think, the Freudian interpretation does not contradict the text (see n. 36), it does go beyond the textually explicit, and once more the problem lies in the limited evidence that Shakespeare has provided us. In an actual therapeutic situation, the analyst might hypothesize hostility underlying the patient's extreme praise of his father, as Jones does with Hamlet. But in actual analysis the therapist can verify his hypothesis with the data that further analysis may uncover—and, ultimately, with the cure of the patient. Such verification, of course, is denied us in *Hamlet*. We are not told the precise contents of Hamlet's bad dreams. The question, then, is whether psychoanalysis can offer any supplementary evidence to verify its interpretation.

In fact, Jones offers two such supplementary verifications. The first of these is a biographical study of Shakespeare himself: "It has been found," he says, "that with poetic creations this critical procedure [of intellectual appreciation] cannot halt at the work of art itself: to isolate this from its creator is to impose artificial limits to our undersanding of it."[37] This passage makes it sound as if Jones is in the critical tradition of Taine and Carlyle, but that is not quite so. The psychoanalytic correspondence between artist and artifact, as we shall see, ultimately involves an entirely new way of "understanding" a poetical text, as well as a new variation on the old theme of the "artist's intentions" in creating this text. In any case, to Jones it seems likely that *Hamlet* expresses the state of Shakespeare's own soul at the turn of the sixteenth century: that it marks a revival in him of his own oedipal problems, which the writing of the play alone could purge. The evidence that Jones adduces for this revival is threefold. To begin with, there is the celebrated "strain of sex-nausea" that appears in the plays that Shakespeare wrote after 1600, beginning in *Hamlet*.[38] Secondly, in 1601 occurred the deaths of Essex and, more important, of Shakespeare's father,[39] so that *Hamlet* may have been written, as Freud suggests, "under the immediate impact of his bereavement and, as we may well assume, while his childhood feelings about his father had been freshly revived."[40] Finally, Jones surmises that Shakespeare was under the influence of his betrayal, described in the Sonnets, by his mistress and his closest friend, a betrayal analogous to what Hamlet felt and to what Shakespeare presumably felt as a child towards his parents, for it is the feelings of childhood that determine the relationships of the adult.[41] (Whether the Sonnets are truly auto-biographical is, as Jones admits, impossible to determine. Nevertheless, what the poet imagines himself as doing may be as much a fact of his personality as what he actually does.)

This biographical argument, though not entirely implausible, is scarcely convincing. There is simply not enough evidence, and such evidence as we have might be contradicted by facts of which no evidence has survived. It is debatable, moreover, that the so-called "sex-nausea" of the middle plays is autobiographical, and the death of Shakespeare's father (September, 1601) may well have occurred after the composition of *Hamlet*, although, as Jones suggests, he might have suffered long from a fatal illness.[42] Moreover, Otto Rank has found the same oedipal themes in *Julius Caesar* as in *Hamlet*, and also in other plays composed long before the death of John Shakespeare.[43] It is true that the oedipal situation seems more overt in *Hamlet* than in other plays; however, as Jones himself admits, "the dates and circumstances . . . are too indeterminate to allow us to regard Freud's supposition from being any more than an inspired guess, which, however, may be greatly inspired."[44] In any case, even though some biographical information does seem to support a Freudian interpretation of *Hamlet*, Jones would certainly not have undertaken to psychoanalyze one his own patients on the basis of such slight evidence.

This biographical approach, we may note in passing, obviously does not consider the creative process to spring from deliberate artistic intent; rather, it stresses the artist's "unawareness of the ultimate source of creation."[45] The poet's primal purpose in creation may be personal and preconscious, his consideration of the audience secondary. Thus, for instance, Ella Sharpe can state: "The poet is not Hamlet. Hamlet is what he might have been if he had not written the play of *Hamlet*. The characters are all introjections thrown out again from his mind. . . . He has ejected all of them symbolically and remains a sane man, through a sublimation that satisfies the demands of the super-ego and the impulses of the id."[46] There is, of course, no reason why the final form this catharsis takes cannot be a popular drama. Indeed, as we shall see, personal catharsis and popularity may go hand in hand.

If the biographical interpretation is inadequate, Jones's other extra-textual approach to the play stands on firmer ground. This approach is to explore the psychological relationship of *Hamlet* and the Hamlet legend with other myths. Indeed, Jones says, "to anyone familiar with the modern interpretation, based on psychoanalytic researches, of myths and legends, that [psychoanalytical] explanation of the Hamlet problem would immediately occur on the first reading of the play."[47] According to this comparative mythology, *Hamlet* is a latter-day, highly elaborate variation of that group of myths whose main theme is the displacement of the rival father by the young hero, with a correspondent intimacy, actual or symbolic, between hero and mother—a particularly significant theme when we consider the Freudian view of myths as derived from infantile fantasy.[48] A common feature of this group of myths is the "repression" of the actual fratricide: the hero kills a father figure, not his real father. (The psychological mechanism here is essentially the same as that which disguises the meaning of a dream that might otherwise offend the conscience.) Thus, the father is "decomposed" into two persons—commonly, the real and tender father and the cruel tyrant. Frequently, these two are related, so that the villain is the hero's grandfather, grand-uncle, or—less often— uncle, as in the Hamlet legend. But, unlike the legendary Amleth, Shakespeare's hero shrinks even from killing the father symbol: "Shakespeare's marvelous intuition has, quite unconsciously, penetrated beneath the surface of the smooth Amleth version. He lifts for us at least one layer of the concealing 'repression' and reveals something of the tumult below."[49] Moreover, in the various relations between Hamlet and the Polonius family (as well as between Claudius and Laertes, and also in the entire Fortinbras situation) we see simply further manifestations of this same myth.[50]

This comparative mythology is based on much the same sort of hypothesis that permits the psychoanalyst to detect Hamlet's unexpressed emotions. If comparative mythology does permit us to state with some assurance that "repressed" forms of the myth are closely related to overt forms of the oedipal theme, and if, furthermore, psychoanalysts have found it useful to employ in actual therapy concepts derived from study of these myths, then we have a large body of independently derived knowledge that links life and literature (including Shakespeare's ultimate sources) and serves to corroborate the Freudian interpretation of Hamlet, to make it appear less arbitrary than it may seem at first.

The answer to Weitz's question of textual evidence, then, is that under certain circumstances it may be legitimate to regard *Hamlet* as more than simply a text. To the psychoanalyst it is, in fact, the center of a theoretical nexus that includes Shakespeare, the Elizabethan audience, and the modern reader—for what Shakespeare created, so, in its essentials, have we. *Hamlet* moves us, Jones can assert, only

> because the hero's conflict finds its echo in a similar inner conflict in the mind of the hearer, and the more intense is this already present conflict the greater is the effect of the drama. Again, it is certain that the hearer himself does not know the inner cause of the conflict in his own mind, but experiences only the outward manifestations of it. So we reach the apparent paradox that the hero, the poet, and the audience are all profoundly moved by feelings due to a conflict of the source of which they are unaware.[51]

The Freudian interpretation is not simply an interpretation of the play, but also an interpretation of mankind's reaction to it. To confute or verify Jones we must turn from the text to psychoanalytic introspection. The question psychoanalysis ultimately poses is not whether the psychological facts that the analyst describes are present in the text, nor even whether they were present in Shakespeare's mind, but rather, whether the text provides an effective vehicle for the projection from our own personalities of the same problems and emotions that the analyst detects in *Hamlet*.[52] Comparative mythology, in linking the Hamlet myth with universal fantasies, indicates that the text does indeed serve this function. Jones has moved the interpretation of *Hamlet* into the social sciences. The professional aesthetician may limit his own approach to a rational analysis of a text by itself; recent criticism, at least, has tended to do so.[53] Jones is not, I think, as violently "antitextual" as Weitz says, but even if he were, it does not follow that "that way lies chaos"—especially if the putative misreading of the textual data is not so arbitrary but that many or most people "misread" the text in exactly the same way. Jones has tacitly raised the possibility that subjectivity, if universal, is a legitimate basis of interpretation—perhaps, with *Hamlet,* the only one. However distasteful such an approach may be to most critics, to insist too stringently on overt textual data is to beg an important question.

4

We are now in a position to observe how, in seeking the roots of the play in myth and fantasy, psychoanalysis suggests a resolution of the paradox that *Hamlet* is at once popular and profound. Thus, before continuing with further problems to which psychoanalytical criticism gives rise, we might look at this paradox. To my knowledge, Schlegel was the first to notice it: "*Hamlet* is singular in its kind: a tragedy of thought inspired by continual and never-satisfied meditation on human destiny and the dark perplexity of the events of this world, and calculated to call forth the very same meditation in the minds of the spectators. . . . What naturally most astonishes us, is the fact that with such hidden purposes, with a foundation laid in such unfathomable depth, the whole should, at a first view, exhibit an extremely popular appearance."[54] But the evolutionists have since stressed that *Hamlet* was, after all, a popular stage drama, and that the theatergoer could not possibly perform the sort of criticism that Schlegel at once describes and exemplifies: "This enigmatical work resembles those irrational equations in which a fraction of unknown magnitude always remains, that will in no way admit of solution."[55] The thoroughness of a Coleridgean reading, the subtlety of a Bradleian analysis, or the medical erudition of an Adams would be beyond the grasp of the average spectator as he sat in the theater, and we are left with a dilemma: if *Hamlet* is as psychologically and morally subtle as the main-line critics have found it, then its great popularity on the stage must be irrelevant to its true significance. Schlegel appeared quite willing to accept this conclusion, but, with our growing respect for the Elizabethan stage, we are liable to find it unpalatable today.[56]

Our dilemma exists because former critics have tacitly equated "understanding" the play with conscious understanding, and on the conscious level it will appear impossible to reconcile the play's complexity with its melodrama. Jones, however, posits a subconscious comprehension on the part of the audience, a comprehension of which each member of the audience is immediately capable—to which, indeed, each is compelled. Thus, the play is at once subconsciously understandable to the popular audience and yet profound in that it deals with experiences at the hidden core of human nature. To the psychoanalyst *Hamlet* is popular precisely because it is profound.

Psychoanalytic criticism also offers a solution to another aspect of Schlegel's dilemma: if the play is profound, why does it also contain so many elements of the melodramatic? It is one of the bloodiest of dramas, and it has its source in the violence of Scandinavian fable, a violence that would hardly have been played down by Kyd and evidently suffered little at the hands of Shakespeare. What is Shakespeare's subtlest character doing in such a work? Critics have long seemed to be tacitly aware of this problem and have proposed, like Coleridge, to ignore the plot and treat the play as a portrait of the hero or, like Stoll, to ignore the hero as a separate entity and treat the play as a vehicle for the melodrama inherent in the plot. From Jones, however, comes a new suggestion: the plot, the basic Hamlet story, is a mythical expression of the very problem that besets Hamlet. Both plot and character reflect a single psychological conflict, and both have the same effect—not diverse ones, as critics had tacitly assumed—on the minds of the audience.

Finally, psychoanalysis suggests that *Hamlet* is a unified whole.

The evolutionists—and particularly Robertson—charged that Shakespeare failed to assimilate his material perfectly and that the signs of this failure were the "excrescences" on the plot, comprised primarily of the episodes dealing with Polonius and Fortinbras. Rank and Jones, however, treat Polonius and Fortinbras as variations in the changes that Shakespeare rings on the oedipal theme. The "superfluous" scenes show rebellion against the father or father figure and, conversely, the father trying to stem the "licentious" behavior of his son or keeping the hero's beloved from him.[57]

5

Another important charge often leveled at psychological criticism in general is that a dramatic character is purely fictional and, having no independent existence, cannot be explained the way one explains a real person.[58] John Dover Wilson applies this rule specifically to psychoanalytic criticism: "Apart from the play, apart from his actions, from what he tells us about himself, and what other characters tell us about him, there is no Hamlet. . . . [Those who] attribute his conduct to a mother-complex acquired in infancy, are merely cutting the figure out of canvas and sticking it in the doll's-house of their own invention."[59] This rule, if applied too stringently, would of course render almost any interpretation impossible—including that of Dover Wilson, who assumes that Hamlet has doubts during his two-month delay about the honesty of the Ghost, whereas by Dover Wilson's own dictum Hamlet ceases to exist during this hiatus. A certain amount of inference beyond the text is inevitable. The question, of course, is how much.

In fact, a fictional character is quite likely to have an independent existence in the mind of his creator, and even against the creator's will—a fact attested to by E. M. Forster among others. "I wonder what will happen with Pendennis and Fanny Bolton?" Thackeray wrote to Mrs. Brookfield about his own creations. "Writing it and sending it to you somehow it seems as if it were true—I shall know more about them tomorrow. . . ."[60] That some such process went on in Shakespeare's mind is, of course, impossible to say, but it is scarcely an incredible hypothesis. Do the same unconscious forces that affect the author's creation also affect the audience's reaction? Psychoanalytic criticism assumes that they do.

The character's independence of the text may in fact be quite great if, as psychoanalysis suggests of Hamlet, he exists not simply on paper but also in the minds of the author and audience. Hamlet's "mother-complex acquired in infancy," is really our own. T. S. Eliot makes much the same objection as Dover Wilson when he says that *Hamlet* is an artistic failure because the Prince "is dominated by an emotion which is in *excess* of the facts as they appear." Eliot apparently accepts the psychoanalytic suggestion that there is a hidden, repressed meaning in *Hamlet*, but he ignores the corollary that this meaning is common human property, and Jones can answer: "As they appear, yes, but not as they actually exist in Hamlet's soul. His emotions are inexpressible not for that reason, but because there are thoughts and wishes that no one dares to express even to himself."[61] "As they actually exist": the psychoanalyst sees literature as a part of life, Hamlet as a part of ourselves.[62]

Because it is so much centered in universal audience reaction, the psychoanalyst's interpretation may go far beyond what is overt in the text, often to the dismay of more conventional critics. "If Hamlet has a complex," complains A. J. A. Waldock, "what business is it of ours? When a complex is made into dramatic material it becomes our business, not before"[63]—the tacit assumptions being that artistic creation is a wholly conscious process, that the artist puts into the play no more than the anti-impressionistic critic perceives, and that the audience's view of the work is essentially the same as the critic's, only perhaps not quite so perceptive. But if art can be largely unconscious both in its conception and its communication, then perhaps we cannot keep Hamlet's complex from being our business. Freud even suggests that if Hamlet's complex *is* to be our business, then it cannot be shaped too explicitly into dramatic material:

> It appears as a necessary precondition of this form of art [i.e., the sympathetic portrayal of the highly neurotic character, such as Hamlet] that the impulse that is struggling into consciousness, however clearly it is recognizable, is never given a name; so that in the spectator too the process is carried through with his

attention averted, and he is in the grip of his emotions instead of taking stock of what is happening. A certain amount of resistance [i.e., to forbidden impulses] is no doubt saved in this way. . . . It would seem to be the dramatist's business to induce the same illness [as the hero's] in us.[64]

In short, Freud raises the paradoxical possibility that, in order to communicate Hamlet's complex, Shakespeare had to avoid any overt explanation, had to avoid making the complex into explicit dramatic material for the very sake of the audience's sympathetic comprehension. Otherwise, Freud says, the audience's reaction would be either to dismiss Hamlet as incomprehensible or, if the neurosis is too explicit, to suggest sending for the doctor.

The current critical disavowal of character studies, if carried to extremes, becomes as extravagant as the subtlest nineteenth-century motive hunting that it reacts against. Of course Hamlet is merely ink on paper—but if it comes to that, a real person (to anyone but himself) is merely an aggregate of sound and light waves. In either instance the perceiver, from long human habit, shapes his sense impressions into some more or less coherent pattern in his own mind. Provided that he remain true to these impressions, the one action may be no more reprehensible than the other. When someone speaks of Hamlet as if he were a real person (or about a real person as if he were a real person), he is not making a statement about objective fact but about subjective reaction—his own and, in the case of the psychoanalyst talking about Hamlet, ours.

There are limits. In an earlier treatment of *Hamlet,* for example, Jones amazingly suggests that Hamlet's attraction to Ophelia never flowers "because Hamlet's unconscious only partly desires her; in part Ophelia is felt to be a permitted substitute for the desired relationship with Laertes."[65] Evidently such veiled homosexuality may occur in real-life cases that resemble Hamlet's. Jones has simply made a statement about analytical theory disguised as a statement about Hamlet, one scarcely required by the Freudian theory and leading nowhere in the play itself, however far it may sometimes lead on the couch.

Of course, a fictional character when viewed from the standpoint of the consciously shaping artist—or, more to the point, of the structural critic—will be seen as a mere part of the artistic organism. But that is not the standpoint of the theater audience. (Aristotle, we should remember, says that dramatic action must determine character only that it may appear to the audience that the character determines the action.) The artist gives his character no alternatives, but the audience must, if only to comprehend the moral significance of the character's deeds. As artifact, Macbeth has no free will, but when Macbeth kills Duncan, the man in the gallery will not say that the choice was Shakespeare's. If a stage character *seems* real to us, we cannot help responding to him as if he *were* real.

That is a big "if," of course. A character does exist in his own artistic world, and often (some critics will say always) this world obviates our responding to him as if he were real. No one, I suppose, has ever tried to psychoanalyze Everyman. And, to be sure, virtually everyone recognizes that what he sees in the theater is not reality but a highly formalized representation of reality, one that makes its own rules and establishes its own probabilities.[66] This is a problem that many psychoanalytic critics have ignored, often to the detriment of their work, but it has not always gone unheeded. We have already seen, for instance, that Jones seeks to bridge the gap between realism and the internal logic of the artistic universe when he says that Shakespeare's contribution to the Oedipus myth was to subject the hero himself to the same inner conflicts that the basic story expresses. Here, not only does *mytho*s determine character but the two independently express the same thing. Legend and psychological realism are brought face-to-face, to the enrichment of both. Jones may not be right, of course, but at least he is not a naïve character-monger.

Not all psychoanalytic criticism is so careful. A case in point is Dr. A. Andre Glaz's article *"Hamlet, Or the Tragedy of Shakespeare."*[67] One would almost guess this interesting work to be a parody were it not so long. To Glaz, *Hamlet* represents the hero's (and the author's) own self-analysis. Hamlet's basic problem seems to be concern over his own illegitimacy, a concern called to the fore when his idealized mistress (who appears in the Sonnets but not the play) betrays him. Moreover, Gertrude was guilty of adultery during Hamlet's early childhood. Since Hamlet was illegitimately conceived, his legal father (represented in the play by Polonius) was bribed to marry Gertrude to avoid scandal, and when Hamlet kills Polonius, he is freed from a sense of guilt towards this false father, who embodies Hamlet's oppressive superego. There is more,[68] but this will do. Here, surely, Weitz's complaints about antitextualism are in order.

One problem among many in this article immediately presents itself: how could Hamlet's legal father be bribed to marry Gertrude? How does one bribe a king? The problem exists, however, only on the realistic level of the text, and at the outset of his essay, Glaz dispenses with an interpretation that follows logical order, chronological sequence, cause and effect: "There is no realistic explanation to *Hamlet* which includes all its parts."[69] The realistic level is simply for the entertainment of the audience, while Shakespeare is concerned with the underlying "silent drama" of Hamlet himself.[70] The characters, split in time and space, can shift from one level to another; only Gertrude and Hamlet are three-dimensional, and the play is essentially an extended conversation between mother and son, often played out by the other characters, who are projections of Hamlet's personality.[71]

What is happening here? For one thing, it seems as though Glaz is taking a real-life medical case and applying it willy-nilly to Hamlet. One suspects that another analyst, using the same method, might have come up with a much different interpretation. Glaz's method completely lacks the external verification that Jones attempts to provide in his own study. In addition, Glaz appears to be making an error that is peculiar to psychoanalytic criticism. As we have seen, he chooses to ignore chronological sequence and to ignore cause and effect. Psychoanalysis has described very interestingly the relationship between artistic creation and dreaming and has suggested that the ultimate psychic sources of dreams and of art are identical. It is the dream that dispenses with chronological sequence and causal reality. What Glaz has done is to treat *Hamlet* as if it were simply a dream of Shakespeare's (or of Hamlet's, since he rather confusingly identifies the two). But art is not dream. Few are the artists who do not wish to have an audience, and few are the dreamers who, if they knew the significance of what they dreamed, could easily tolerate one. Here, then, is a clear example of psychoanalytic interpretation that is suspect because it distorts the mimetic nature of its subject. Drama does not communicate in precisely the same way as the dream. If it did, its function in the psychological nature of things would be the same as the dream's, and we would not write plays or go to the theater: we would sleep. Thus, the ultimate objection to Glaz—as, in one way or another, to many critics before him—is that in his hands *Hamlet* ceases to be a play.

Like any other school of interpretation, psychoanalysis can not only overextend itself, as with Glaz, but can also present varying solutions to a given problem. One point in Jones's interpretation of *Hamlet* has seemed especially debatable. In the Jonesian Hamlet, the will to death is very strong and never relinquishes its hold on the Prince until its final victory: "He is caught by fate in a dilemma so tragically poignant that death becomes preferable to life. Being unable to free himself from the ascendancy of his past he is necessarily impelled by Fate along the only path he can travel—to Death."[72] This interpretation fails to explain why *Hamlet* is not a depressing play—as to many, I think, it is not. The Hamlet that Jones describes, whatever his other qualities, is a morbid figure, and his fate is a morbid fate. But that is not the impression that the play very often conveys (and impression, after all, is crucial in psychoanalytic interpretation). The issue, of course, is the change, noticed by many critics, that comes over the Prince towards the end of the play—"a slight thinning of the dark cloud of melancholy," Bradley calls it,[73] though he is skeptical that it means much. To Granville-Barker, Hamlet returns from England purged of his madness,[74] and even the psychoanalyst Slochower detects the same serenity, while K. R. Eissler sees in Hamlet's soliloquies a progression from blind obedience of his father to ethical autonomy, with a concommitant freedom from oedipal compulsion.[75] While Jones considers acceptance of the duel with Laertes an irrelevant pretext for inaction,[76] Geoffrey Bush says that in accepting the challenge Hamlet "reaches a point of perfect quiet and complete possibility."[77] We see signs of this change in the new feeling of resolution that Hamlet seems to possess ("It will be short; the interim is mine") and, perhaps more important, in his confidence that he is working in cooperation with providence, compared to his earlier rebellion against his fate, his unhappiness that ever he was born to set the time right. The change in Hamlet's attitude toward providence, moreover, may be of considerable psychoanalytic significance, in that it constitutes a sort of religious conversion, a realignment of Hamlet's soul with the will of God. According to Freud such conversion may be indicative of a psychoanalytic conversion as well. The concept of the father is linked with the concept of God in the mind of the child, and the restoration of balance after an inner rebellion against the father may take the form of a new submission to the will of God.[78] Psychoanalysts less reductionistic than Freud, or more open to existentialism, may see in Hamlet's new attitude a transcendence of old values rather than a capitulation to them, a moral autonomy that accepts what it finds valuable in the old and incorporates it, as Slochower says, into the "emancipated ego."[79] Either way, it is significant that Hamlet seems to submit to calmly and that he now seems to be prompted, not by heaven and hell, but by heaven alone. Even from the psychoanalyst's point of view, then, Hamlet seems to have reached some solution of his unconscious problem, and it is hard to agree with Jones that at the end he is still "caught in coils from which there is no escape" or that in him we feel "no sense of consistent power."[80]

A final objection to the psychoanalytic interpretation of *Hamlet* is that it limits rational contemplation of the play to the medical specialist, since the meaning of Hamlet's struggle is communicated to the average spectator subconsciously. However, psychoanalysis does not exclude other forms of interpretation. Freud himself says of *Hamlet* (and with rather more modesty than many critics show) that "all genuinely creative writings are the product of more than a single impulse in the poet's mind, and are open to more than a single interpretation. In what I have written I have only attempted to interpret the deepest layer of impulses in the mind of the creative writer."[81] The fact remains that psychoanalysts are inclined to regard other themes of the play as subsidiary to the analytical. Some general clinical comments that Jones makes are easily applied to *Hamlet*:

> We have there [in the repression of sexual impulses] the explanation of the clinical experience that the more intense and the more obscure is a given case of deep mental conflict the more certainly will it be found on adequate analysis to centre about a sexual problem. On the surface, of course, this does not appear so, for, by means of various psychological defensive mechanisms,

the depression, doubt, despair, and other manifestations of the conflict are transferred on to more tolerable and permissible topics, such as anxiety about worldly success or failure, about immortality and the salvation of the soul, philosophical considerations about the value of life, the future of the world, and so on.[82]

Whether the more conscious themes of *Hamlet* coexist with the unconscious in a sort of interpretative plurality, as Freud suggests, or whether they are derivative, as Jones implies, they are worth studying. After all, the play takes place largely on the conscious level, and its philosophical, religious, and political content is considerable. And if such themes as these are indeed derivative from the unconscious meaning of the play, then perhaps we cannot fully understand the play, even from the psychoanalytic point of view, without understanding how Hamlet's inner problem (or Shakespeare's main impulse) finds expression in these external institutions and ideas that body forth the deeper workings of the mind. To my knowledge, such an interpretation has not been done.

Hamlet as Universal Anagoge

6

1

We turn now to those critics who, like the psychoanalysts, seek to explain *Hamlet* in terms of universal human experience, but who, like the students of Elizabethan thought, are not concerned so much with character as with the relevance of the play as a whole to the moral life of man. Schlegel, in his contrast of Classic and Romantic, fore-shadows this school and provides what could serve as its manifesto in his description of Shakespeare as a Romantic poet:

> Romantic poetry . . . is the expression of the secret attraction to a chaos which lies concealed in the very bosom of the ordered universe. . . . [Classical poetry] is more simple, clear, and like to nature in the self-existent perfection of her separate works; the latter, notwithstanding its fragmentary appearance, ap-proaches more to the secret of the universe. . . . it embraces at once the whole of the chequered drama of life with all its circumstances; and while it seems only to represent subjects brought accidentally together, it satisfies the unconscious requisi-tions of fancy,[1] buries us in reflections on the inexpressible signif-ication of the objects which we view blended by order, nearness and distance, light and colour, into one harmonious whole; and thus lends, as it were, a soul to the prospect before us.[2]

We may have to make some allowance for Schlegel's Romantic pre-dilections in order to make him the spokesman for a school that in-cludes the classicist H. D. F. Kitto.[3] Nevertheless, we may observe

that this group of critics generally assumes that there is a central meaning, a "soul," underlying the diversity and apparent disunity of
Shakespearean drama, a meaning that lies near the secrets of the
universe and farther than in classical poetry from the formulations of
the intellect—a meaning that may even lie close to the heart of primal
chaos. What Schlegel provides for, then, is an allegory of nature, of
human morals in their most profound sense, as opposed to the allegory
of those critics who deal with an historically limited expression of
morals. It is this concentration on the moral nature of man that permits
Kitto to liken *Hamlet* to religious drama.[4] The allegory is commonly
drawn from universal human experience, unlimited in space or time.
G. Wilson Knight at one point draws analogies to Hamlet's situation
from Taoism, Greek culture, Nietzsche, and the life of Christ.[5]

Schlegel's conception of Shakespearean drama is echoed by modern
writers of the present school, particularly by their most original and
thoroughgoing spokesman, G. Wilson Knight, who finds the apparent
diversity and inconsistency in the action of Shakespearean tragedy
subsumed under a "spatial" unity: "A Shakespearean tragedy is set
spatially as well as temporally in the mind. By this I mean that there
are throughout the play a set of correspondences which relate to each
other independently of the time-sequence which is the story. . . .
This I have sometimes called the play's 'atmosphere'. . . . Perhaps it
is what Aristotle meant by 'unity of idea'."[6] Inconsistency and irregular-
ity, in character or plot, are only apparent: all parts of the drama stem
from its anagogic meaning, "that burning core of mental or spiritual
reality from which each play derives its nature and meaning."[7] D. A.
Traversi too insists that in Shakespeare "each event and each character
has just its part *and no more* to play in an organic whole which
transcends their separate significance. . . . and the key to this creation lies in the feeling which underlies every part of it."[8] It is this
search for an anagoge, this attempt to relate the drama, thematically
and structurally, to an ultimate fact of man's moral being, that char-
acterizes the critics with whom we are now dealing.

It is not surprising that the anagogical school has reacted to the
main-line school of character analysis, since to the anagogist the play's
center lies far beyond character portrayal. We see this reaction in the
quotation just given from Traversi. We see it again in the very title of

C. S. Lewis's celebrated lecture "Hamlet: The Prince or the Poem?" and in his suggestion that studies of Hamlet's character in itself are no more significant than the concern of a certain pedagogue with the precise breed of Chaucer's Chauntecleer and Pertelote.[9] We see it most explicitly in Kitto's insistence that "we should not try to consider everything in the play as something that reveals or influences the mind and the fate of the one tragic hero, Hamlet; rather should we contemplate the characters as a group of people who are destroyed, and work each other's destruction, because of the evil influences with which they are surrounded."[10] Indeed, it is worth noting that although the *Hamlet* interpretations of Coleridge and Schlegel are commonly deemed similar (so similar that Coleridge felt it necessary to deny the charge of plagiarism), Coleridge's stress is on straight character-study, on Hamlet as a portrait, while Schlegel emphasizes the anagoge: "*Hamlet* is singular in its kind: a tragedy of thought inspired by continual and never-satisfied meditation on human destiny and the dark perplexity of the events of this world, and calculated to call forth the very same meditation in the minds of the spectators."[11]

Other approaches find equally short shrift at the hands of the anagogists. It is not surprising that treatments of *Hamlet* in terms of action alone, and particularly of melodrama, receive little sympathy. The spatial element which Knight describes is independent of action, and the limitation of significance to action alone (which is supposedly the nature of melodrama) is incompatible with an approach that seeks an underlying profundity. (Note that in the quotation on p. 102 Schlegel likens Shakespearean drama to painting, in which the artifact is complete at any given moment in time, while Stoll likens the same drama to music.)[12] Knight in particular rejects interpretations involving the artist's putative ethical intentions or the study of sources, as these "impose on the vivid reality of art a logic totally alien to its nature":[13]

> The tale of Cleopatra married to a Hardy's imagination would have given birth to a novel very different from Shakespeare's play: the final poetic result is always a mystery. That result, and not vague hazards as to its 'source', must be the primary object of our attention. It should further be observed that, although the purely 'temporal' element of Shakespearean drama [i.e., plot]

may sometimes bear a close relation to a tale probably known by Shakespeare, what I have called the 'spatial' reality is ever the unique child of his mind.[14]

By extension, most historical criticism must go by the board, as well as the ethical character studies prevalent in the nineteenth century, for they cannot express the magic of the poet's insight.

Closely involved with the anagogic approach is the insistence by some of its proponents on what might be called interpretative neoimpressionism, an insistence that the commentator be "true to his own imaginative reaction."[15] If we yield ourselves up to the imaginative experience of the play, difficulties in the work which resist the power of the intellect disappear: "We should not, in fact, think critically at all: we should interpret our original imaginative experience into the slower consciousness of logic and intellect, preserving something of that child-like faith which we possess, or should possess, in the theatre."[16] Likewise, Kitto complains that agility of intellect may limit our power of imaginative response,[17] and C. S. Lewis attempts "to recall attention from the things an intellectual adult notices to the things a child or peasant notices": concrete, imaginative detail.[18] It is almost as though Wordsworth were resurrected and allowed to wander through the pages of Shakespearean criticism, saving it from those who murder to dissect.

Such impressionism is, ideally, neither haphazard nor even totally uncritical, since the final interpretation theoretically combines ease of response with full consciousness, after the fact, of the nature of that response.[19] The point in any case that the anagogic meaning transcends workaday common sense and its theatrical equivalent, the demand for consistency of cause and effect. It is the imagination that perceives transcendental relationships, that permitted Wordsworth to see Death resting in a grove of yew trees—or Knight, Kitto, and Lewis to see him lurking in the poetry of *Hamlet*.[20] Insistence on imaginative impression serves the same function in anagogic criticism that unconscious reaction serves in psychoanalytic: to provide a link between a meaning, often profound and apparently recondite, and the average spectator, who is moved by *Hamlet* without being able to explain why. Again, a corollary of this insistence on "a wise passiveness" is to stress the spiritual immediacy of Shakespeare's work. Thus, imagination furnishes one of the weapons in the war against recondite allegory, notably of the various historical schools and of the main line. In its more extreme form—particularly in the hands of Knight—this neo-impressionism can at times become an antiallegorical allegory, so to speak: an attempt to do away with the ordinary media of interpretation and to establish an immediate communication between text and reader, stage and viewer, to which subsequent critical statement is purely incidental. In this respect, too, anagogic criticism sometimes resembles psychoanalytical criticism.

The trouble with impressionism, of course, is that different people have different impressions. Thus, Knight's imagination perceives the essential healthy-mindedness of Claudius and his court, while this impression seems to have completely eluded Kitto and Roy Walker.[21] On the whole, however, it is striking to what degree the critics of this school have achieved unanimity. Their chief differences, it seems to me, lie in the aspects of the play that they stress; their interpretations tend to overlap rather than conflict.

2

There are several related approaches to the play analogous to the anagogic school proper. These, too, deal with a central, underlying meaning whose roots lie deep in human experience. The ultimate allegory of these interpretations, however, lies not in static theme, or image, or "atmosphere," but in an anagogically significant action: in myth or ritual. We have already seen one example: the comparative mythology of Otto Rank and Ernest Jones. In fact, psychoanalytic criticism belongs in the anagogic school insofar as it treats *Hamlet* as a particular realization of a universal story.

Another treatment of *Hamlet* as myth is Gilbert Murray's celebrated essay "Hamlet and Orestes: A Study in Traditional Types." Comparing *Hamlet* with the Greek myth of Orestes, Murray goes to cultural anthropology to find the lowest common denominator between them, seeking their basic allegory "in some original connexion between the myths, or the primitive religious rituals, on which the dramas are ultimately based."[22] He continues: "We finally run the Hamlet-saga to earth in the same ground as the Orestes-saga; in that prehistoric and world-wide ritual battle of Summer and Winter, of Life and Death, which has played so vast a part in the mental development of the human race."[23] Like Rank and Jones, Murray sees *Hamlet* as an allegory of stories and situations "deeply implanted in the memory of the race, stamped, as it were, upon our physical organism."[24]

Gilbert Murray, of course, deals primarily with Hamlet himself and has little to say about the play *Hamlet* as a whole. It is Francis Fergusson, in *The Idea of a Theater*,[25] who attempts to show how the myth of Orestes and Oedipus is expressed through Elizabethan dramaturgy, how Shakespeare's tragedy is a complex reworking of this myth, and how this complexity gives the play structural unity.

The central myth of *Hamlet* for Fergusson is that of the scapegoat and the purgation of a rotten society. But now it is seen as a myth told and retold, examined and reexamined from many angles. The subplots, the minor characters, even what Fergusson calls Hamlet's "improvised" movements—his sallies of wit, his monologues, his commentaries extraneous to the literal world of Denmark, as in his comments on the War of the Theaters—all these are "reflectors" (Fergusson borrows the term from Henry James) of the central myth, as are the various ceremonial scenes, "lamps lighting the rottenness of Denmark."[26] The meaning of *Hamlet*, Fergusson states, is too complex to be completely subject to schematic reasoning:

> The situation, the moral and metaphysical "scene" of the drama, is presented only as one character after another sees and reflects it; and the action of the drama as a whole is presented only as each character in turn actualizes it in his story and according to his lights. This is as much as to say that the various stories with their diverse casts of characters are analogous, and that the drama as a whole is therefore "one by analogy" only. . . . we must be prepared to follow these shifting perspectives, as we move from character to character and from story to story, trying, as we go, to divine the supreme analogue, the underlying theme, to which they all point in their various ways.[27]

Given this concern with the play as a complex expression of an underlying "supreme analogue," it is understandable that Fergusson cares little for psychological probings into Hamlet's character alone. The protagonist's actions are not the heart of the play: they are to help reveal this heart. Prince Hamlet is the chief reflector of the situation in Denmark, and "the adequate response to the rottenness of Denmark, as he sees it, is not a simple, purposive course of action, but a bearing-witness and a suffering-for-the-truth."[28] As Fergusson describes it, Hamlet's reaction to his situation is a more philosophical, even religious, reaction than that described by a psychological critic such as Ernest Jones. While Jones concentrates on the provenance of Hamlet's vision of evil and the nature of Hamlet's inclusion in the corruption he sees around him, Fergusson concentrates on the results, on Hamlet's reaction to his situation. Once again, the interpretation of the whole play determines what is singled out for examination in the parts.[29]

3

Yet another approach to the play is represented by those critics who seek Shakespeare's meaning in the very verbal patterns of his plays, in what Caroline Spurgeon has likened to a Wagnerian leitmotif.[30] This approach is closely related to the anagogical school proper and may in fact be considered a subsidiary of that school. It differs not so much in terms of its allegory as in the part of the artifact studied: the poetry itself as image or rhetoric. It thus may be said to lay a certain empirical groundwork for the more far-reaching interpretations of critics such as Knight and Kitto, concentrating as it does on immediate verbal fact. Especially in the hands of Spurgeon, who has painstakingly tabulated all the images in the Shakespearean canon, this form of analysis has had considerable influence.

Spurgeon's quest is for a revelation of the central meaning of the play in Shakespeare's repetition of imagery, in what she calls the "undersong": "It is quite clear that it is his habit of mind to have before him, as he writes, some picture or symbol, which recurs again and again in the form of images throughout a play, and . . . these leading motives, for instance in the tragedies, are born of the emotions of the theme, and shed considerable light on the way Shakespeare himself looked at it."[31] In *Hamlet,* images of disease and blemish predominate, and "we discover that the idea of an ulcer or tumour, as descriptive of the unwholesome condition of Denmark morally, is, on the whole, the dominating one."[32] This datum Spurgeon expands, in an often-quoted passage, into an interpretation of the play as a whole:

> To Shakespeare's pictorial imagination, therefore, the problem in *Hamlet* is not predominantly that of will and reason, of a mind too philosophic or a nature temperamentally unfitted to act quickly; he sees it pictorially *not as the problem of an individual at all,* but as something greater and even more mysterious, as a *condition* for which the individual himself is apparently not responsible, any more than the sick man is to blame for the infection which strikes and devours him, but which, nevertheless, in its course and development, impartially and relentlessly, annihilates him and others, innocent and guilty alike. That is the tragedy of *Hamlet,* as it is perhaps the chief tragic mystery of life.[33]

For Spurgeon the play is an allegory of the poet's mind, and the "undersong" reveals the central mental picture that gives rise to the dramatic mimesis. Knight, we have seen, arrives at a similar view in his treatment of the "spatial reality" of a play as the unique child of the poet's mind. Both critics assume a personal involvement of the poet with his work, though Knight stresses the impact of the work on the audience, while Spurgeon is interested primarily in penetrating into the mind of Shakespeare himself—which like all such attempts, involves pure hypothesis. It is one thing simply to observe a set of recurring images and another to insist that they result from a static conception in the mind of the poet rather than from the mimetic contingencies of the play. Spurgeon makes her allegorical hypothesis quite clear: even an "objective" artist like Shakespeare "unwittingly reveals his own innermost likes and dislikes, observations and interests, associations of thought, attitudes of mind and beliefs, in and through the images, the verbal pictures he draws to illuminate something quite different in the speech and thought of his characters."[34] Significantly, Spurgeon uses her technique not only to interpret the plays of Shakespeare but his life as well.[35]

Equally important for our purposes is Spurgeon's stress on the poet's pictorial imagination as part of the formal cause of the play. Hamlet himself ceases to be the *primum mobile* of the play, as he is in main-line criticism, and his place is taken by the undersong of infection, which, like Knight's spatial reality, embodies the play's meaning and precedes characterization. Here we depart from the concept of mimetic realism. As with the evolutionists, Shakespeare himself once more protrudes into the world of his artifact—only this time it is not Shakespeare the theater-owner and speculator in dramatic commodities, but Shakespeare the poet, Shakespeare the man of imagination.

However, Spurgeon does not make the connection between the undersong and the play as a whole clear. In the passage last quoted, for instance, she makes Shakespeare's process of creation sound like an elaborate process of repression: the poet "unwittingly reveals" himself as if he were a subject in Freud's *Psychopathology of Everyday Life* or as if a computer might be the best tool to unlock Shakespeare's imagination. It is reassuring to those sympathetic to Spurgeon's interpretation, therefore, that critics such as Knight and Kitto can arrive at somewhat similar readings on the force of imagination alone.[36]

Instead of analyzing imagery, Harry Levin, in *The Question of Hamlet,* examines rhetoric. Since, he argues, the play is, "primarily and finally, a verbal structure, our scrutiny is most concretely rewarded at the level of phrase and emphasis," and he finds the play an expression of rhetorical questions, of ultimate doubt and irony. Once more, the characterization of the hero is subordinate to the wider metaphysical problems of author and audience: "Hamlet is not so much a perplexing personality as he is a state of perplexity into which we enter, the very personification of doubtfulness." The action, too, presents metaphysical perplexity. The early parts of the plot comprise "two separate lines of questioning" (those of Claudius and of Polonius) ending in failure, while the catastrophe is seen as the culmination of the rhetorical framework: "With Shakespeare the dramatic resolution conveys us, beyond the man-made sphere of poetic justice, toward the ever-receding horizons of cosmic irony." Again, like Spurgeon, only in smaller detail, Levin traces themes through the repetition of a word or image, through Shakespeare's use "of tagging his ironies through the use of images relating to an earlier statement to a changed situation"— as in Laertes' trap image after the duel ("as a woodcock to mine own springe" hearkening back to Polonius's "Ay, springes to catch wood-cocks!"). "Neither the father nor the son," Levin concludes, "has recked his own rede."[37] Once more we see, behind the mimetic facade, the poet carefully shaping the play to fit the pattern of his own moral awareness.

4

When critics treat *Hamlet* as an illustration of Elizabethan ethics, the effect of the play may be seen as rhetorical: to inculcate in the spectator an adherence to the ethical code. We must now turn to the anagogic critics' treatment of *Hamlet* as an imitation of the mysteries of man's moral nature, the effect of which is to heighten our aware-ness of this nature. The scope of these critics is wider than that of the ethical historians, their interpretation of *Hamlet* leading beyond historical codes of behavior to the overarching moral nature of man. We may note, for example, that Levin's treatment of rhetoric scarcely reveals Elizabethan ethical or didactic concerns. One would be hard put to imagine Roger Ascham discussing how that august art conveys us "toward the ever-receding horizons of cosmic irony."

We have seen that the anagogists turn their backs on character study for its own sake as centrifugal, as tending, Knight would say, to flee from the play's spiritual core on the wings of ethics. The result of this reaction is to turn from the soul of Hamlet to the rottenness of Denmark; to find, as Kitto does, that everything in the play is related to the disastrous growth of evil; to find, as Walker does, that the original crime of Claudius assumes cosmic proportions, that the un-happy king "has poisoned the whole ear of Denmark."[38] C. S. Lewis and Maynard Mack frankly turn their backs on character study and deal exclusively with the world of *Hamlet*: the "imaginative environ-ment," as Mack puts it, "that the play asks us to enter when we read it or go to see it"[39]—a conception closely akin to Knight's "atmosphere."

To Kitto, especially, *Hamlet* appears as an imitation not so much of character as of the working out of *dikê*, the cosmic force of justice. Evil races through the universe, and until it has run its course and order is reestablished, humanity must suffer: "The impression with which [Shakespeare] leaves us is not the tragedy that one so fine as

Hamlet should be ruined by one fault; it is the tragedy that one so fine should be drawn down into the gulf; and, beyond this, that the poison let loose in Denmark should destroy indiscriminately the good, the bad and the indifferent."[40] It is the original crime of Claudius, says Kitto, that spreads its poison throughout Denmark and is the direct cause of the ills that ensue. It is this crime that corrupts the court, destroys the love of Hamlet and Ophelia, and corrupts Laertes;[41] it is in the working out of *dikê* that Polonius meets his death, and also Claudius and Gertrude: all are involved in a tragedy for which "The King, the King's to blame."[42]

In Kitto we see an interpretation of *Hamlet* as revealing the laws of justice at work against the suprapersonal corruption of evil—a treatment of *Hamlet* as an allegory of absolute moral forces. The result is to exculpate Hamlet from the deaths that he brings about—the deaths of Polonius and Ophelia, of Rosencrantz and Guildenstern: "Denmark is rotten, Polonius is rotten; his death, and the death of seven others, are the natural outcome."[43] Hamlet is not blameless, but the question of his blame, of his character, is not the central issue of the play. Polonius's death was decreed by heaven; Rosencrantz's and Guildenstern's stem ultimately from the scheming of Claudius. Hamlet is seen as an instrument caught in a vise between the initial evil of Claudius and its catastrophic purgation wrought by heaven. In *Hamlet*, Kitto concludes, "Shakespeare draws a complete character, not for the comparatively barren purpose of 'creating' a Hamlet for our admiration, but in order to show how he, like the others, is inevitably engulfed by the evil that has been set in motion, and how he himself becomes the cause of further ruin."[44] Hamlet is a "complete character"—there is no getting around Shakespeare's psychological genius—but this character is simply one figure among many in Shakespeare's grand depiction of the workings of evil.[45]

To Kitto, evil functions in a world governed, however mysteriously, by providence. Other critics, however, have treated *Hamlet* as the expression of a universe from which the hand of God has been withdrawn. G. Wilson Knight undertakes such a treatment, and the extravagance of which he has often been accused stems from his picture of the world of *Hamlet*, a picture in whose background looms, not heaven and *dikê*, but the nihilistic vision of Nietzsche.

To Knight, as to Kitto, Denmark is rotten. Knight, however, finds the source of rottenness in Hamlet himself—Hamlet, who spreads death and the consciousness of death throughout the otherwise healthy commonwealth:

> Except for the original murder of Hamlet's father, the *Hamlet* universe is one of healthy and robust life, good-nature, humour, romantic strength, and welfare: against this background is the figure of Hamlet pale with the consciousness of death. He is the ambassador of Death walking amid Life. . . . [This consciousness of death] insidiously undermines the health of the state, and adds victim to victim until at the end the stage is filled with corpses. It is, as it were, a nihilistic birth in the consciousness of Hamlet that spreads its deadly venom around. That Hamlet is originally blameless, that the King is originally guilty, may well be granted. But if we refuse to be diverted from a clear vision by questions of praise and blame, responsibility and causality, and watch only the actions and reactions of the persons as they appear, we shall observe a striking reversal of the usual commentary.[46]

The people of the court, Claudius included, are of the world—"with their crimes, their follies, their shallownesses, their pomp and glitter; they are of humanity, with all its failings, it is true, but yet of humanity. . . . Whereas Hamlet is inhuman, since he has seen through the tinsel of life and love."[47] Had it not been for Hamlet, Claudius might have lived down his crime, "and all would have been well."[48] Knight's position is rather like that of Erasmus's Folly, whose arguments in favor of herself are unimpeachable—they are the arguments of a well-fed, oblivious humanity—so long as she maintains a completely secular frame of reference. As soon as she introduces thoughts of God and heaven, however, the unworldly, who in the secular world seemed foolish, now appear wise. "When ignorance is bliss, 'tis folly to be wise"—Knight comes close to making this the moral of *Hamlet;* it is, I think we shall see, one-half of his interpretation. The court of Claudius is of humanity then—humanity with all its crimes, says Knight, rather complacently. But where no higher standard exists, humanity will do, and in Knight's imaginative reaction no other standard is given. Where critics set the play against a background of moral absolutes, on the other hand, Hamlet becomes an everyman, a hero with whose plight in a world of evil and uncertainty the spectator can identify himself. "I would not cross the room to meet Hamlet," C. S. Lewis states. "It would never be necessary. He is always where I am."[49] Knight, of course, must dismiss such a possibility: our identification with Claudius is too strong, Hamlet's awareness of death too repellant—as indeed they would be in a universe without a transcendent moral vision.

While to Kitto *Hamlet* reveals a moral universe, in Knight the result of the play is moral perplexity. Claudius, guilty but vital, is faced with Hamlet, innocent but morbid: "The drama aims to penetrate beyond good and evil by relating the opposition to life and death, using a complex design in which the positive of one opposition is alined with the negative of the other, so sharply stimulating our sense of incongruity and dissatisfaction."[50] To Kitto the problem of *Hamlet* is the problem of evil, while in Knight we go "beyond good and evil" and see Hamlet destroyed by awareness not of evil but of death. Where there are no absolute moral standards, there can be no evil in itself. Society alone provides the norms, and death is simply the ultimate in maladjustment. To Kitto, it is impossible to go beyond good and evil: they are moral facts of the universe. To Knight, however, they are functions of temporal ethics, the very ethics that true interpretation must avoid. To praise Hamlet, Knight might well say, "is to behave like a judge, one who must stand outside the drama and sum up from a neutral point of view; the critic who tries to do this would be better employed in a police-court than in criticism." These are not Knight's words, however; they are Kitto's,[51] and they are used against those who seek to enumerate Hamlet's faults. The metaphysical background that each critic provides, then, colors his interpretation of textual fact. Knight says that the beautiful side of Hamlet's nature struggles, but unsuccessfully, against his morbidity; while Claudius's later crimes are forced upon him. Conversely, Kitto says that Claudius struggles, but unsuccessfully, against his sin; while the evil in which Hamlet partakes is forced upon him.[52] There is no arguing with impressions.

The issue, however, is not one of impression alone; it is also one of allegory. If *Hamlet* is an allegory of ontological values, it is hard to approve of Claudius; if *Hamlet* is not, it is hard to approve of Hamlet. The question is whether these values are included in the form of the play, or whether, as Knight argues, they are foisted on the play by the quotidian ethics of the critic. The text itself, I think, is on the side of Kitto. There are too many references to God and providence in the play to allow us, as good-hearted, tolerant pragmatists, to dismiss Claudius's sins as better off forgotten.[53] If something is rotten in the state of Denmark, then "Heaven will direct it." "Foul deeds will rise" to be purged by Heaven's minister and scourge. Significantly, to Knight it is not providence that intervenes in the final catastrophe, but "fate."[54]

An absolute moral vision of the universe, evoked and accepted from the outset, exculpates Hamlet. If we can accept Walker's assertion that Hamlet is no more maladjusted than Dante was in Hell,[55] then we can also condemn the society of Claudius as superficial and hypocritical and see Polonius, Rosencrantz, and Guildenstern as the authors of their own deaths: ". . . Polonius meets his fitting end. Unable to see through the curtain of appearances behind which he has cleverly concealed himself he does not see the reality of death rushing upon him. His reunion with reality is the agony of the sword in his heart."[56] Knight, meanwhile, is complacent about Polonius's morality. It is superficial, to be sure. "But it has another side. It is tolerant. Polonius accepts the ordinary flux of human affairs, human conventions, without probing below the surface."[57] Yet if heaven is in the play, tolerance is not enough. Perhaps the crux of the matter lies in Knight's statement: "Ethics are essentially critical when applied to life; but if they hold any place at all in art, they will need to be modified into a new artistic ethic which obeys the peculiar nature of art as surely as a sound morality is based on the nature of man."[58] Such a position, however, is by no means self-evident, and if Shakespeare has, in fact, introduced a moral standard into his play, then surely this is the artistic ethic we must follow. It might not be going too far to say that in his substitution of maladjustment for metaphysics, Knight is in fact committing an anachronism by substituting his own ethics for those of the play.

It must be noted that despite the differences just examined, Knight and Kitto are largely agreed: Claudius is healthy enough; Hamlet certainly is not. In addition, they do not differ much in their conceptions of Hamlet's disease. The difference lies in the moral lessons they draw from these basic facts, a difference that depends on their allegorical hypotheses and, perhaps, on Knight's lack of sympathy with certain religious passages in the text.

To summarize: Knight and Kitto present two distinct allegories of *Hamlet*, one relativistic, the other absolutist. We must not ignore a third interpretation: that Hamlet himself is torn between these two views of the moral universe. This is a problem we have already touched on in the discussion of ethical history, and we shall return to it in the next section.

5

There remains the question of Hamlet's delay. The solution which the anagogic critics follow is closely related to Bradley's treatment of Hamlet as a "tragedy of moral idealism," of disillusionment leading to paralysis of the will. Disillusionment itself, of course, will not necessarily lead to loss of will, as Ernest Jones points out, but simply to a "simplification of motive in general, and to a reduction in the number of those motives that are efficacious; it brings about a lack of adherence to certain conventional ones rather than a general failure in the springs of action."[59] What Bradley has in mind, however, is something stronger: a violent shock to Hamlet's entire moral being.[60] The classical treatment of such disillusionment is found, however, not in Bradley but in Nietzsche's *Birth of Tragedy*, where Hamlet is treated as one who has suffered the ultimate disillusionment, one who has returned to the world from the ecstasy of the Dionysian state, who "has penetrated into the very heart of the terrible destructive processes of so-called universal history, as also into the cruelty of nature, and who is in danger of longing for a Buddhistic negation of the will."[61] The Dionysian finds everyday reality "nauseating and repulsive":

> In this sense the Dionysian man resembles Hamlet: both have for once penetrated into the true nature of things,—they have *perceived*, but it is irksome for them to act; for their action cannot change the eternal nature of things; the time is out of

joint and they regard it as shameful or ridiculous that they should be required to set it right. Knowledge kills action, action requires the veil of illusion—it is this lesson which Hamlet teaches, and not the idle wisdom of John-o'-Dreams who from too much reflection, from a surplus of possibilities, never arrives at action at all. Not reflections, no!—true knowledge, insight into the terrible truth, preponderate over all motives inciting to action, in Hamlet as well as in the Dionysian man. . . . existence with its glittering reflection in the gods or in an immortal beyond is abjured. In the consciousness of the truth once perceived, man now sees everywhere only the terror or the absurdity of existence.[62]

"Not to be born surpasses all philosophy," Sophocles wrote and, the Nietzschean would argue, Hamlet unknowingly echoes this idea in his curse that he was ever born to set the time right.

Almost in chorus, the anagogic critics have taken up the cry. Thus Knight: "Hamlet, when we first meet him, has lost all sense of life's significance. To a man bereft of the sense of purpose there is no possibility of creative action, it has no meaning. No act but suicide is rational. Yet to Hamlet comes the command of a great act—revenge: therein lies the unique quality of the play—a sick soul is commanded to heal, to cleanse, to create harmony."[63] Hamlet has seen "the utmost horror of evil and death at the heart of life."[64] To L. C. Knights, Hamlet's problem stems from "a sterile concentration on death and evil."[65] And Walker, commenting on the "To be, or not to be" soliloquy, finds that "like Peer Gynt peeling his onion, Hamlet has stripped away the layers of human experience and found at the centre —nothing. . . . from his chaotic nightmare of a godless world and a godless afterlife Hamlet can find no cause or will or strength or means to carry through a great enterprise, or any enterprise worth attempting."[66] Fergusson finds that the simple murder of Claudius would not cure the wider evil that Hamlet sees,[67] a conclusion echoed by Kitto, who goes on: "What he sees, as he peers into this abyss [i.e., to which the Ghost leads him], is . . . evil so appalling, so unfathomable, that he has no foundations left either for action or for passion. . . .

he suddenly finds himself in a world in which 'your philosophy' is no guide."[68] And finally Maynard Mack: "The ghost's injunction to act becomes so inextricably bound up for Hamlet with the character of the world in which the action must be taken—its mysteriousness, its baffling appearances, its deep consciousness of infection, frailty, and loss—that he cannot come to terms with either without coming to terms with both."[69]

It is no coincidence that the anagogists should choose such an explanation of Hamlet's behavior. Dionysian revelation provides the ideal link between plot and theme—specifically between Hamlet's delay and the dark view of the universe presented by the play as lyric. The link is stressed by Traversi: in Hamlet himself

> we are presented with a central figure whose motives penetrate the action at every point, seeking clarification through contact with it and illuminating it, in turn, by the centrality of its presence. In pursuing the duty laid upon him by his father's ghost, Hamlet brings to light a state of disease which affects the entire field presented to his consciousness; and, in the various stages through which this infection, this "impostume," is exposed, he explores progressively the depths of his own infirmity.[70]

The same vision of evil that forces Hamlet's delay also reveals the universe in which action is impossible. "Deep consciousness of infection, frailty, and loss," in Mack's phrase, characterize, not Hamlet's soul, but the world. Of course, the vision of death or evil is common to relativist and moral absolutist alike, but whereas Knight treats this vision as symptom of a wit diseased, Kitto and Walker treat it as a sign of ultimate spiritual health.

The relativist and the absolutist will part company, however, on the question of whether or not Hamlet ever recovers from his vision of evil. "The world of *Hamlet* is a world where one has lost one's way," says C. S. Lewis in a famous passage. "The Prince also has no doubt lost his, and we can tell the precise moment at which he finds it again,"[71] namely, when he observes that there is a special providence in the fall of a sparrow—that is, when he once more grasps the world of absolutes which to a religious man must always lie behind even the most horrifying vision of evil. From the nihilistic viewpoint of Nietzsche the gods are but a "glittering reflection" of existence itself. There is nothing beyond the Dionysian vision.

According to the relativist, then, Hamlet can overcome his vision and proceed to act only through an essentially psychological change. To Knight, the possibilities are twofold: Hamlet at first aspires to the Nietzschean "superstate" wherein "the personality is beyond the antinomies of action and passivity. . . . In this state one is beyond fear of death since life and death have ceased to exist as antinomies."[72] Such is Hamlet's aspiration at the time of the "To be, or not to be" soliloquy. The second solution is what we see in Hamlet's repose at the end of the play, and especially in his courtliness at the outset of the duel scene. There, he accepts the world on its own terms; he is at last "willing to stop being profound," to take on "a love which is humility before not God's ideal for the race but God's human race as it is, in one's own time and place."[73] I must leave it to the reader to see if he can find any direct evidence of *love* on Hamlet's part for the court of Claudius; I cannot. That Hamlet seems to *accept* the uses of this world, however, appears in his courtly address to Laertes and to the King.[74] In addition, of course, there is the possibility that Hamlet does not change at all. This is the interpretation that Knight gives in his earlier essay, "The Embassy of Death." At the end of the play, according to Knight, "fate steps in, forces him to perform the act of creative assassination he has been, by reason of his inner disintegration, unable to perform."[75]

Action is possible only when the Dionysian vision is overcome. To the Nietzschean it may be overcome either by the progression of the soul into a state of poise beyond the vision or, on the other hand, by simple acceptance of the vision. To Knight (in one of his interpretations) Hamlet acts when he backs down from his vision and comes to know himself "neither saint nor soldier, but a Renaissance gentleman of finely tuned sensibility; and that is saying a lot."[76] In the religious view of C. S. Lewis, on the other hand, Hamlet's problem is that of "man—haunted man—with his mind on the frontier of two worlds, man unable either quite to reject or quite to admit the supernatural,"[77] and the resolution comes at the moment when, in the words of Walker, Hamlet attains "the divine spontaneity in which humanity is transfigured into the image of a divinity that shapes our ends."[78]

In these two views, interpretation of the Ghost's role plays an important part. To Knight, the Ghost adds to Hamlet's Dionysian revelation; it is, indeed, a symbol of death itself, "a thing of hideous spiritual nakedness, tormented for his 'foul crimes'. Absolute death, absolute evil, disease and horror, and all life now but a tale told by a ghost . . . this is Hamlet's vision."[79] To Walker, on the other hand, the Ghost stands as a symbol for the truths that Hamlet alone represents in the rotten world of Elsinore.[80] Here, I think, we simply see further examples of allegory foisted on the text; the Ghost, as though his burden were not great enough already, is now required to support interpretations beyond the power of his lines to carry. He certainly is a rather poor purveyor of death-visions, coming as he does (barring the subtler points of doctrine) from a rather conventional purgatory, about which, in any case, he refuses to talk. Knight, it is true, likens this purgatory to hell itself, and thus to "essential death"[81]—which ignores the purgatorial nature of the confinement: the Ghost's sentence is for a "certain term"; heaven is implicit in his revelation.[82] But only implicit—the fact remains that he is a condemned sinner, a spirit doomed to walk the night and for the day confined to fast in fires. Turning to Walker we may ask on what grounds the Ghost symbolizes the transcendental values which Hamlet must render once more effectual in Denmark. His sole words on this subject are his injunction that Gertrude be left to Heaven, and, as to Elsinore:

> Let not the royal bed of Denmark be
> A couch for luxury and damned incest. (I.v.82–83)

Here then, we see allegory going beyond the text. It does not follow, however, that the choice between Knight and Walker is a thing indifferent. Of these two views, the nihilistic and the religious, the text seems to support the second. If something is rotten in the state of Denmark, then, as Horatio points out, heaven will direct it. If the time is out of joint, the very image implies the ultimate existence of a more ideal state, a time in joint.

There's a divinity that shapes our ends,
Rough-hew them how we will.

The image is of cooperation between earth and heaven. The only legitimate way to get around this religious vision in the play is either to reduce it merely to a projection of inner psychological resolution or to dismiss it, with Knights, as "truth glimpsed in defeat"[83]—disheartening alternatives.

6

In *Hamlet*, Shakespeare has often seemed completely oblivious to unity of action. We have seen in the second chapter how the presence of "superfluous" scenes such as Polonius's colloquy with Reynaldo or the entire Fortinbras subplot, led Robertson to the assumption that Shakespeare never managed to control his material sufficiently to impose dramatic unity on it, and how Schücking argued that such unity was not even Shakespeare's goal. Robertson, especially, concluded that the mystery and profundity of the play actually stemmed from the critics' attempts to supply what Shakespeare himself had omitted. But we must note that what the evolutionists mean by "unity" is unity of action alone, causal unity, and we must note equally that such unity is not the only criterion of an artistically conceived whole. In the present chapter we have dealt with critics who have treated questions of artistic wholeness in terms of unity of idea, and here we have an approach that makes far more sense of *Hamlet* at the same time that it appears more faithful to the actual principles of Elizabethan dramaturgy.

Francis Fergusson's notion of a "supreme analogue" to which all the elements in the highly variegated plot point is a key feature of anagogical criticism, a feature that allows us to find unity in *Hamlet* where critics such as Robertson have found none. In fact, Fergusson points out that when Robertson finds "excrescences" on the plot he is tacitly assuming that Shakespeare was employing a principle of dramaturgy followed in the theater from Corneille to William Archer, namely that the plot should form a logical causal whole; this is the principle that culminated in the "well-made play" of the late nineteenth century.[84]

But Fergusson has been at pains to show that such was not Shakespeare's mode of construction. In so doing he follows in the footsteps of Schücking, whose principle of episodic intensification was an attempt to describe Shakespeare on his own terms. But episodic intensification itself is less a principle of construction than an explanation of why Shakespeare's plays lacked the structure that Schücking was accustomed to seek, and Fergusson abandons the concept of causal unity for that of unity by analogy. What is central to the play for Fergusson is not a clearly conceived, causally linked plot, as in Robertson, but an underlying analogue, and a scene, a character, a speech gains relevance to the play not through its relationship with the main plot, but through its relationship with this analogue.

Again in Kitto and in Walker (whose book is in part a rebuttal of Robertson) we see the attempt to treat the "excrescences" on the plot as parts of the whole. Thus, the Reynaldo episode extends the theme of subterfuge and espionage from the court to the home, to family and servants, and thereby renders the corruption of Denmark clearer and more universal. The actors, using show to convey reality, stand in contrast with the court, which uses show to conceal reality, while in the madness and death of Ophelia we see the evil of Elsinore poisoning innocence and beauty.[85] Fortinbras, bringing with him a new order, provides a foil to the corruption of Elsinore.[86] Fortinbras and Horatio alone are not caught up in the general corruption, and it is Horatio who lives to tell Hamlet's story to the next king of Denmark. "The minutest markings of the surface," Walker says, "help to reveal the unseen central reality."[87] We have seen in the last chapter how the psychoanalytical approach to theme reveals much of the same sort of unity in the play.

In their treatment of structural unity in *Hamlet*, the anagogical critics support the findings of modern students of Elizabethan dramaturgy. Bernard Beckerman, for example, states:

> At the core of each play there seems to be a point of reference of which the individual scenes are reflections. Though a play moves temporally toward a conclusion, each scene may like a glass be turned toward a central referent. . . . Since, to the Elizabethan, the world was a manifold manifestation of a God whom

he was unable to compress into one idea or image, in a similar way the Shakespearean play was a manifold reflection of a theme irreducible and unseen.[88]

7

Two brief qualifications may be made to the anagogic approach to *Hamlet*. First, concentration on theme *alone* is liable to result in a conception of *Hamlet* as a lyric poem, and under the spell of Knight we may forget that Shakespeare has forged a play filled with suspense and frankly melodramatic excitement as well as poetry and thought. There need be no contradiction between these two aspects of the play; their coexistence simply serves to point out that the anagogic school, like any other, is partial.

Second, and perhaps more serious, is the question of the connection between the Dionysian vision and inaction. Once more we are faced with the proposition, difficult in the post-Bradleian era to maintain, that Hamlet is suffering from a general aboulia. "His will," Knight says, "is snapped and useless, like a broken leg. Nothing is worth while"[89]—which leaves us somewhat as a loss to explain how Knight's Hamlet could be any more active than Goethe's. We are brought back to the Freudian (and Bradleian) suggestion that it was not so much the Ghost himself—the Ghost qua ghost or symbol of death—as it was the information he imparted and the task he imposed that so stunned the young Prince. The relation of the specific oedipal vision and the wider-reaching Dionysian vision is a matter we shall turn to in the last chapter.

Conclusion

7

Now let any man iudge if it be a matter of meane art or wit to containe in one historicall narration, either true or fained, so many, so diuerse, and so deepe conceits. . . .

Sir John Harington, Preface to *Orlando Furioso* (1591)

1

It needs no extensive study to show that there is widespread disagreement about the meaning of *Hamlet*. Why this disagreement is not merely evident but also inevitable is not so obvious, however, nor is the precise nature in which varying interpretations conflict or concur. The cynic might suspect that interpretation has more to do with the interpreter than with the text, and he would not be far from wrong—even though that, as we shall see, is no slur on interpretation. *Hamlet* criticism, at any rate, has passed through at least three fairly distinct periods, and each has produced its own characteristic corpus of interpretation. The relationships of these, and of varying interpretations within any given period, depend only in part—even only in small part—on the text itself.

In this century interpretation has shunned the hasty and the impressionistic in favor of care and research, sometimes to the point where modern critics invoke scientific objectivity as their guide in interpreting a literary text. But complete objectivity is impossible, barred by the very relationship of the literary work to the natural world that is the object of science.

Inasmuch as interpretation seeks correspondence between art and actuality, it can never give a completely adequate description of the literary work it treats. By its very nature the artifactual world, even in the most thoroughly representational art, does not correspond perfectly to actuality, and when interpretation has done its utmost there will yet remain an aesthetic residue that lies beyond—and, for that very reason, may lie at the heart of our aesthetic experience. When we look at Michelangelo's David, we recognize it, despite its size and color, as the representation of a young man: the mimetic conventions of Renaissance statuary are second nature to us—though perhaps not to someone from another culture,[1] while to a baby or a dog the statue would be simply a mammoth and inanimate block. Proceeding to interpretation, we may discuss the statue's religious significance, its iconographical dimensions. But in doing so we have noted nothing that we would not find just as well in a cheap six-inch replica, and if we stop here in our commentary we belie our aesthetic experience, for we ignore the glory of this man-artifact, a glory immanent in the marble itself, in its contours, in its size, its texture, and color, so that what makes the statue un-man and therefore uninterpretable is also what makes it more-than-man and therefore a masterpiece, a glorification of the very humanity that is inadequate to its description. A crucifixion by Cimabue and a crucifixion by Dali represent the same Christ; even the most scrupulous theological interpretation cannot account for the difference between our responses to the two paintings. The sense is immanent in the sensible, the form is inherent in the matter, and these are things which interpretation cannot quite touch.

Since its realm is art in its representational aspect, interpretation always begins—and often ends—by treating the objects expressed in art as if they were objects *in se*. But representative art does not show us objects *in se*, it shows us objects as objects of imaginative consciousness. A flower in a painting is not a flower, it is the artist's *grasp* of a flower. In responding to the painting, we do not respond to the flower, we respond to the grasp, we make it our own. David is neither man nor marble: it is our grasp of man-in-marble. "L'art libère un étrange pouvoir dans les plus humbles choses qu'il représente," says the philosopher Mikel Dufrenne, "parce que la représentation se dépasse vers l'expression, ou, si l'on préfère, parce que le sujet y devient symbole."[2] The object qua representation is seen *through* the work, while the object qua expression is seen *in* the work: it is the object of our aesthetic experience, while the object as representation is the object of our literary analysis, of interpretation. Even the historical critic, who often seems to look beyond the represented objects to the artist who produced them, and who thus seems to describe the artistic grasp itself, is really talking about the artist's grasp of objects in his actual, historical milieu, not the objects expressed in his work.

The universe of *Hamlet* as analyzable object is not identical to the prior universe of *Hamlet* as aesthetic object. The law of the first is adherence; of the second, coherence. In the first case, the resemblance of *Hamlet* to actuality is the object of our examination; but in our aesthetic experience of *Hamlet,* the play's resemblance to actuality is at the service of its own autonomous structure, which is not the structure of reality, any more than the time of its action necessarily corresponds to the time spent watching the play. The work exists in its own time and space—we relinquish our categories in order to live *its.* Consider the hiatus between Act I and Act II—if the play represented reality, we would explore this gap, and we would have to withhold judgment on the entire action until we found out precisely what Hamlet was doing during all that time. But in the aesthetic world of Elsinore, that lapse has no real presence: it is merely part of the horizon of the action surrounding it. The aesthetic precludes consideration of what, in the real, would be crucial. Between Act I and Act II, literally nothing happens. Not only does Hamlet not act, but he undergoes no spiritual movement beyond what is inferable from the prior and subsequent action—clearly a realistic impossibility, were it not that the time separating Act I and Act II is not real time, in which things must occur, but rather time subordinate to the mode of consciousness that is the play. It exists, therefore, only in that we are aware that it has passed; it has no content, because we are not conscious of its content.

Yet many of the interpretations we have already examined implicitly provide this space with content. From them we infer a Hamlet in the grips of oedipal paralysis; a Hamlet, his excitement waning, increasingly prey to doubts about the Ghost; or an active Hamlet casting about for means to approach the King and kill him. Nor are such inferences fallacious, so long as we recognize that the world of *Hamlet* they describe is posterior to our direct aesthetic experience, correlative to it, but not identical.

This relationship of representation to expression in art suggests that interpretation often performs its most useful work precisely where it begins to point out its own inadequacy. We appreciate David all the more fully in examining how far our experience of actual men falls short in comparison with the statue. Robert H. West has shown how Renaissance demonology cannot fully explain the Weird Sisters in *Macbeth,* and has then put this very inadequacy to critical use:

> Shakespeare does not look behind these mysteries, and he does not suggest that we may do so. Rather he looks *into* them, shows us the phenomena in a piercing way that conveys a sense of their ghastly significance without bringing us much the nearer to a rational account of them or of it.[3]

Not all objects expressed in art resist interpretation as much as do the Weird Sisters in *Macbeth,* but there is always a limit beyond which the rational accounts of interpretation cannot go. The best interpretation may spend much of its time exploring this very limit, tacitly calling to our attention that there is no necessary eidetic connection between the world of fact and theory that is its realm and the unique world that the artist and his audience share. This is not to say that we should be able to understand all art without having recourse to interpretative studies; rather it is to delimit precisely what it means in this context to "understand." The categories of interpretation do not *derive* from the world of our aesthetic experience, and they do not *apply* directly to it; rather, *they arrange our minds in the face of* art. They are not part of what we carry away from the work, they are part of what we bring to it. Our knowledge of nature does not govern the artistic vision but is at its service.

The responsible modern critic, then, can show that his interpretation is more or less adequate and plausible, but beyond that he cannot go. What sets the responsible critic apart from the irresponsible is not objectivity but that he approaches the work with other spectators in mind. He seeks what they too may see, and the final test of his work will be whether it draws sparks from other perceiving consciousnesses. Coleridge's bland statement that he fancied he had a touch of Hamlet in himself would be anathema today because it turns its back on the reader who feels no such kinship with Hamlet whatever. Where the scientist relies on experiment and demonstration, the interpreter of literature aspires to consensus; his equivalent of objectivity is inter-subjectivity.[4]

But this consensus may be as much historical or sociological in origin as aesthetic. If responsible interpretation necessarily appeals to a collective response, the nature of the collective can vary from critic to critic and from era to era. A major revolution in *Hamlet* interpretation (and, perhaps, in interpretation generally) occurred toward the end of the eighteenth century, and modern *Hamlet* interpretation is a child of that revolution.

One major reason that the eighteenth-century critics found little of the arcane or the unique in *Hamlet* was simply that they were not interested in the arcane or the unique. Dr. Johnson praised Shakespeare for creating personages who "act and speak by the influence of those general passions and principles by which all minds are agitated," for creating not individuals but species, and for approaching, in his comedies, the immutable quintessence of the English language. Such praise seems somewhat strange to us today, though conforming to eighteenth-century aesthetic values.[5] But critics in the time of Johnson were working from the postulate that men are interesting in proportion to their exemplification of well-established moral truths. Our own premises are different: the current popularity of a Dostoevsky or a Sartre does not stem from our finding in their pages what oft was thought, but ne'er so well expressed. One wonders how many details that we find significant Johnson sweeps under the carpet in his complaint that Shakespeare often ignores the obvious moral implications of his actions, that he "carries his persons indifferently through right and wrong, and at the close dismisses them without further care, and leaves their examples to operate by chance."[6] From such a point of view, interpretation becomes largely a matter of course, and *Hamlet* critics in the eighteenth century commonly turned their attention to evaluation.[7]

The Romantic movement reversed that trend. Prizing the individual-
istic, the alienated, and the mysterious, the Romantics quickly found
such qualities in Hamlet, qualities that precluded ready interpretation
in terms of the old norms. A whole new world in *Hamlet* was opened
up by postulates such as Schlegel's that the play was inspired by "continual and never-satisfied meditation on human destiny and the dark
perplexity of the events of this world."[8] The Neoclassical consensus
had broken down.

Clearly owing much to the Romantic revolution, modern *Hamlet* interpretation continues to flourish in an age that remains out of touch
with a universe built on generally accepted and accessible truths. We
are still in a period whose literature stresses individuality and isolation,
and Hamlet's spiritual alienation is the theme of critics today as
much as it was a century and a half ago.

> The death of his father, the marriage of his mother, have sick-
> ened him with the world, with man and woman; then comes the
> apparition of his father, and lifts the gates of his soul, as it were,
> quite off their hinges. . . . Hamlet now looks, as from another
> world, at everything in this. . . .

This passage might be from Nietzsche, Knight, or Walker; in fact, it
is from Herder and was published in 1800.[9] And though we have
largely turned away today from the recondite character-analyses that
Romanticism spawned, we continue to use its basic postulate that the
core of life may be nonrational and mysterious. G. Wilson Knight,
Gilbert Murray, and Ernest Jones evoke our darkest imagination to
bring us in touch with a play that Dr. Johnson felt was the heritage
of all rational men.

Modern historical interpretation also seems to have its roots in the
reaction against Neoclassicism. Johnson clearly feels that the more
things change, the more they remain the same, and he considers it no
small sign of Shakespeare's greatness that he has survived for so long,
that his works "have past through variations of taste and changes of
manners, and, as they devolved from one generation to another, have
received new honours at every transmission." The topical, the fashion-
able, the eccentric is worn away by time as Shakespeare passes out of
the hands of his contemporaries, and the residuum comprises "just

representations of general nature."[10] But while today Hamlet's spiritual isolation in Elsinore is attractive to many critics, others find him—and Elsinore itself—isolated from the twentieth century, and this historical relativism is at odds with the notion that the essential in art is timeless. Jan Kott's assertion that Shakespeare is our contemporary is made with a sense of paradox that Johnson would not have appreciated. The historical critic sees himself and his audience as isolated by time from the ideal, original audience of *Hamlet*, while Johnson felt that the passage of time, by weeding out the extraneous, would bring him closer to the essential Shakespeare. It would be a mistake to say that Johnson was wrong; he knew how distance of time can affect the response of an age to the art of the past, though he might have considered attempts to bridge the historical gap wasteful or even pernicious.[11] Modern historical critics would not always have supplied him with the truths he sought in art. They seek different truths, however, and Shakespeare is vast enough to accommodate both sides.

The prospects today are for further expansion of interpretative schools, whose adherents will be governed by their own interests and predilections in careful dialectic with the words that Shakespeare wrote. Within basic limits of critical responsibility, there is nothing wrong with this process—it is, after all, the process that has brought us to our present position. The greatest enemy of interpretation is dogmatism, and it is well to remember that while a given interpretation may be demonstrably wrong, it can never be demonstrably right.

Man has long felt the need to bring *Hamlet* into rapport with his own life, whether it is the life of the scholar in his study, the psychologist in his office, or even the mystic absorbed in his private vision. Even the numerous historical approaches, which sometimes seem to say that the true *Hamlet* has all but slipped beyond the grasp of the nonspecialist, are a product of our own acute and peculiarly modern sense of historical perspective and, at times, of the rather sad sense that we are isolated from something valuable in the past. To all men who react deeply to *Hamlet*, then, the text does not so much *contain* the meaning as serve as a vehicle for the meaning. In the Romantic era, the will to interpret was (we now feel) subjective in its source, and it is generally acknowledged that a critic such as Coleridge was re-creating Hamlet in his own image. We need look no further for another example than the *Hamlet ist Deutschland* school that pervaded a melancholy Germany a century ago. If modern critics have painted what seems to us a more accurate picture of Hamlet, it is perhaps because modern man, seeking scientific objectivity, has become more self-effacing. Coleridge would never have dreamed of trying to see *Hamlet* as the Elizabethans saw it: he thought he knew better.

We live in an age that prides itself on being scientific, and many of the interpretations we have been studying are the result of more or less scientific research. *Hamlet* is particularly liable to such treatment. Granting that the play is one of mystery, the critic may follow one of two tracks: to assume that the mystery has arisen only with the passage of time and may be solved by literary archaeology, or to assume that the play is mysterious because it depicts something that is mysterious in nature, in which case to understand *Hamlet* we must understand the world. Increasingly, critics have had recourse to the methods of history and the social sciences, the prejudice of the age perhaps being that it is in these fields that true significance resides. The insights—often inaccurate but almost always beautiful—of a Goethe, a Coleridge, or a Hazlitt have been replaced by the clinical analyses of Adams or Jones, the historical investigations of Campbell or Craig, or the tabulations of Spurgeon, sometimes to the extent that the universally significant in criticism has been replaced by the esoteric.

2

Art lies beyond meaning, and meaning itself depends in part on the era or person seeking it. "Ultimate interpretation" is a contradiction in terms. Accordingly, in the remainder of this last chapter we shall investigate the possibility of critical pluralism, the possibility that although no interpretation can explain *Hamlet* utterly, many may be coordinate and that interpretative difference need not be interpretative conflict. I cannot attempt a complete synthesis; my goal is simply to indicate the most general conditions of coordination or conflict between critical schools, and also to suggest that the possibilities of cooperation are great and the impediments less than many seem to feel.

In fact, one critic's arguments against another often contain more rhetoric than logic, and a critic is likely to be at his most vulnerable

precisely where he seeks to make his own criticism preeminent. For
example, to consider the melodramatic aspects of *Hamlet,* as E. E. Stoll
does, is certainly useful, if for no other reason than to dispense once
and for all with the delicate prince of Goethe and later Romantics.
Stoll calls attention where attention has long been overdue: to the
external action of the play, to the contention of mighty opposites. He
runs into difficulty, however, when he considers the play merely
melodramatic, no more than improved Kyd for an audience that
wanted no more than that. In order to explain away Hamlet's admission
of delay and his self-laceration, Stoll must invent an audience and a
commercial theatrical situation for whose existence there is no proof
and little likelihood. J. M. Robertson's use of the palimpsest theory
functions similarly. Robertson allows Hamlet a psychosis but dismisses
its significance by placing it in the undigested, non-Kydian part of the
play. Meanwhile, D. A. Traversi, insisting that the plays of Shakespeare are most reliably approached through their language and verse,
is inclined to sneer at the "partiality of outlook" of Victorian sub-
jectivism[12]—an outlook no more partial, perhaps, than his own; while
G. Wilson Knight, as we have seen, would subordinate character
study to "spatial" interpretation and, in case of a conflict between the
two, would dismiss character study as misleading—a position backed
up by little more than forceful assertion. And while Spurgeon's tabula-
tion of Shakespeare's imagery does provide a considerable body of
fact, her hypothetical introduction of Shakespeare's "pictorial imagination" serves largely to defend her interpretation against others equally
plausible. If, as she says, to Shakespeare's pictorial imagination the
situation in *Hamlet* is one for which the individual is not responsible,[13]
then we are left in the awkward position of having to explain away the
considerable feelings of responsibility and guilt that both Hamlet and
Claudius give voice to. Like Stoll's audience, Spurgeon's idea of the
pictorial imagination is a hypothesis that may be used to deny the
significance of a great deal of textual evidence. Both writers are
attempting to make their own academic specialty seem more central
to the play than it really is.

Interpretative pluralism was probably more widely accepted in the
Renaissance than it is now—in fact, it could be *de rigueur* in a time
when critics followed the formula of seeking, even in earthy works,

not only a literal, but also a moral, an allegorical, and an anagogic meaning. Thus, in the myth of Perseus slaying the Gorgon and ascending to heaven, Sir John Harington found depicted the virtuous man overcoming sin, the child of God overcoming his earthly nature and rising "vp to the vnderstanding of heauenly things," heavenly nature severing itself from earth corruption, and, finally, the soul "killing and ouercomming all bodily substance" and ascending to heaven.[14] We think we know better now than to follow such a didactic path, a path that leads to a reading of *Orlando Furioso*, for example, as above all else a collection "of Christen exhortation, doctrine, & example."[15] What we have lost, perhaps, is the willingness to accept more than one meaning for one work—except when dealing with an overt allegory such as *The Faerie Queene*. Spenserians show no unwillingness to discuss "allegorical levels," and manage to discuss them cogently, but such phrases are rare on the lips of Shakespeare scholars, and particularly students of *Hamlet*. It is felt, perhaps, that *Hamlet* is a riddle and that a riddle can have but one right answer.

Yet even one answer may be expressed in different ways. Harington's multiple versions of the Perseus myth are not as diverse as they seem. They all reflect an essential Christian doctrine: the conflict of body and spirit, of the temporal and the eternal. This basic conflict underlies and renders significant the actions of the moral man in society as well as of the immortal soul in its prison of clay. And in *Hamlet*, though the levels of allegory are supplied by separate critics, yet they can often complement each other, as in Harington the anagogic complements the moral.

Both complementation and conflict in interpretation involve more than the literary text alone, although much interpretative conflict stems from an initial disagreement over mimetic data; in this instance— and perhaps in this instance only—conflict can often be resolved, as Bradley's impressive defeat of the Romantic Hamlet illustrates. Where, however, two interpretations both take the mimetic data of the text into adequate account, their relationship is governed primarily not by the text but by the ulterior relationship of their own respective fields of derivation. Indeed, if *Hamlet* criticism has been taken over increasingly by the social sciences and their sister arts, then the social sciences by very virtue of their preestablished disciplines have made it increasingly clear that interpretative issues are frequently extraliterary: that such issues stem not only from ambiguity in the text but equally from conflicts among the various disciplines applied to the text. The *Hamlet* problem involves far more than *Hamlet*.

3

It would be folly to argue that all interpretative conflict can be resolved. Still, many disputes are more apparent than real. To begin with, critics may disagree because they are examining different parts of the play. One of the major differences among *Hamlet* interpretations, for instance, is between those critics who concentrate on the external struggle, the agon between hero and villain, and those who treat the play primarily in terms of the struggle within the soul of the protagonist himself. We see the first of these approaches most clearly in Stoll, who treats Hamlet as a melodramatic hero of undivided will and the action of the play as an expertly maintained structure of suspense culminating in the death of the villain. Other critics have varied this basic theme. Draper has described *Hamlet* as the struggle between Prince and regicide, between the good man and the corrupt society, while Gilbert Murray sees the play as an expression of "that prehistoric and world-wide ritual battle of Summer and Winter, of Life and Death,"[16] and Ernest Jones treats *Hamlet* as a variation of the oedipal theme of youth's revolt "against the restraint imposed by the jealous eld."[17] (That these four interpretations themselves appear to conflict is a problem that we shall turn to shortly.)

Most critics, of course, do not see *Hamlet* as simply an external struggle. Indeed, a persistent conclusion of *Hamlet* interpretations, a conclusion appearing over and over in one critical guise after another, is that Hamlet has assimilated in some degree the bad qualities of the villain. Gilbert Murray himself observes that although he is the slayer of Winter, Hamlet "has the notes of the Winter about him,"[18] and Jones bases his interpretation on Hamlet's coveting what Claudius gained. In the ethical interpretation of Lily B. Campbell, where sinful yielding to passion marks the villain, Hamlet, too, has yielded to passion; while to the anagogic critic such as Knight or Kitto it is Hamlet's vision of evil that renders him capable of doing "such bitter business as the day would quake to look on" (III.iii.409–10). In this general context, too, we must read Bowers's statement that Hamlet treads dangerously the line between minister and scourge. In his tirade against Ophelia, Hamlet takes time out to accuse himself of such things that it were better his mother had not borne him (III.i.125–26).

That Hamlet's conflict is in part internal does not mean, however—the Romantic critics to the contrary notwithstanding—that we can dismiss the external agon as unimportant. Rather, the external conflict of good and evil is repeated within the soul of the hero. The conflict with Claudius loses no importance but simply becomes part of a more complex artistic expression. The verbal pattern of corruption that Carolyn Spurgeon finds in *Hamlet,* for instance, easily complements Fergusson's allegory of the scapegoat or Kitto's of *dikê,* just as the illness in Thebes complements similar allegories in *Oedipus Rex.* Internal and external struggles, psychomachy and agon run parallel courses through the play, and an interpretation of one need not exclude an interpretation of the other.

More severe differences may occur among critics with mutually exclusive allegorical hypotheses. An allegorical hypothesis involves, after all, not merely a statement about the play, but also a statement about the world (or about Shakespeare's supposed conception of the world), and some views are simply not to be reconciled with others. Irreconcilable allegorical conflicts occur most frequently between historical and "universal" interpretations, and interpretative pluralism can often fall flat here. If, for instance, Hamlet is suffering from the adustion of black melancholy, then he cannot be suffering from a Freudian neurosis. The first is an Elizabethan convention about nature, while the second professes to be a universally true concept: the two do not exist in the same universe, and if Shakespeare erred along with his contemporaries, then we cannot apply our better knowledge to his plays. Historical criticism at its best helps us approach the works of the past by making the apparently archaic both clear and relevant. But wherever modern man has utterly ceased to accept the Elizabethan conventions with which the historic critic often deals, we become faced with two completely irreconcilable systems of ideas, and here all the student of criticism can do is recognize the conflict and choose sides.

Conflict also occurs between historical critics themselves, of course, though it is rarely as radical as that between historical and universal critics. Hardin Craig interprets the Elizabethan moral reaction to *Hamlet* in the light of the gentle Cardan, while Lily B. Campbell glosses the play with the more somber *Mirrour for Magistrates*. Whereas Campbell and Ernest Jones as psychologists work within two different and utterly irreconcilable bodies of fact, Campbell and Craig as historians work within the same one, Elizabethan culture, disagreements about which may stem either from incoherence in the data which that era has passed on to us or from incoherence in the era itself. Conflict here is moot, not absolute, and suggests the need for further research into Elizabethan moral attitudes or, indeed, the possibility that Elizabethan culture and *Hamlet* itself allow for a certain range of moral reactions.

On the other hand, the gap between the historical and the universal critic may be bridged when the first expresses the concepts of the second in terms of the institutions of Shakespeare's own day. Such, we shall see, is the relationship of Theodore Spencer to Nietzsche. In such instances the historical critic is less an archaeologist than a translator. He sees Shakespeare's time not as utterly foreign to our own, nor yet as identical, but as analogous.[19]

For the remainder of this chapter, then, I would like to examine the key issue in interpretative pluralism: the relationship of allegorical hypotheses. I would suggest that a significant number of these may be used coordinately, the result being a more comprehensive view of *Hamlet* than any one of them alone can supply, and I would like to sketch roughly the course such a synthesis might take and to suggest its possibilities and limitations.

In the interpretations of Stoll, Draper and Joseph, Murray, and Jones that we glanced at above, we have seen what appears to be an allegorical conflict. These views, however, are not essentially different. If the melodramatic hero is a prince and the villain the corrupt chief of a corrupt society, then Joseph's interpretation simply enlarges upon Stoll's by extending personal melodrama into the political sphere: Hamlet is all the more heroic for being a prince; Claudius is all the more villainous for being a usurper. If, moreover, the hero is young and the villain old (or older), and if Murray and Jones are right in their assumption that certain basic stories of youth and age are but analogues to a basic human myth, then the melodrama of the first two critics may also incorporate the deeper meanings of the latter two: the battle of young hero and old villain may lie at the core of what we think about ourselves. (We might ask ourselves why the hero in melodrama is almost always younger than the villain.) There is no conflict here: only an enlargement of theme. Any single human action may be representative of a species of action, and what we see here is one case of the struggle between good and evil being placed in a larger context in turn by the historian of the drama, the student of political thought, the psychoanalyst, and the cultural anthropologist. Each sees the struggle in a different light, yet the basic struggle remains, just as surely as behind Harington's different interpretations of the Perseus myth there stands the idea of Christian dualism.[20] It could, of course, be argued (and Stoll unquestionably would argue) that melodrama by its very nature precludes deep psychological significance, but Jones and Murray would argue the precise opposite: that melodrama invariably derives from basic myths that express man's inmost nature. The issue leads us away from the study of literature proper and into the realm of audience psychology. The question is moot, although the psychologists and anthropologists seem to be carrying the day. At any rate, the possibility remains that we can accept much of Stoll without rejecting all of Gilbert Murray.

Among the critics whose chief interest is Hamlet's struggle with his own soul, three of the most important—Nietzsche, Theodore Spencer, and Ernest Jones—treat *Hamlet* as a depiction of disillusionment. In confronting his father's ghost, Hamlet confronts one of his own ideals.[21] In the Freudian interpretation the result of the interview is to make Hamlet consider himself alienated from this ideal, to make him subconsciously aware that he is guilty in his own imagination of the sin which, as his father's agent, he must punish in another. In the Nietzschean view, the confrontation reveals fully to Hamlet the death and evil underlying the smooth surface of his society; while according to Spencer, Hamlet cannot reconcile the evil revealed to him with orthodox theodicy. In each interpretation, the revelation of evil paralyzes Hamlet's will and embitters his spirit.

In Freudian psychology the young man's assimilation into society results largely from idealization of the father, from which germinates the young man's idealization of social norms. It is in idealizing the father that the boy controls his oedipal passions, and without this control socialization is difficult. To Freud the archetypal revelation of evil is the young man's realization that he does not fit the role that his father assigns him but, on the contrary, desires to take over, through passion and violence, the role of the father himself. From the Freudian viewpoint, Hamlet's sin is Lucifer's.[22] Strict Freudian interpretation, then, treats the breakdown of idealism in relation to the very genesis of ideals, while Knight and Nietzsche treat this breakdown in relation to ideals already established by the adult, and Spencer in relation to historically specific ideals: the institutions of the Elizabethan age. According to Spencer, Hamlet is abruptly confronted with a new and horrifying duality in man. Man's capacity for evil is greater than conventional theodicy allows for, and thus the gap between man and God, which once seemed a temporary estrangement, now seems forever impossible to bridge—just as in Freud, Hamlet's distance from his father suddenly becomes immense. From the Nietzschean point of view, *Hamlet* shows the shattering of the myths that man builds up to make mortal life bearable; historically, these center about the myth that man is essentially godlike despite his inherent animality. To the psychoanalyst, the shattered myth is that built up by the child: that man is rational and not subject to the desires that he must in fact repress in order to live in society. To summarize: in Nietzsche, Hamlet is overcome when he sees through the Apollonian myth that is the anodyne of man's existence; in Spencer, when he perceives evil that violates the specific "myth" of orthodox theodicy; and in Freud, when he is forced to regress from the myths he has built up in order to make his childhood emotions tolerable to himself and his father.

I suggested earlier that the text will not bear out the nihilistic view of Nietzsche that ideals are in fact no more than false myths; it is not so much the lassitude of disillusionment as the tension between ideal and fact that torments Hamlet. If I am right, then Hamlet's providence speeches show him accepting a transcendent ideal despite fact. The theme of regicide (although I think Draper has greatly exaggerated its importance) also fits into this tension between ideal and fact, for

Claudius is not only a regicide in fact but he embodies at the same time the institution of kingship, just as he is at once Hamlet's father and the murderer of Hamlet's father. Gertrude presents a similar problem; T. S. Eliot has criticized the discrepancy between what she is in herself and what she seems to represent to Hamlet: "To have heightened the criminality of Gertrude would have been to provide the formula for a totally different emotion in Hamlet; it is just *because* her character is so negative and insignificant that she arouses in Hamlet the feeling which she is incapable of representing."[23] But this discrepancy is precisely what she represents. In herself she is so little, yet to Hamlet she means so much. It is this tension that Hamlet must cope with to the end, and that lends poignancy to such lines as

> No, by the rood, not so!
> You are the Queen, your husband's brother's wife,
> And (would it were not so!) you are my mother. (III.iv.14–16)

To Freud, this tension within Hamlet, specifically between his father-ideal and his parricidal ego, causes his delay. Fortinbras's freedom from this tension, his willingness to ignore all else for honor's sake, elicits Hamlet's praise. And it is Fortinbras who must logically succeed to the Danish throne—Fortinbras, who obeys his "uncle-father" and is rewarded by inheriting his father's lost kingdom, as Hamlet could not, and as Oedipus did only at great cost. Perpetually, Hamlet is forced to distinguish between father-king and Claudius, between mother-queen and Gertrude, between the Everlasting and Fortune the strumpet, and, most important of all, between son and Hamlet. These are distinctions that he has never had to make before, and it is making them that is his problem. He must live with people, including himself, who used to embody ideals and no longer do, yet who continue to exist. Each of the three interpretations that we have been examining deals with this same problem, which each seeks to clarify and restate according to the knowledge at its disposal. To say that each view may be valid is to say that disillusionment is a complex experience.

All of which is not to say that these three approaches are completely compatible. There is at least one important difference. In the Freudian view, the immobilizing vision of evil begins as an awareness of personal evil, as a feeling of guilt, and then is projected outward upon the universe. In the Nietzschean and Spencerian views, the evil is objective: a veil is drawn from the world and universal evil is revealed. It is the awareness of this objective evil that infects Hamlet's soul. What to Freud is guilt, to Knight, for example, is "negative consciousness." One may agree, of course, with William James's politic compromise:

> In the psychopathic temperament we have the emotionality which is the *sine qua non* of moral perception; we have the intensity and tendency to emphasize which are the essence of practical moral vigor; and we have the love of metaphysics and mysticism which carry one's interests beyond the surface of the sensible world. What, then, is more natural that that this temperament should introduce one to regions of religious truth, to corners of the universe, which your robust Philistine type of nervous system, forever offering its biceps to be felt, thumping its breast, and thanking Heaven that it hasn't a single morbid fiber in its composition, would be sure to hide forever from its self-satisfied possessors?[24]

Yet the possibility that revelation has psychological roots is a sore point with philosopher and theologian alike. Both Nietzschean and Christian may object that the Freudian approach makes *Hamlet* into a medical case history, no matter how interesting or universal a case history, and so reduces questions of good and evil, of God and the universe, to matters of therapeutic fact, much to the indignity of man, God, and the universe. The Freudian may reply that he describes *Hamlet* as an imitation of the world as he sees it and that, like Bacon, he refuses to justify God with a lie.

In fact, neither the Freudian subjective projection of evil nor its Nietzschean opposite are actual parts of the play. Shakespeare does depict personal guilt and universal evil, but he does not connect them causally. Sticking strictly to the text, we can achieve no more certainty than the neutrality of Traversi—if, indeed, as much:

> By the end of the play Hamlet has revealed all the evils which surround him and has shown them to be variously, if obscurely, related to the stresses . . . in his own soul.[25]

The play itself cannot solve the argument, since it cannot tell us whether the Ghost is essentially a father or essentially a reporter of evil or even something else altogether, nor can the play tell us Hamlet's precise inner reaction to the Ghost. The most our three critics can say, then, is simply that *Hamlet* is an allegory of life (or Elizabethan life), and that in life the vision of the Ghost would necessarily entail such-and-such characteristics.

The issue here is analogous to the conflict we have already discussed between the historical critics Craig and Campbell. We do not know enough about human nature to formulate unvarying rules concerning what happens in man's deepest soul to make him profoundly disillusioned, just as we do not know enough about Elizabethan culture to be certain what the Elizabethans' moral response to *Hamlet* would be, or even if there would be any single response. The first soliloquy links Hamlet's dejection with his disgust at his mother's remarriage, but we cannot be certain whether this disgust stems from his own subconscious sexual involvement with his mother or whether the o'erhasty marriage has shattered a moral abstraction to which he had lent his faith. Is the sexual problem a symptom of the moral one, the moral one a projection of the sexual, or do the two coexist, mutually influencing each other? We have left the realm of criticism proper and entered that of psychology and metaphysics. Conflict there is, as there must always be when the psychologist and the metaphysician get together, but it is conflict that involves far more than the play itself. It is this sort of conflict that will, perhaps, make clearer the old saw that because *Hamlet* is true to life, it partakes of the mystery of life itself.

Of making many books on *Hamlet* there is no end. The task of future critics will doubtless be to relate the play to a continuous succession of ideas yet unborn. But this process need not be so much one of revolution and supersession of ideas as of addition and consolidation, however tentative and however varying from reader to reader. When a new book on *Hamlet* appears and we have read it, our work has only begun. We have still to ask whether and how this book fits in with others of its school and of other schools, not so much to ask whether it overturns old opinion and establishes new as to discover how much it adds to what we already have and thus expands our horizons.

Appendix A

Doubt of the Ghost

The aim of the ensuing discussion is not to set forth a new view of the Ghost in *Hamlet* or to support an old one, but rather to illustrate with a key issue the problems that may arise when interpretation confronts a genuinely ambiguous text.

Stoll, Draper, Dover Wilson, Campbell, Prosser, and others have observed that Elizabethan demonology left considerable room for doubt of the Ghost's true identity. He might as easily be a devil as the spirit of Hamlet's father. Prosser, of course, goes farthest, arguing that the Ghost is really the Devil. Her argument is based largely on a strictly Protestant view of apparitions, of which Lavater is the chief spokesman. This view denies the existence of spirits returning from the dead: God will not send them from heaven, they cannot return from hell, and purgatory is a popish imposture.[1] What might seem to be a ghost, then, is in fact either an angel or a devil, in the guise of the dead man. The *locus classicus* of the dispute in the Renaissance was the raising of Samuel to Saul by the Witch of Endor (I. Sam. 28: 7–20), the strict Protestant position on this being that the Witch of Endor had raised a demon in the shape of Samuel.[2] And if, following the Protestant argument, the apparition of Hamlet's father must be either angel or devil, then the argument for devil is strong: the Ghost brings no words of Christian consolation, it enjoins revenge, and it fades upon the crowing of the cock. (See further arguments above, p. 57.)

But it is open to question whether Shakespeare's audience on the whole was nearly as strict as Lavater in its views on ghosts. A considerable body of testimony, both from popular ballads and from the writings of learned men, suggests that it was not. The ballads, especially, indicate not only that pagan ghost lore had continued uninterrupted into the seventeenth century,[3] but moreover that in the popular imagination pagan ghost lore and Christian doctrine had largely merged. If, as has often been argued, *Hamlet* requires a Christian context, the context of Shakespeare's Protestant audience need not rule out considerable ambiguity.

Ballad after ballad tells of ghosts, with no hint whatsoever that they are anything more than the spirits of the dead. Many ghosts, indeed, are sufficiently far from the spiritual as to stress their own corporeal coldness or decay, as does the ghost of Clerk Saunders:

> "My mouth it is full cold, Margaret,
>   It has the smell, now, of the ground;
> And if I kiss thy comely mouth,
>   Thy days of life will not be long. . . .
>
> "There's nae room at my head, Marg'ret,
>   There's nae room at my feet;
> My bed it is full lowly now:
>   Amang the hungry worms I sleep.
>
> "Cauld mould is my covering now,
>   But and my winding-sheet;
> The dew it falls nae sooner down,
>   Than my resting place is weet."[4]

The ballads seem comfortable enough with theological anomaly. Numerous ghosts, for instance, descend from heaven, and some of these return at cock-crow.[5] One broadside of 1616 tells of three ghosts arising from their graves in Holdt, Germany to announce the imminence of doomsday. The first, "most semly clear and white," praises the Lord; the second, "all in fire," calls for repentance, and the third, "gnashing of his teeth together," hideously cries, "Woe, woe vnto you, wicked men!"[6] It seems clear that the first and third ghosts are from heaven and hell, while the second, though the ballad is for Protestant consumption, is from purgatory. Another broadside, describing the ghost of a murderous midwife, is equally undogmatic if more cautious:

> She having now reveal'd her mind,
>   did vanish in a Flash away,
> And none doth know where she's confin'd,
>   until the General judgement-day.[7]

The ballads are not alone in promoting belief in the existence of actual ghosts, and some of their anomalies seem orthodox enough in other circles. Numerous seventeenth-century British theologians and men of letters, including Henry More, Joseph Glanvill, George Sinclair, and John Aubrey, mustered arguments and collected numerous accounts to prove that the spirits of the dead often revisited the earth. Both More and Glanvill maintained that it was the genuine ghost of Samuel that appeared to Saul,[8] Glanvill observing that in this celebrated debate "there are *Papists* and *Protestants* on both sides of the Question."[9] Yet more relevant to *Hamlet* is More's statement that departed souls "have a faculty and a right to move of themselves," that "they have a power of appearing in their own personal shapes to whom there is occasion," and that it was Saul's "deep distress" and "agony of mind" that called the ghost, just as "a keen sense of Justice and Revenge" made a contemporaneous ghost appear to her murderer.[10] Aubrey, indeed, avers that "so certainly does the revenge of God pursue the abominated murderer, that, when witnesses are wanting of the fact, the very ghosts of the murdered parties cannot rest quiet in their graves, till they have made the detection themselves,"[11] and cites examples.

One particular seventeenth-century account of a ghost is worth examining in some detail because it was so widespread, appearing in several pamphlets and books as well as a ballad,[12] and because it illustrates the difficulty of treating ghosts as necessarily angels or devils. In it the ghost of one Edward Avon appears to his son-in-law Thomas Goddard, whom he asks to pay a debt that he had disavowed in his own lifetime; he then confesses a murder he had committed and asks Goddard to take from Avon's son a sword stolen from the murdered man which has since been bringing the son ill fortune. At one time the ghost's appearance is foreshadowed by the likeness of a hare, and in Glanvill's account Avon is accompanied by a mastiff: clearly, a demonic familiar spirit is implied; the ghost is not an angel. But it is not a devil either, for its purpose is to right several wrongs committed in Avon's lifetime, it appears in the daytime, it praises (in Glanvill) God's great mercy, and it responds when enjoined to speak in the name of God.[13]

Most of the material I have cited above was written well after the composition of *Hamlet,* but there seems no reason to doubt that it reflects a body of thought common in Shakespeare's time and, indeed, much earlier—all the more so as belief in ghosts was getting weaker as the seventeenth century progressed. This material indicates that the issue of ghosts was confused indeed: that among the learned, the Catholic-Protestant lines of contention, though clearly drawn, were not always observed, and that beyond the pale of theology superstition ran loose. It is true that an angel would not speak as the apparition of Hamlet's father does, and that a devil might, but so might the actual warlike spirit of a murdered king and wronged husband, and that is how many Elizabethans, learned and unlearned, Catholic and Protestant, would have responded to the Ghost.

The diversity of Elizabethan ghost lore seems incorporated into Shakespeare's initial treatment of the Ghost in Hamlet. I have already spoken of the disparate frames of reference provided by Horatio's reference to the non-Christian ghosts that "did squeak and gibber in the Roman streets" prior to Caesar's assassination, versus Marcellus's Christian speech on the crowing of the cock (see above, p. 60.) The explicit doubts of the Ghost's identity and intentions are obvious and have been frequently discussed, but the manner in which Hamlet and Horatio respond to the Ghost is even more ambiguous than has generally been observed. Horatio at first clearly takes the Ghost to be a devil who "usurps" the time of night and the "fair and warlike form" of the late King (I.i.46-49), but in his triple exhortation to the Ghost later in the same scene, he seems to lean toward the assumption of a bona fide ghost:

> If thou hast any sound, or use of voice,
> Speak to me.
> If there be any good thing to be done,

> That may to thee do ease, and grace to me,
> Speak to me.
> If thou art privy to thy country's fate,
> Which happily foreknowing may avoid,
> O, speak!
> Or if thou hast uphoarded in thy life
> Extorted treasure in the womb of earth
> (For which, they say, you spirits oft walk in death),
> Speak of it! (I.i.128–39)

Clearly Horatio does not impute diabolical motives to the Ghost here, nor does he treat him as an angel (whose plight would not have to be eased), and the motif of hidden treasure is common in folklore, as Horatio's "they say" implies: the Ghost begins to resemble the ghosts of the ballads.

Hamlet's first address to the Ghost shows the same ambiguity. His initial frightened exclamation implies the demonic theory, which, however, he quickly expands to embrace the demonic-angelic alternative:

> Angels and ministers of grace defend us!
> Be thou a spirit of health or goblin damn'd,
> Bring with thee airs from heaven or blasts from hell,
> Be thy intents wicked or charitable,
> Thou com'st in such a questionable shape
> That I will speak to thee. (I.iv.39–44)

But as he continues to speak, he begins to treat the apparition as a real ghost, and his words reflect the motif of spirits rising from their graves that we heard earlier from Horatio and that we have also seen in the ballads:

> Let me not burst in ignorance, but tell
> Why thy canoniz'd bones, hearsed in death,
> Have burst their cerements; why the sepulchre
> Wherein we saw thee quietly inurn'd,
> Hath op'd his ponderous and marble jaws
> To cast thee up again. What may this mean
> That thou, dead corse, again in complete steel,
> Revisits thus the glimpses of the moon . . . ? (ll. 46–53)

In conclusion, it would seem that the varied views of his audience gave Shakespeare a free hand to shape the Ghost in what form he would, just as he did the fairies in *A Midsummer Night's Dream*.[14] But, far from artistically resolving the ambivalences and ambiguities of his time, he incorporated them into the play. Clearly Shakespeare's handling of the Ghost opens up numerous roads of interpretation, none of which, however, are exclusively indicated by the text.[15]

In any case, doubt of the Ghost provides a perfectly reasonable motive for Hamlet's delay up to the time when the play-within-the-play ends his doubts once and for all. Planning his trap, Hamlet himself states the motive:

> The spirit that I have seen
> May be a devil; and the devil hath power
> T'assume a pleasing shape; yea, and perhaps
> Out of my weakness and my melancholy,
> As he is very potent with such spirits,
> Abuses me to damn me. (II.ii.626–31)

But other critics, following stage effect rather than pneumatology, have attacked this view of the Ghost—H. B. Charlton perhaps most vociferously:

> One thing is certain. When Hamlet sees and listens to the ghost, there is not even the faintest hint of possible deception. He takes the spectre for what it really is, the spirit of his dead father. Moreover, the tale which the ghost tells him fits exactly into his instinctive sense of the wickedness of his uncle. 'O, my prophetic soul, my uncle!' is his immediate conviction of the truth of the ghost's evidence. . . . Hamlet's acceptance of the ghost is instantaneous and absolute: and in the relative calm following the encounter, he assures his friends, 'It is an honest ghost'. The first intimation from Hamlet that he is apparently wavering in this confidence comes only after the lapse of considerable time, and therefore when Hamlet must feel self-reproach at his tardiness.[16]

Indeed, the general dramatic strategy up to this point may be seen as supporting our belief in the Ghost. It is a dramaturgical adage that the best technique for overcoming an audience's doubt is to introduce that doubt in the characters and have them overcome it onstage. In the first scene of the play we move, through Horatio, from doubt of the very existence of the Ghost to frightened acceptance. In the fourth and fifth scenes, we move from highly stressed and repeated doubts of the Ghost's intentions to full acceptance of these intentions in Hamlet's obvious and trusting sympathy: "Alas, poor ghost!" (I.v.4). Had Shakespeare wished us to doubt the Ghost, it could be argued, he would have taken precisely the opposite tack.

Moreover, the time sequence of events in II.ii. indicates that Hamlet's specific doubt of the Ghost is a false rationale. First he asks the player to insert in *The Murther of Gonzago* a speech "of some dozen or sixteen lines," and then, having prepared for the Mousetrap, he proceeds bitterly to accuse himself of inaction in the soliloquy "O, what a rogue and peasant slave am I." If he had doubted the Ghost all along, these self-accusations would be unnecessary, especially since he has at last taken steps to verify the Ghost's words (see Charlton, pp. 88–89). Dover Wilson, it is true, claims that "though the soliloquy is actually uttered after the players have gone out, it is in effect a dramatic reflection of what has already taken place." That is, it "recapitulates Hamlet's emotions as the Player's recitation proceeds."[17] Dramatic convention, Wilson argues, makes such an interpretation possible. However, Hamlet begins by observing, "Now I am alone"; the effect of these words is to isolate the soliloquy in time rather than to apply it to Hamlet's thoughts before he was left alone. It would be possible to argue that this entire question of time sequence in II.ii would hardly be noticed by the audience, as it has eluded the notice of all but a handful of critics. Even so, Hamlet's doubt comes on us with awkward abruptness.

Thus, the interpretation that stresses Hamlet's doubt of the Ghost has to hypothesize that the audience would doubt the Ghost so strongly as to render probable Hamlet's sudden doubt, which the text itself leaves rather awkward. In short, the critic's allegory will largely determine his own attitude toward the Ghost's part in the delay.

Appendix B

The Closet Scene

An embarrassment for those critics who insist on a psychological hindrance to Hamlet's revenge is the promptitude with which he slays the concealed Polonius at the outset of the closet scene. Stoll eagerly calls attention to the fact:

> Despite the minor contrasts and differences, the three situations hold like the stones of an arch together,—the words about the bitter business, the sparing of the King for a more fearful end, when he shall be about an act that hath no relish of salvation in it, and the killing of him (as Hamlet thinks) when in the bed-chamber he has at last caught him about it, on the spot. One centripetal force holds all three—the identity of Hamlet's revengeful spirit. The last two situations, indeed, are to each other as question and answer, promise and promise-keeping. If we doubted him at the beginning, we wholly believe in him here at the end.[1]

Lily B. Campbell has to hypothesize that Hamlet is subject to moments of anger—anger which, however, has nothing to do with her diagnosis of Hamlet's slothful grief and which she brings up almost *en passant*.[2] Ernest Jones, following Loening, observes—probably with more quickness of thought than either Hamlet or the spectator possesses—that the figure behind the arras could not possibly be the King, whom Hamlet had just left behind, and that Hamlet, unconsciously realizing this, can go ahead and kill the intruder and yet remain free of the psychological threat that killing Claudius would involve.[3] This interpretation, however, not only goes far beyond anything that the text indicates, but would also be quite impossible to stage.

Most critics have assumed that at the moment when he runs his sword through the arras, Hamlet believes that Claudius is on the other side. But the textual evidence is ambiguous, and the possibility exists that Hamlet at that moment has no such idea. "O me," the Queen asks, "what hast thou done?" To which Hamlet replies, "Nay, I know not. Is it the King?" It should be noted that his first reply is that he does not know what he has done. *Then* he asks if it is the King, and it is quite possible that such an idea has only now occurred to him.[4] A sufficient pause between the two sentences plus an appropriate change in the tone of his voice would make such an interpretation perfectly clear on the stage: suddenly (and praised be rashness for it) all his problems are at an end; unwittingly he has accomplished the deed that—according to many critics—he could never done deliberately. Such an interpretation could explain some of his bitterness when he lifts up the arras and sees that his victim is only Polonius:

> Thou wretched, rash, intruding fool, farewell!
> I took thee for thy better.

Hamlet took him for his better, the argument would run, not during the murder, but only afterwards, in the brief period while the victim lay unidentified.

Such an interpretation accords with other facts of the play as well. The eagerness which he evinces on his way to see Gertrude—eagerness which makes him go on with the interview as if the death of Polonius had not intervened—would make him impatient of interruption. (His detection of Polonius behind the arras, according to a traditional staging, is what moves him to fierce anger during his interview with the other woman whom he loves.) Hamlet enters his mother's chamber able, by his own admission, to drink hot blood, and his behavior is sufficiently alarming to make his mother call out for help. The sudden awareness as he hears Polonius's voice that once more his confidence has been betrayed would be sufficient to move him to murderous frenzy and to stab blindly at the "rat." This interpretation, moreover, leaves no need to explain away (as Stoll and Draper must) the Ghost's almost immediately subsequent reprimand:

> Do not forget. This visitation
> Is to whet thy almost blunted purpose.

For it was not Hamlet's purpose, in slaying the man behind the arras, to kill the king. Finally, if Hamlet killed Polonius in a state of frenzy, then Hamlet need not suffer under Dr. Johnson's accusation that when he "uses some gentle entertainment" to Laertes before the duel, he justifies himself with a lie:

> Was't Hamlet wrong'd Laertes? Never Hamlet. . . .
> Who does it then? His madness. If't be so,
> Hamlet is of the faction that is wrong'd;
> His madness is poor Hamlet's enemy. (V.ii.244–50)

This would, in fact, be the truth. Hamlet's would be a classic case of what a modern court would call temporary insanity.

I am not arguing that this interpretation is required by the text but only that it is a possible reading. Obviously, it fits better into some interpretations than into others. In the rather extreme form I have given it, it blends best with the Freudian approach and in any case would require a Hamlet with considerable emotional imbalance. The point once more is that what goes on in *Hamlet* is largely a matter of the critic's own allegory.

References and Notes

Chapter 1.   Critical Method and Critical Schools

1. Morris Weitz, *Hamlet and the Philosophy of Literary Criticism* (Chicago: University of Chicago Press, 1964), p. 258.

2. Lily B. Campbell, "Bradley Revisited: Forty Years After" [1947], Appendix to *Shakespeare's Tragic Heroes: Slaves of Passion* (New York: Barnes & Noble, 1963), p. 241.

3. Northrop Frye, *The Anatomy of Criticism* (Princeton: Princeton University Press, 1957), pp. 86–89.

4. E. E. Stoll, "Hamlet the Man," *Shakespeare and Other Masters* (Cambridge, Mass.: Harvard University Press, 1940), p. 188.

5. See Elder Olson, "Hamlet and the Hermeneutics of Drama," *Modern Philology* 61 (1964): 225–37; and Weitz's distinction between description and explanation in *Philosophy of Literary Criticism*, pp. 244–45.

Chapter 2.   The Evolutionist School

1. E. E. Stoll, "Hamlet the Man," *Shakespeare and Other Masters* (Cambridge, Mass.: Harvard University Press, 1940), p. 128.

2. Karl Werder, *Vorlesungen über Shakespeare's Hamlet* (Berlin, 1875), p. 40; quoted and translated by H. H. Furness in his New Variorum edition of *Hamlet,* 10th ed., 2 vols. (Philadelphia: J. B. Lippincott & Co., 1877), 2:357.

3. Charlton M. Lewis, *The Genesis of Hamlet* (New York: Henry Holt & Co., 1907), pp. 1–19; for a further summary of the "objective" and "subjective" solutions to the delay, see J. M. Robertson, *The Problem of "Hamlet"* (London: George Allen & Unwin, 1919), pp. 11–23.

4. See Robertson, *Problem of "Hamlet,"* pp. 57–63, 84; Robertson, *"Hamlet" Once More* (London: Richard Cobden-Sanderson, 1923), pp. 132–33; and Levin L. Schücking, *The Meaning of Hamlet,* trans. Graham Rawson (London: Oxford University Press, 1937), pp. 54–66. A number of these anomalies were originally noticed by the German Roderich Benedix in his book *Die Shakspearomanie* (Stuttgart, 1873), quoted and translated in Furness, New Variorum *Hamlet,* 2:351–54.

5. Robertson, *Problem of "Hamlet,"* p. 30.

6. Lewis, *Genesis of Hamlet*, pp. 20–21.

7. See Lewis, *Genesis of Hamlet*, chaps. 3–4; Robertson, *Problem of "Hamlet,"* chap. 2. To this already complex picture Robertson adds two additional touches: that the *Ur-Hamlet* was a play in two parts, some of the "excrescences" being the result of inadequate abridgement, and that the hand of George Chapman intervenes between Kyd and Shakespeare, inserting anomalies that Shakespeare himself let stand or only partially revised (*Problem of "Hamlet,"* pp. 52–62). Schücking replaces the classic palimpsest theory with one of his own: that the "extraneous" episodes of the play are Shakespeare's interpolations by way of expansion for publication; thus, they become literary virtues, not theatrical vices (*Meaning of Hamlet*, pp. 175–86). This view scarcely corresponds to Schücking's treatment of the play in *Die Charakterprobleme bei Shakespeare* [1919], trans. as *Character Problems in Shakespeare's Plays* (London: George G. Harrap & Co., 1922). It is with this earlier book that we are most concerned.

8. Robertson, *Problem of "Hamlet,"* p. 44.

9. Lewis, *Genesis of Hamlet*, pp. 91–92.

10. Ibid., p. 86.

11. Ibid., p. 96.

12. Ibid., p. 80.

13. Johann Peter Eckermann, *Gespräche mit Goethe*, 4th ed. (Leipzig: Brockhaus, 1876), part I, p. 175, conversation of July 26, 1826; my translation.

14. Robertson, *"Hamlet" Once More*, p. 116.

15. Ibid., pp. 71–72.

16. Robertson, *Problem of "Hamlet,"* p. 73.

17. Robertson, *"Hamlet" Once More*, p. 162.

18. August Wilhelm von Schlegel, *A Course of Lectures on Dramatic Art and Literature* [1808], trans. John Black, rev. A. J. W. Morrison (London: Henry G. Bohn, 1861), p. 404.

19. Robertson, *Problem of "Hamlet,"* pp. 75, 86–87; see also Robertson, *"Hamlet" Once More*, pp. 174–75, 180–82.

20. Robertson, *Problem of "Hamlet,"* p. 86.

21. T. S. Eliot, "Hamlet and his Problems" [1919], in *Selected Essays: 1917–1932* (New York: Harcourt, Brace and Co., 1932).

22. Ibid., p. 124.

23. Ibid., p. 125.

24. Ibid.

25. Lewis, *Genesis of Hamlet*, p. 20.

26. Goethe, for instance: ". . . all his plays revolve around that secret point which no philosopher has yet been able to see and to determine, and in which the peculiar quality of our *Ego,* the pretended freedom of the will, comes into conflict with the inevitable course of the whole" (*Criticisms, Reflections, and Maxims of Goethe,* trans. W. B. Rönnfeldt [London: Walter Scott, n.d.], p. 43). See also Thomas Campbell: "When we know how unlike the action of Shakespeare's mind was to our own,—how deep and unboundedly various his

beholdings of men's minds, and of all manifested existence . . . how can we tell that we have attained the purposes of his mind?" (*Blackwood's Magazine*, February 1818, p. 505; quoted in Furness, New Variorum *Hamlet*, 2:158.

27. Eliot, "Hamlet and His Problems," p. 124.

28. My discussion of Schücking is based primarily on his work in *Character Problems in Shakespeare's Plays*. His later book *The Meaning of Hamlet* presents some second thoughts on certain problems, notably Shakespeare's workmanship and the dignity of Hamlet's suffering.

29. Schücking, *Character Problems*, p. 201.

30. Schücking, *Meaning of Hamlet*, p. 1.

31. Schücking, *Character Problems*, p. 114.

32. Ibid., p. 19.

33. See ibid., pp. 19, 37, 68; and Schücking, *Meaning of Hamlet*, p. 62.

34. Schücking, *Meaning of Hamlet*, p. 1.

35. Schücking, *Character Problems*, p. 172.

36. Schücking, *Meaning of Hamlet*, p. 66.

37. Unlike Lewis and Robertson, Schücking credits Kyd with inventing the complex, half-mad Hamlet that Shakespeare was to apotheosize; Kyd had, after all, done much the same thing in his Hieronimo (*Character Problems*, pp. 152–53). Thus, Shakespeare's conception may be more of a piece than Lewis and Robertson find.

38. Ibid., pp. 153–59.

39. Ibid., pp. 159–60, 165; *Meaning of Hamlet*, pp. 28, 31.

40. Schücking, *Character Problems*, pp. 159–60, 165, 170; *Meaning of Hamlet*, pp. 28, 31.

41. Schücking, *Character Problems*, p. 8.

42. E. E. Stoll, *Art and Artifice in Shakespeare: A Study in Dramatic Contrast and Illusion* (Cambridge: Cambridge University Press, 1933), p. 121.

43. A. C. Bradley, *Shakespearean Tragedy*, 2nd ed. (London: Macmillan & Co., 1906), p. 89.

44. E. E. Stoll, *Hamlet: An Historical and Comparative Study*, Research Publications of the University of Minnesota, vol. 8, no. 5 (Minneapolis: University of Minnesota Press, 1919), p. 6.

45. Stoll, *Hamlet: An Historical and Comparative Study*, p. 7.

46. Ibid., pp. 3–4.

47. See E. E. Stoll, "Hamlet the Man," *Shakespeare and Other Masters* (Cambridge, Mass.: Harvard University Press, 1940), p. 184.

48. E. E. Stoll, "The Dramatic Texture in Shakespeare," *Shakespeare and Other Masters*, pp. 23–24.

49. E. E. Stoll, *Shakespeare Studies* (New York: Macmillan Co., 1927), p. 131.

50. Stoll, "Dramatic Texture," p. 25.

51. Stoll, *Shakespeare Studies*, p. 125.

52. Stoll, *Hamlet: An Historical and Comparative Study*, p. 71.

53. Stoll, "Hamlet the Man," p. 141.

54. Stoll, *Hamlet: An Historical and Comparative Study*, p. 9.

55. Stoll, *Shakespeare Studies*, pp. 131–32.

56. Stoll, *Hamlet: An Historical and Comprehensive Study*, p. 17.

57. Stoll, "Hamlet the Man," p. 179 and, in general, pp. 147–51; and *Hamlet: An Historical and Comparative Study*, pp. 47–60.

58. Stoll, *Hamlet: An Historical and Comparative Study*, p. 42.

59. Stoll, "Hamlet the Man," p. 152.

60. Stoll, *Hamlet: An Historical and Comparative Study*, pp. 31–35. Insofar as the contents of the soliloquy have any significance, it is as sententious speech common in Elizabethan tragedy and analogous to the choral ode of the Greek drama, which does not enter into the plot (ibid., pp. 36–37).

61. Ibid., p. 73.

62. Ibid.

63. Robertson, *"Hamlet" Once More*, pp. 6–7; Schücking, *Character Problems*, pp. 7, 27. "The impression is the play" Schücking cites from the critic Walter Raleigh.

64. See George Ian Duthie, *The 'Bad' Quarto of Hamlet; A Critical Study* (Cambridge: Cambridge University Press, 1941), p. 269. Professor Virgil Whitaker has argued more recently for a textual genesis hearkening back to the evolutionists (*Shakespeare's Use of Learning* [San Marino, Cal.: The Huntington Library, 1953], pp. 251–65, 329–46). Albert B. Weiner, in a study seconded by Hardin Craig, argues that Q_1 represents an adaptation from a somewhat earlier version than that represented by Q_2; Shakespeare may thus have done some revision, but nothing on the scale suggested by the evolutionists (*Hamlet: The First Quarto* [New York: Barnes and Noble, 1962]).

65. Peter Alexander, *Shakespeare's Henry VI and Richard III* (Cambridge: Cambridge University Press, 1929), esp. p. 143.

66. Stoll, *Hamlet: An Historical and Comparative Study*, pp. 7–8.

67. See Alfred Harbage, *Shakespeare's Audience* (New York: Columbia University Press, 1941), esp. chap. 3 and pp. 135–36, 146–47.

68. In the last quarter of the seventeenth century, Davenant excised in performance some 841 lines "prejudicial to the Plot of Sense," including most of the "excrescences" that Robertson mentions and, perhaps more important, twenty-seven lines of the self-incriminating soliloquy "O what a rogue and peasant slave am I." Thus, self-accusation is muted and the revenge action thrown into bold relief. Since Davenant left out Fortinbras until the end of the play, as well, presumably he left out the soliloquy "How all occasions," too. Betterton did, and so, to judge by the First Folio, did Burbage. (See George C. D. Odell, *Shakespeare from Betterton to Irving* [New York: Charles Scribner's Sons, 1920], 1:25.) The same practice was followed by the actors responsible for editions of the play appearing a generation later (*The Tragedy of Hamlet Prince of Denmark: As it is now Acted by Her Majesties Servants* [London, 1703] and *Hamlet, Prince of Denmark, A Tragedy, As it is now Acted by his Majesty's Servants* [London, 1718].) Significantly missing from the stage (in addition to much of the "superfluous" business with Fortinbras, Rosencrantz and

Guildenstern, the actors, and the closet scene) are much of the soliloquy "O what a rogue and peasant slave am I," all of the soliloquy "How all occasions," the Polonius-Reynaldo scene (which indicates a lapse of time sufficient for Laertes to have reached Paris and run out of money), the return of the ambassadors from Norway (also an index of time lapse, since they were sent there in Act I) and much of Hamlet's manic behavior after the play. Thus, most of the evidence for the delay, much of Hamlet's erratic behavior, philosophizing, and self-recrimination are missing. An audience seeing this play might well refrain from commenting on Hamlet's problems: they have been all but left out of the production. The resulting play combines unity of time with singleness of purpose in the hero—but both are contributions of the eighteenth century, not of Shakespeare.

69. See James Boaden, *Life of J. P. Kemble* (London, 1825), 1:110, quoted by Furness, New Variorum *Hamlet*, 2:244–45:

> Hamlet bursts in upon the King and his court, and Laertes reproaches him with his father's and his sister's deaths. The exasperation of both is at its height when the King interposes; he had commanded Hamlet to depart for England, and declares that he will no longer bear this rebellious conduct, but that his wrath shall at length fall heavy on the Prince. 'First,' exclaims Hamlet, 'feel you mine!' and he instantly stabs him.

70. *Boswell's London Journal*, 1762-1763, ed. Frederick A. Pottle (New Haven: Yale University Press, 1950), pp. 234-35.

71. *The Birth of Tragedy*, trans. Clifton P. Fadiman, *The Philosophy of Nietzsche* (New York: Modern Library, 1954), p. 1008.

72. *Coleridge's Shakespearean Criticism,* ed. Thomas Middleton Raysor (London: Constable & Co., 1930), 2:192.

73. Stoll, *Hamlet: An Historical and Comparative Study,* p. 66.

Chapter 3.   Elizabethan Psychology

1. A generation earlier, Richard Loening anticipated this school in *Die Hamlet-Tragödie Shakespeares* (Stuttgart, 1893), chap. 10, and "Ueber die physiologischen Grundlagen der Shakespear'schen Psychologie," *Shakespeare Jahrbuch,* 31 (1895): 1–37, but he seems to have had little influence on his successors.

2. Except for John W. Draper, who argues that Hamlet's melancholy is the *result* of inaction, and that the inaction is due to objective causes (*The "Hamlet" of Shakespeare's Audience* [Durham, N.C.: Duke University Press, 1938], pp. 175-82).

3. Theodore Spencer, *Shakespeare and the Nature of Man,* 2nd ed. (New York: Macmillan Co., 1949), p. 24.

4. Richard Hooker, *Of the Laws of Ecclesiastical Polity,* I. vii. 3.

5. See Hardin Craig, "Shakespeare's Depiction of Passions," *Philological*

Quarterly 4 (1925): 289–301. For a description of the commonplace transformation of sorrow into a desire for revenge, see Ruth Leila Anderson, *Elizabethan Psychology and Shakespeare's Plays* (Iowa City: University of Iowa Press, 1927), pp. 97–98.

6. Timothy Bright, *A Treatise of Melancholie* (London, 1586), reprinted by the Facsimile Text Society, publication no. 50 (New York: Columbia University Press, 1940), p. 115.

7. Anderson, *Elizabethan Psychology*, pp. 168–69 and n. 76. Murray W. Bundy argues that Hamlet's indecision is the result of an overactive imagination ("Shakespeare and Elizabethan Psychology," *Journal of English and Germanic Philology* 23 [1924]: 516–49); this is saying much the same thing, for the imagination would be governed by the passions unless reason held tight sway, as Bundy observes (p. 549).

8. Bright, *Treatise of Melancholie*, p. 110. Phlegm, being cold and moist, was not generally considered subject to adustion; see Lawrence Babb, *The Elizabethan Malady; A Study of Melancholia in English Literature from 1580 to 1642* (East Lansing: Michigan State University Press, 1951), p. 22.

9. See Bright, *Treatise of Melancholie*, p. 111 and Babb, *Elizabethan Malady*, p. 21. Excessive natural melancholy can also be caused by strong emotion (Babb, p. 24); the effect would be the same as that of adustion, only possibly less severe.

10. Bright, *Treatise of Melancholie*, p. 135. See also Mary Isabelle O'Sullivan, "Hamlet and Dr. Timothy Bright," *Publications of the Modern Language Association* 41 (1926): 667–79. Sir Thomas Overbury also observed that the melancholiac "is all contemplation and no action" (*The Overburian Characters*, ed. W. J. Paylor [Oxford: B. Blackwell, 1936], p. 22). See also Babb, *Elizabethan Malady*, p. 108 and n. 23. Draper's insistence that melancholy characterized the man of action (*The "Hamlet" of Shakespeare's Audience*, pp. 145–46) is irrelevant: such melancholy would not be the extreme form under question here.

11. Lily B. Campbell, *Shakespeare's Tragic Heroes: Slaves of Passion* [1930] (New York: Barnes & Noble, 1963).

12. Ibid., p. 111.

13. See Prince Hal's comment: "Falstaff sweats to death/And lards the lean earth as he walks along" (*I Henry IV*, II.ii.115–16). Sweat was thought to emanate from the subcutaneous fatty tissue.

14. Campbell, *Slaves of Passion*, p. 112.

15. Bright, *Treatise of Melancholie*, pp. 114–15.

16. Ibid., pp. 111, 134, 163.

17. Campbell, *Slaves of Passion*, p. 141.

18. *The French Academie*, trans. T. B. C. (London, 1618), p. 467; quoted in Babb, *Elizabethan Malady*, p. 105. Bright, also, speaks of the "heauiness without cause" brought about by black melancholy adust, though he also considers "monstrous terrors of feare" as symptoms (*Treatise of Melancholie*, p. 111),

and these we do not see in Hamlet. Lily B. Campbell applies this same passage to Hamlet, apparently without realizing its inconsistency with her own diagnosis (*Slaves of Passion*, p. 118).

19. Babb, *Elizabethan Malady*, p. 106. Campbell proffers Hamlet's observance to Laertes in the graveyard scene that he is not "splenitive and rash" as evidence that he does not suffer from the melancholic humor, which lodges in the spleen (*Slaves of Passion*, pp. 111–12). But the heavy melancholy that La Primaudaye describes would scarcely make Hamlet rash. Hamlet is probably referring to a malfunctioning of the spleen, which would permit vapors to rise to the head and obscure reason (see Babb, *Elizabethan Malady*, p. 29, and Bright, *Treatise of Melancholie*, pp. 102–03). In general, one cannot be splenetic without being melancholy, but one can be melancholy without being splenetic (see Burton, *The Anatomy of Melancholy*, 1.1.2.4; 1.1.3.4; 1.2.5.4; and 1.2.5.7).

20. Physical lassitude is a symptom of melancholy that Babb simply writes off as irrelevant—legitimately enough, since the symptoms of the disease vary so much. Yet the lack of these symptoms would make Hamlet all the less typical (see Babb, *Elizabethan Malady*, pp. 105–06). Schücking insists on physical weakness, Hamlet's action thus being the result of excitement (see *Character Problems*, pp. 160, 170; and this book, p. oo). But this is an a priori argument; besides, a man suffering such weakness would be more proof against excitement than Hamlet appears to be. Campbell, too, mentions Hamlet's activity without integrating it into her diagnosis (*Slaves of Passion*, p. 144).

21. II.ii.309, 322. There is also the problem of Hamlet's sincerity to Rosencrantz and Guildenstern. It is possible that he is being deliberately academic in his description of his symptoms so that they will be quick to form a conventional diagnosis.

22. Levinus Lemnius, *The Touchstone of Complexions*, trans. Thomas Newton (London, 1576), fol. 148; quoted in Babb, *Elizabethan Malady*, p. 34.

23. "Lethargy" is a term that Campbell quotes from Sir Thomas More to apply to Hamlet (*Slaves of Passion*, p. 114); equally inappropriate is the term "sloth" (ibid., pp. 114, 144).

24. According, at least, to Hardin Craig ("Shakespeare's Depiction of Passions," p. 301). Babb, perhaps, would disagree (see this book, p. 53). If empiricism did not enter into Elizabethan psychology at all, then the likelihood of Shakespeare's own empiricism increases.

25. Babb, *Elizabethan Malady*, pp. 36–37; for the changeability of the melancholiac, see Bright, *Treatise of Melancholie*, pp. 114–15.

26. Campbell, *Slaves of Passion*, p. 112.

27. Ibid., chap. 12; Babb, *Elizabethan Malady*, p. 109.

28. Campbell, *Slaves of Passion*, pp. 114–18.

29. Ibid., p. 116.

30. Campbell says that in the first soliloquy Hamlet is merely feeding a preexisting melancholy with thoughts of his mother's frailty (ibid., p. 119); thus she takes Claudius's testimony to be more valid than Hamlet's. She ignores the fact that Hamlet's uniform of mourning is an indictment of the court, and that

Claudius would naturally be eager to integrate into his society the lone dissenter: "Be as ourself in Denmark" (I.ii.122). Later on, Campbell treats the introduction of Hecuba, a type of the grief-stricken, as Shakespeare's indictment of Hamlet (ibid., pp. 131–32). But it makes at least as much sense to consider Hecuba an emblem of what Gertrude should have been, an image that Hamlet asks to have brought before him: "Say on; come to Hecuba," he demands of the player (II.ii.524).

31. Juan Luis Vives, *An Introduction to Wisedome,* trans. Rycharde Morysine [1540], quoted in Babb, *Elizabethan Malady,* p. 17. See also Babb, *Elizabethan Malady,* pp. 17–20; Anderson, *Elizabethan Psychology,* pp. 143–45; and Campbell, *Slaves of Passion,* pp. 67–72.

32. Campbell, *Slaves of Passion,* p. 22.

33. Ibid., p. 42.

34. See Madeleine Doran, *Endeavors of Art: A Study of Form in Elizabethan Drama* (Madison: The University of Wisconsin Press, 1954), esp. chaps. 4, 9, 12.

35. Campbell, *Slaves of Passion,* p. 23.

36. See Fredson Thayer Bowers, *Elizabethan Revenge Tragedy* (Princeton: Princeton University Press, 1940), chap. 1, and Eleanor Prosser, *Hamlet and Revenge* (Stanford: Stanford University Press, 1967), chap. 1.

37. Campbell, *Slaves of Passion,* p. 15.

38. For another possible view of fortune in tragedy, see Arnold Hauser, *The Social History of Art* (London: Routledge and Kegan Paul, 1951), pp. 416-17:

> The motifs which Shakespeare and his contemporaries add to the description of this spiritual struggle [of "a tragic conflict of conscience"] consist in the inevitability of the conflict, its ultimate insolubility and the moral victory of the hero in the midst of disaster. This victory is first made possible by the modern conception of destiny, which differs from the classical idea, above all, in the fact that the tragic hero affirms his fate and accepts it as intrinsically significant. A fate becomes tragic in the modern sense only through being accepted. The intellectual affinity of this idea of tragedy with the Protestant idea of predestination is unmistakable; and even if there is perhaps no direct dependence, at any rate, it is a case of parallelism in the history of ideas, which invests with real significance the simultaneity of the Reformation and the origin of modern tragedy.

Hamlet's thoughts on providence could easily be brought into line with such an interpretation, which allows a sharp distinction between providence (a fate that is accepted) and fortune (a fate that is not).

39. Indeed, the opponents of the theater were quick evidently to find mere rationale in the defenses that Campbell cites, defenses that appeared, it seems, on tongues of less worthy men than Sidney, Heywood, or Horace: "Seeke to withdrawe these felowes from the Theater vnto the sermon," one morally concerned Elizabethan complained of theatergoers, "they wil saie, By the preacher they maie be edified, but by the plaier both edified and delighted" (Anthony Munday [?], *A second and third blast of retrait from plaies and Theaters*

[1580], p. 139, quoted in E. K. Chambers, *The Elizabethan Stage* [Oxford: The Clarendon Press, 1923], 4:209). For a further discussion, see William A. Ringler, Jr., "Hamlet's Defense of the Players," *Essays on Shakespeare and Elizabethan Drama in Honor of Hardin Craig,* ed. Richard Hosley (Columbia, Missouri: University of Missouri Press, 1962), pp. 201–11.

40. Hardin Craig, "Hamlet's Book," *Huntington Library Bulletin,* No. 6 (November 1934), pp. 17–37.

41. Craig, "Hamlet's Book," p. 23.

42. Ibid., pp. 30–31.

43. Ibid., p. 31.

44. In *Poison, Play, and Duel: A Study in Hamlet* (London, Routledge & Kegan Paul, 1971), Nigel Alexander adds another dimension to historical character study of Hamlet by examining "the symbolic Renaissance psychology expressed throughout the play in the emblems of the Judgment of Paris, the qualities of the Olympian gods, the battle of memory, understanding, and will within the soul, and the love dance of the three graces" (p. 166). These emblems, which he derives principally from the writings of St. Augustine and Giordano Bruno and the paintings of Raphael and Titian, are all paradigms of balance— of psychological balance, as in the case of the war of memory, understanding, and will; or of ethical balance, as in the Judgment of Paris, which represents the choice among the active, contemplative, and passionate lives—and Alexander maintains that Hamlet cannot take revenge without abandoning "his own memory and understanding to the unrestrained power of his will" (p. 196), without, that is, committing the precise sin of Claudius and Laertes. Thus, whereas the students of faculty psychology see Hamlet's delay as a sign of moral weakness and even of sin, Alexander sees it as a sign of moral strength.

45. Campbell, *Slaves of Passion,* pp. 144–47.

46. Anderson, *Elizabethan Psychology,* pp. 105–06. Schücking's view is similar (*Character Problems,* p. 166).

Chapter 4.   The Elizabethan Ethos

1. For a general view of the medieval influence on Elizabethan culture and imaginative literature at large, see E. M. W. Tillyard, *The Elizabethan World Picture* (New York: Modern Library, n.d.). For brief accounts of the role of medieval thought among Renaissance philosophers, see Walter Clyde Curry, *Shakespeare's Philosophical Patterns* (Baton Rouge: Louisiana State University Press, 1959), chap. 1; and Maurice De Wulf, *Histoire de la Philosophie Médiévale,* 5th ed. (Paris and Louvain, 1925), 2:243–96.

2. Richard Hooker, *Of the Laws of Ecclesiastical Polity,* I.viii.5.

3. Carl Becker, *The Heavenly City of the Eighteenth-Century Philosophers* (New Haven: Yale University Press, 1932), p. 7.

4. Lawrence Babb, "On the Nature of Elizabethan Psychological Literature,"

Joseph Quincy Adams Memorial Studies, ed. James G. McManaway, Giles E. Dawson, and Edwin E. Willoughby (Washington: Folger Library Publications, 1948), pp. 510–11.

5. *The Great Instauration,* "Proemium," in *Selected Writings of Francis Bacon,* ed. Hugh G. Dick (New York: Modern Library, 1955), p. 424. For the relationship of the emerging sciences to "the old metaphysical fantasticalness," see W. Windelband, *A History of Philosophy,* trans. James H. Tufts (New York: Macmillan Co., 1926), pp. 370–77. Copernicus himself founded his system on an ideal mathematical model rather than on empirical observation; see Edwin Arthur Burtt, *The Metaphysical Foundations of Modern Physical Science* (Garden City: Doubleday & Co., 1954), chap. 2.

6. Fredson Bowers, "Hamlet as Minister and Scourge," *Publications of the Modern Language Association* 70 (1955): 740–49.

7. Ibid, p. 745.

8. Ibid.

9. Moreover, Bowers assumes that public justice was impossible at the time of Polonius's death, and that any killing in the hours after the play scene would have constituted private and damnable revenge. But in fact, public justice *was* possible: the King had unkenneled his guilt, not only to Hamlet but to Horatio as well, and it is Horatio's testimony, not the publicness of the revenge, that is finally to exculpate Hamlet and condemn Claudius. (I am assuming that the crux of Horatio's testimony will be about the King's original crime; all other "carnal, bloody, and unnatural acts" are either public knowledge or are described in the document that Hamlet obtained on board ship. The only exclusive knowledge that Horatio possesses is one of the original regicide. It is this knowledge alone that can explain Hamlet's anxiety lest Horatio kill himself.)

10. Bowers, "Minister and Scourge," p. 745.

11. Eleanor Prosser, *Hamlet and Revenge* (Stanford: Stanford University Press, 1967).

12. Ibid., chap. 1. Bowers also finds that "the Elizabethans firmly believed the law of God to forbid private vengeance," though he also claims that "there was a very real tradition existing in favor of revenge under certain circumstances," (such as Hamlet's) where there could be no recourse to law (*Elizabethan Revenge Tragedy* [Princeton: Princeton University Press, 1940], p. 40 and, in general, chap. 1). Dame Helen Gardner suggests that the opinions of preachers and moralists, who say what they are obligated to say, are an uncertain guide to the attitudes of a people (*The Business of Criticism* [London: Oxford University Press, 1963], pp. 36–37. In general, Prosser's conclusion seems reasonable: "We cannot doubt that the average Elizabethan sympathized strongly with a revenger, but we cannot assume that he therefore disregarded all the ethical and religious precepts with which he was daily bombarded, and with which, according to all evidence, he was in general agreement" (*Hamlet and Revenge,* p. 34).

13. Prosser, *Hamlet and Revenge,* p. 72.

14. For a brief survey of the major pneumatological writings of the period, see ibid., p. 101, n.3.

15. Ibid., pp. 133–38.

16. Ibid., p. 155.

17. Ibid., p. 171.

18. About to be executed, Cutwolf gleefully recalls his victim's desperate pleas for mercy: "At this his importunity I paused a little, not as retiring frō my wreakfull resolution, but going backe to gather more forces of vengeaunce. With my selfe I deuised how to plague him double for his base minde: my thoughtes traueld in quest of some notable newe Italionisme, whose murderous platforme might not onely extend on his bodie, but his soul also." He then forces his victim to curse God and renounce salvation: "These fearefull ceremonies brought to an end, I bad him ope his mouth and gape wide. He did so, (as what wil not slaues do for feare?); therewith made I no more ado, but shot him full into the throat with my pistoll: no more spake he after; so did I shoot him that he might neuer speake after, or repent him" (*The Vnfortunate Traveller* [1594], *The Works of Thomas Nashe*, ed. Ronald B. McKerrow [London: A. H. Bullen, 1904], 2:325–26). See also Prosser, *Hamlet and Revenge*, p. 22.

19. We have been corrupted, Prosser argues, by generations of pro-Ghost staging and scholarship, and the critical naïveté of Shakespeare's first audiences is beyond our grasp (*Hamlet and Revenge*, pp. xiii–xiv, 141–42). This notion is distressing, but possibly true. One is inclined to go off and ask one's freshman students whether they distrust the Ghost. The answer they give is that Hamlet is finally convinced and they trust his judgment. It is not a bad answer.

20. Cf. the ghost of Andrugio, speaking to his son, in Marston's *Antonio's Revenge*:

> Thy pangs of anguish rip my cerecloth up;
> And lo, the ghost of old Andrugio
> Forsakes his coffin. Antonio, revenge!
> I was empoison'd by Piero's hand;
> Revenge my blood! Take spirit, gentle boy.
> Revenge my blood! . . .
> Thou vigor of my youth, juice of my love,
> Seize on revenge, grasp the stern-bended front
> Of frowning vengeance with impeised clutch.
> Alarum Nemesis, rouse up thy blood,
> Invent some stratagem of vengeance
> Which, but to think on, may like lightning glide
> With horror through thy breast. Remember this:
> *Scelera non ulcisceris, nisi vincis.*
> [Injuries not exceeded are not avenged.] (III.i.33–51)

If Lodge's famous allusion to "the Ghost which cried so miserably in the theatre, like an oyster-wife, 'Hamlet, revenge!' " is at all accurate, the Ghost in Kyd's *Ur-Hamlet* could not have been much different.

21. Even if the Ghost's demands are diabolical, Hamlet's own reaction to them is excessive. The strongest reproach that the Ghost levels at Claudius is to call him "that incestuous, that adulterate beast" (I.v.41). Compare this with Hamlet's frenzied anger: "O villain, villain, smiling damned villain!" (I.v.106) or "Bloody bawdy villain!/ Remorseless, treacherous, lecherous, kindless villain!" (II.ii.607-08) The Ghost's words may be ambiguous—they are harsher than Lavater allows for, yet mild indeed compared to the Senecan idiom. Of Hamlet's attitude, however, there can be do doubt.

22. Hardin Craig, "A Cutpurse of the Empire," *A Tribute to George Coffin Taylor*, ed. Arnold Williams (Chapel Hill: University of North Carolina Press, 1952), pp. 3–16.

23. Prosser, *Hamlet and Revenge*, p. 229. Prosser finds that "the phrasing suggests the old fury against the man who had whored his mother, the old vindictive purpose," though the typical avenger probably would not pay even lip service to "perfect conscience."

24. John W. Draper, *The Hamlet of Shakespeare's Audience* (Durham, N.C.: Duke University Press, 1938).

25. Ibid., p. 96.

26. Ibid., p. 95.

27. Ibid., pp. 198–99.

28. Ibid., p. 196.

29. Ibid., pp. 166–73. In addition, Draper maintains that the Elizabethan reaction to nervous shock such as Bradley describes "was usually humorous rather than pathetic" (p. 235); in general Draper's notion of the active, robust Elizabethan audience seems to owe much to Stoll: "Shakespeare's audience is an audience of men; and Shakespeare's *Hamlet* is a man's *Hamlet*" (p. 244).

30. Ibid., pp. 175–82. Draper's account is highly documented and certainly represents one important view of melancholy. It fails, however, to take into account the ambiguities of the term.

31. Ibid., p. 188.

32. Ibid., p. 226.

33. Ibid., p. 206.

34. Ibid., pp. 237–38.

35. Bertram Joseph, *Conscience and the King* (London: Chatto & Windus, 1953), pp. 48–49.

36. Draper does admit a more universal appeal in the play:

> [Hamlet] can see but one righteous course; and he struggles single-mindedly against all odds, and at the very moment of victory is a martyr to his cause. The spectators at the Blackfriars or at the Globe, courtier, merchant, prentice and country clown, even such as could hardly comprehend Divine Right and the theory of government, could understand

and honor such a struggle, and follow step by step the efforts of such a hero, and see in him themselves; and so, in his fall, they could experience the universal significance and deep poignancy of highest tragedy. (*Shakespeare's Audience*, pp. 243–44)

This interpretation, of course, still stresses the political side of *Hamlet*.

37. Ibid., p. 240. Understandably, to Draper the important scenes are those in which Hamlet confronts his society. Most important is the play scene, which ends Hamlet's doubt and begins the real action and counteraction of revenge (ibid., pp. 184–88). And this scene is underlined by being "the one great scene with practically all the principal figures on the stage: Hamlet and Horatio, the King and Queen enthroned, and the entire court, including Ophelia and Polonius" (p. 184). The apparent assumption that such a scene is theatrically more effective than one with Hamlet alone—or than the contrast between the two—is simply a corollary of Draper's allegory.

38. Geoffrey Bush, *Shakespeare and the Natural Condition* (Cambridge, Mass.: Harvard University Press, 1956).

39. Ibid., pp. 12–13.

40. Ibid., p. 53.

41. Joseph E. Baker, "The Philosophy of Hamlet," *Essays in Dramatic Literature; The Parrott Presentation Volume,* ed. Hardin Craig (Princeton: Princeton University Press, 1935), pp. 455–70.

42. Ibid., 455.

43. Ibid., 466–67.

44. Ibid., p. 457.

45. Ibid., p. 456.

46. It could be argued that Hamlet's speech here is rhetorical; but Gertrude is already overcome, and if he persists in this vein, it is not because of his words' effect on her, but on him. "The cardinal fact about physical nature for Hamlet," Baker says, "is its impermanence" (ibid., p. 456). If so, his inextricable involvement with it is all the more horrible.

47. Theodore Spencer, *Shakespeare and the Nature of Man,* 2nd ed. (New York: Macmillan Co., 1949), p. 94.

48. Ibid., p. 101.

49. Ibid., p. 45.

50. Ibid., p. 101.

51. Ibid., p. 92.

52. Spencer suggests that the reign of an unworthy king also shatters Hamlet's ideals (ibid., p. 95), but nowhere in his personal utterances do we see Hamlet tormented over the purely political situation in Denmark. Such disillusionment with kingship as he shows would seem more an effect than a cause of his new awareness.

53. E. M. W. Tillyard, *Shakespeare's Problem Plays* (Toronto: University of

Toronto Press, 1950), pp. 19–21. See also Tillyard, *The Elizabethan World Picture* (New York: The Modern Library, n.d.), p. 76.

54. Hooker, *Ecclesiastical Polity*, I.vii.3,7.

55. See III.iv.82–88:

> O shame! where is thy blush? Rebellious hell,
> If thou canst mutine in a matron's bones,
> To flaming youth let virtue be as wax
> And melt in her own fire. Proclaim no shame
> When the compulsive ardour gives the charge,
> Since frost itself as actively doth burn,
> And reason panders will.

The idea of reason pandering will may seem less paradoxical: in their plotting, villains such as Claudius and Lady Macbeth could subject their reason to the purposes of a corrupt will. The word "pander," however, can imply not merely that reason yields to will and serves it, but that reason actually solicits the will to evil—an impossibility in all but a damned universe.

56. Spencer, *Nature of Man*, pp. 95–97.

57. Bush, *Natural Condition*, p. 96.

58. Montaigne, "Apologie de Raimond Sebond," *Essais* (Paris: Bibliothèque de la Pléiade, 1958), p. 555.

59. Baker calls Hamlet's concern with fame an appeal as "an idealist and a humanist" to the "incorruptible element" in man ("Philosophy of Hamlet," p. 461).

60. Spencer, *Nature of Man*, pp. 108–09.

61. Bush, *Natural Condition*, p. 127.

62. Draper, *Shakespeare's Audience*, p. 5.

63. See Joseph, *Conscience and the King*, chap. 5.

64. Spencer, *Nature of Man*, pp. 105–06. If Hamlet's own inaction is a source of this disillusionment, however, then we are in the awkward position of saying that Hamlet's inaction helps to cause Hamlet's inaction. To escape circularity, it would be necessary to say that Hamlet's inaction stems primarily from his disillusionment with Gertrude. Obviously, the nature of disillusionment rather than its results is what mainly interests Spencer.

65. See also Baker, "Philosophy of Hamlet," pp. 456, 464.

66. Spencer, *Nature of Man*, p. 106, n. 7.

67. Joseph, *Conscience and the King*, p. 130.

68. Paul N. Siegel, *Shakespearean Tragedy and the Elizabethan Compromise* (New York: New York University Press, 1957), p. 98.

69. Spencer, *Nature of Man*, p. 106.

70. See De Wulf, *Histoire*, 1:173 and 2:261; and Harold J. Laski, Introduction to *A Defense of Liberty Against Tyrants* (London: G. Bell and Sons, 1924), pp. 44–46.

Chapter 5.   Psychological Interpretation: Main-Line Criticism Since Bradley

1. Coleridge, *Shakespearean Criticism,* ed. Thomas Middleton Raysor (London: Everyman Library, 1961), 1:34.

2. E. K. Chambers, *Shakespeare: A Survey* (London: Sidgwick & Jackson, 1925), p. 182. (The editions of the plays which these essays originally prefaced appeared from 1904 to 1908.)

3. A. C. Bradley, *Shakespearean Tragedy,* 2nd ed. (London: Macmillan & Co., 1906), p. 113.

4. W. F. Trench, *Shakespeare's Hamlet, A New Commentary* (London: Smith, Elder & Co., 1913), pp. 77–79.

5. Bradley, *Tragedy,* p. 122.

6. Ibid., p. 121.

7. Actually, the most famous of these, the Freudian interpretation, has its source in a footnote to Freud's *The Interpretation of Dreams,* published in 1900, four years before Bradley.

8. Ernest Jones, *Hamlet and Oedipus* (London: Victor Gollancz, 1949), p. 16.

9. F. L. Lucas, *Literature and Psychology,* 1st American ed., rev. (Ann Arbor: University of Michigan Press, 1962), pp. 16–17.

10. Joseph Quincy Adams, commentary to his edition of *Hamlet* (Boston: Houghton Mifflin Co., 1929), p. 195. Cf. Bradley, *Tragedy,* pp. 117–20. Adams differs somewhat from Bradley in deeming the crushing blow to have been the revelation by the Ghost of Gertrude's adultery and (as Hamlet thinks) her complicity in the murder (Adams, *Hamlet,* pp. 213–16.)

11. Adams, *Hamlet,* p. 196.

12. Emmanuel Régis, *Manuel pratique de médicine mentale,* trans. H. M. Bannister (1895); quoted in Adams, *Hamlet,* p. 198.

13. Adams, *Hamlet,* p. 197.

14. Richard von Krafft-Ebing, *Psychiatry,* trans. Chaddock (1905); quoted in Adams, *Hamlet,* p. 197. See also Adams, pp. 225–26.

15. Bradley, *Tragedy,* p. 124. Bradley fails, however, to offer any explanation of precisely *why* Hamlet's feelings should center on killing Claudius—especially as elsewhere Bradley states that "though Hamlet hates his uncle and acknowledges the duty of vengeance, his whole heart is never in this feeling or this task," but rather in his concern over his mother (*Tragedy,* p. 138). In Freud, of course, Hamlet's feelings toward Claudius and toward Gertrude are most meaningfully linked. Meanwhile, Bradley leaves us asking why, if Hamlet was capable of being "suddenly stimulated" (*Tragedy,* p. 123), he did not kill the praying Claudius; at that moment, after all, Hamlet was, by his own admission, capable of drinking hot blood.

16. Sigmund Freud, *A General Introduction to Psychoanalysis,* trans. Joan Riviere (New York: Liveright, 1935), p. 22.

17. Adams, *Hamlet,* p. 195. Bradley, too, copes with this problem:

I have dwelt thus at length on Hamlet's melancholy because, from the psychological point of view, it is the centre of the tragedy, and to omit it from consideration or to underrate its intensity is to make Shakespeare's story unintelligible. But the psychological point of view is not equivalent to the tragic; and, having once given its due weight to the fact of Hamlet's melancholy, we may freely admit, or rather be anxious to insist, that this pathological condition would excite but little, if any, tragic interest if it were not the condition of a nature distinguished by that speculative genius on which the Schlegel-Coleridge type of theory lays stress. (*Tragedy*, p. 127)

18. And had occurred to Freud three years earlier, in 1897.

19. Notable modifications and additions include Ella Freeman Sharpe, "The Impatience of Hamlet," *International Journal of Psycho-Analysis* 10 (1929): 270–79, and "An Unfinished Paper on *Hamlet*," ibid. 29 (1948):98–109; Otto Rank, *Das Inzest-Motiv in Dichtung und Sage* [1912], 2nd ed. (Leipzig: Franz Deuticke, 1926); Erik H. Erickson, "Youth: Fidelity and Diversity," *Daedalus* 91 (1962): 5–27; Maud Bodkin, *Archetypal Patterns in Poetry* (London: Oxford University Press, 1934), chap. 1; Harry Slochower, "Hamlet: The Myth of Modern Sensibility," *American Imago* 7 (1950): 197–238; and K. R. Eissler, *Discourse on Hamlet and "Hamlet"* (New York: International Universities Press, 1971). This last work, one of the most extensive and most interesting of psychoanalytic studies of *Hamlet,* appeared too recently for me to treat it as fully as it deserves. For a full account of the highly varied corpus of psychoanalytic *Hamlet* studies, see Norman N. Holland, *Psychoanalysis and Shakespeare* (New York: McGraw-Hill, 1966), pp. 163–206. This highly useful book appeared only after I had completed this chapter in its first version; I am pleased to find corroboration in it for many of my points.

20. See Holland, *Psychoanalysis,* pp. 177–78, 183–84, 192.

21. E. E. Stoll, *Hamlet: An Historical and Comparative Study,* Research Publications of the University of Minnesota, vol. 8, no. 5 (Minneapolis: University of Minnesota Press, 1919), p. 74.

22. G. K. Chesterton, "Hamlet and the Psycho-analyst," *Fancies Versus Fads* (New York: Dodd, Mead and Co., 1923), p. 27.

23. Jones, *Hamlet and Oedipus,* p. 43.

24. Ibid., p. 44.

25. Sigmund Freud, *The Interpretation of Dreams,* trans. James Strachey, in *The Standard Edition of the Complete Psychological Works of Sigmund Freud,* ed. James Strachey (London: Hogarth Press, 1953), 4:265. In the first edition (1900) this passage was in a footnote. From 1914 on it was incorporated into the text.

26. Jones, *Hamlet and Oedipus,* p. 90. For a more detailed exposition of the Freudian interpretation, see ibid., pp. 69–70, 88–91; and Holland, *Psychoanalysis,* pp. 59–61, 164–65.

27. Jones, *Hamlet and Oedipus,* p. 78.

28. See Lily B. Campbell, *Shakespeare's Tragic Heroes: Slaves of Passion* [1930] (New York: Barnes & Noble, 1963), pp. 114–18 and above, pp. 43–44; Slochower, "Modern Sensibility," p. 218; Jones, *Hamlet and Oedipus,* pp. 83–87.

29. Jones, *Hamlet and Oedipus,* pp. 54–55.

30. E. E. Stoll, *Art and Artifice in Shakespeare: A Study in Dramatic Contrast and Illusion* (Cambridge: Cambridge University Press, 1933), p. 102.

31. Jones, *Hamlet and Oedipus,* p. 54.

32. Ibid., p. 88.

33. Ibid., p. 50.

34. The evidence for this identification is the association of himself with Claudius in the first soliloquy (I.ii.152–53) and with his designation of Lucianus, the regicide in *The Murther of Gonzago,* as "nephew to the King" (III.ii.254). But the evidence of the first soliloquy may indicate no more than mere self-contempt, and while the identification with Lucianus might be seen as a Freudian slip, it might just as well be seen, for instance, as a deliberate, desperate taunting of the King to make him drop his mask, or as a moment of spontaneous insolence. (See Harley Granville-Barker's account, in *Prefaces to Shakespeare* [Princeton: Princeton University Press, 1946], 1:91.)

35. Lucas, *Literature and Psychology,* p. 52.

36. Morris Weitz, *Hamlet and the Philosophy of Literary Criticism* (Chicago: University of Chicago Press, 1964), pp. 24–25. "I find it incredible," Weitz states, "that Jones does not even *mention* this fact of the text, i.e., Hamlet's own words concerning his father" (p. 23). It would be incredible if it were true. But see Jones, *Hamlet and Oedipus,* p. 79:

> If . . . the "repression" [of the son's hostility towards the father] is considerable, then the hostility towards the father will be correspondingly concealed from consciousness; this is often accompanied by the development of the opposite sentiment, namely of an exaggerated regard and respect for him.

and p. 87:

> It is here [in Hamlet's treatment of Polonius] that we see his fundamental attitude towards moralizing elders who use their power to thwart the happiness of the young, and not in the over-drawn and melodramatic portrait in which he delineates his father: "A combination and a form indeed, where every god did seem to set his seal to give the world assurance of a man."

See also ibid., 122–24. We need not accept Jones's judgment of Hamlet's poetry as melodramatic to accept his major point: even if Hamlet's love for his father is genuine and profound, it need not negate the possibility of a coexistent jealousy and hostility, which, because of that very love, must be repressed. Finally, the apparent disrespect Hamlet shows the Ghost in the cellarage scene can be taken as textual evidence that Hamlet's attitude toward his father is ambivalent (see Eissler, *Discourse*, p. 104, n. 84)—providing one assumes that the Ghost is indeed Hamlet's father.

37. Jones, *Hamlet and Oedipus*, p. 11.

38. Ibid., p. 104.

39. Ibid., pp. 112–13.

40. Freud, *Interpretation of Dreams*, p. 265.

41. Jones, *Hamlet and Oedipus*, pp. 114–18.

42. Ibid., p. 113.

43. Otto Rank, *Inzest-Motiv*, cited in Jones, *Hamlet and Oedipus*, pp. 121-26.

44. Jones, *Hamlet and Oedipus*, p. 113. Of course, Rank's detection of recurring incest themes in Shakespeare's earlier works itself supports the oedipal interpretation of *Hamlet*, though it makes it less plausible to connect *Hamlet* with specific events in Shakespeare's adult life.

45. Ibid., p. 14.

46. Sharpe, "The Impatience of Hamlet," p. 272. On the other hand, Kenneth Muir, in an otherwise sympathetic account, thinks otherwise:

> Shakespeare, being a dramatist to his finger tips, was able to utilise and magnify the infantile Oedipus wishes which are common to us all. In real life and in an ordinary man such repressed wishes would doubtless reflect an unresolved Oedipus complex; but as they have been segregated and intensified by the poet for the purposes of his play, we cannot assume that he himself suffered from the neurosis he depicted in his hero. There are other plays as great as *Hamlet*, though Jones regards it as his masterpiece; and it is clear that *Macbeth*, *Othello*, *King Lear* cannot be explained in terms of the Oedipus complex, and would give us no hint that Shakespeare suffered from it. (Kenneth Muir, "Some Freudian Interpretations of Shakespeare," *Proceedings of the Leeds Philosophical and Literary Society* [Literary and Historical Section], 7 [1952]:44)

47. Jones, *Hamlet and Oedipus*, p. 127.

48. Ibid., pp. 128–29. Jones here draws heavily on Rank's *Der Mythus von der Geburt des Helden* (Leipzig and Vienna: Franz Deuticke, 1909). Oedipus, incidentally, is a good example of this form.

49. Ibid., p. 135.

50. Ibid., pp. 137–42.

51. Ibid., pp. 50–51.

52. See ibid., p. 68: "What we are essentially concerned with is the psychological understanding of the dramatic effect produced by Hamlet's personality and behaviour."

53. D. A. Traversi echoes anti-Bradleian critics such as Dover Wilson and A. J. A. Waldock when he claims:

> We all know . . . that to discuss Hamlet's life *outside* the limits of the

play, to attempt to deduce the manner of his upbringing to account for his behavior on the stage, is an illegitimate extension of the critic's proper function. (*An Approach to Shakespeare*, 2nd ed. rev. [Garden City: Doubleday Anchor Books, 1956], p. 2)

54. August Wilhelm von Schlegel, *A Course of Lectures on Dramatic Art and Literature* [1808], trans. John Black, rev. A. J. W. Morrison (London: Henry G. Bohn, 1861), p. 404.

55. Ibid.

56. At least one modern psychological critic has vitiated his interpretation by insisting that Hamlet's motives are hidden and yet that no interpretation is valid that would not be immediately clear to the theater audience; see Arthur Clutton-Brock, *Shakespeare's "Hamlet"* (London: Methuen and Co., 1922). Connoisseurs of literary mayhem will enjoy J. M. Robertson's rebuttal of Clutton-Brock in *"Hamlet" Once More* (London: Richard Cobden-Sanderson, 1923).

57. Such subthemes would be quite in keeping with Elizabethan dramaturgical practice, in which the theme of the main plot was commonly reflected in the themes of the subplots. See Bernard Beckerman, *Shakespeare at the Globe* (New York: Macmillan Co., 1962), pp. 45–48. See also below, chap. 6.

58. This position, highly influential since its adoption by the evolutionists, has its *locus classicus* in A. B. Walkley, "Professor Bradley's *Hamlet*," in *Drama and Life* (London: Methuen and Co., 1907), pp. 148–55.

59. John Dover Wilson, Introduction to his edition of *Hamlet* (Cambridge: Cambridge University Press, 1934), p. xlv.

60. Letter of 18–20 March, 1850 in Gordon N. Ray, ed., *The Letters and Private Papers of William Makepeace Thackeray* (Cambridge, Mass.: Harvard University Press, 1945–1946), 2:652, item 690. "I have been surprised at the observations made by some of my characters," Thackeray remarked elsewhere. "It seems as if an occult Power was moving the pen. The Personage does or says something, and I ask, how the dickens did he come to think of that?" ("De Finibus," *Roundabout Papers,* in *Miscellanies* [Boston: James R. Osgood, 1873], 4:354). A French novelist gives a particularly vivid account of the experience, which with him takes the form of an "alter-ego" beyond his control: "Pour vous donner un example: tout récemment, lors d'un événement qui a ébranlé la conscience du monde, au lieu de se revolter, l' 'autre' s'est mis à écrire une nouvelle, intitulée: 'Un tremblement de terre.' C'est l'histoire d'un personnage louche que continue à jouer aux cartes pendant que la maison s'écroule. El de surcroît, il triche. Quant [sic] j'ai fait des reproches à l' 'autre' pour son attitude insensible et égoiste, il s'est contenté de hausser les épaules" (Ladislas Dormandi, "La genèse d'un roman," *Revue du Ciné-Photo-Club de l'Éducation Nationale,* Nouvelle Série, Nos. 32–33 [Octobre 1958–Mars 1959], pp. 9–18).

61. Jones, *Hamlet and Oedipus,* p. 100.

62. See Holland, *Psychoanalysis,* p. 321: "To talk about the character's

mind is to talk about the audience's; to talk about the audience's is to give the character a mind."

63. A. J. A. Waldock, *Hamlet, A Study in Critical Method* (Cambridge: Cambridge University Press, 1931), p. 55.

64. Sigmund Freud, "Psychopathic Characters on the Stage" (1904–05?), in *Works,* ed. Strachey, 7:309–10. Thus, too, Eissler maintains that "while the action that takes place on the stage is extremely realistic, it is nevertheless so loose and wide-framed that nearly all of man's major, typical unconscious fantasies can be projected onto it" (*Discourse,* p. 132). On the other hand, Eissler also maintains that "even if it could be shown that a psychoanalytic interpretation of a character has never yet found an equivalent process in a member of an audience, that interpretation could still be correct" (p. 18)—but it is not clear what he means by "correct," if not simply that the interpretation provides explanation for the mimetic data of the text without being contradicted by them. But whereas such adequacy is suitable for other modes of interpretation, which function by asking us to consider the literary work under the aspect of theory, Freud here suggests that such rational consideration will seriously distort our aesthetic reaction—that, in fact, the ontological locus of psychoanalytical interpretation is, precisely, in the unconscious. If so, then the mode of psychoanalytical interpretation Eissler defends may be of great academic or clinical interest, but it is of no aesthetic value whatever. Eissler's own study moves somewhat disconcertingly, I think, from apt consideration of audience response (as when he describes Shakespeare's technique in creating an emotional climate "that conveys a feeling [about the relationships of women and castration] such as could not have been easily reproduced by direct verbalization" [p. 114]) to theorization whose appeal is not to any conceivable aesthetic response but rather, one senses, to actual case history. ("My guess is that if Gertrude had been brought to the point of being forced to choose between Claudius's welfare and Hamlet's she would under all circumstances have decided in favor of the latter" [p. 87]).

65. Ernest Jones, Introduction to Vision Press edition of *Hamlet* (London, 1947), p. 20. Fortunately, the suggestion is dropped in *Hamlet and Oedipus,* and the whole discussion of which it formed a part is relegated to a footnote.

66. For a fuller account of this problem in relation to psychoanalysis, see Holland, *Psychoanalysis,* chaps. 10–11.

67. A. Andre Glaz, *"Hamlet,* Or the Tragedy of Shakespeare," *American Imago* 18 (1961): 129–58.

68. For instance, Ophelia represents Hamlet's fixation on the young Gertrude, Yorick represents public opinion, and Hamlet has a younger brother.

69. Ibid., p. 130.

70. Ibid., p. 132.

71. Ibid., pp. 132, 140.

72. Jones, *Hamlet and Oedipus,* p. 156.

73. Bradley, *Tragedy,* p. 144.

74. Granville-Barker, *Prefaces,* 1:134.

75. Slochower, "Modern Sensibility," p. 226; Eissler, *Discourse,* pp. 93–120.

76. Jones, *Hamlet and Oedipus,* p. 53.

77. Geoffrey Bush, *Shakespeare and the Natural Condition* (Cambridge, Mass.: Harvard University Press, 1956), p. 127.

78. See, for instance, Freud's brief article, "A Religious Experience," *International Journal of Psycho-Analysis* 10 (1929): 3. The common Elizabethan analogy of God-king-father makes this sort of meaning all but overt in Elizabethan thought—though an Elizabethan would of course deny the reductions of Freudian cosmology.

79. Slochower, "Modern Sensibility," p. 206.

80. It is interesting that peace of mind similar to Hamlet's at the end of the play is seen in patients with suicidal tendencies once they have finally decided to take their own lives. If Hamlet has achieved calmness and power, the strict Freudian might say, it is because he is prepared to sacrifice his guilty self to the behest of his father—in clinical terms, his ego to the demands of his superego. Certainly he senses that death is near—all is ill about his heart, but "the readiness is all."

81. Freud, *Interpretation of Dreams,* p. 266; see also Jones, *Hamlet and Oedipus,* p. 51, n. 1.

82. Jones, *Hamlet and Oedipus,* pp. 59–60.

Chapter 6.   *Hamlet* as Universal Anagoge

1. "Fancy" (in German, *Phantasie*) might better be translated by the more august term "imagination."

2. August Wilhelm von Schlegel, *A Course of Lectures on Dramatic Art and Literature* [1808], trans. John Black, rev. A. J. W. Morrison (London: Henry G. Bohn, 1861), pp. 343–44.

3. Though in likening Shakespeare to Aeschylus, Kitto treats Aeschylus as, in effect, a Romantic.

4. H. D. F. Kitto, *Form and Meaning in Drama* [London: Methuen & Co., 1956] (New York: Barnes and Noble, University Paperbacks 1960), p. 329 and chap. 8.

5. G. Wilson Knight, *"Hamlet* Reconsidered," *The Wheel of Fire,* 5th ed. rev. (Cleveland: Meridian Books, 1963), p. 311. *"Hamlet* Reconsidered" [1947] was written after the publication of the first edition of *The Wheel of Fire* (London: Oxford University Press, 1930).

6. G. Wilson Knight, "On the Principles of Shakespearean Interpretation," *Wheel of Fire,* p. 3.

7. Ibid., p. 14.

8. D. A. Traversi, *An Approach to Shakespeare,* 2nd ed. rev. (Garden City: Doubleday Anchor Books, 1956), p. 6.

9. C. S. Lewis, "Hamlet: The Prince or the Poem?" The British Academy Annual Shakespeare Lecture, 1942, in *Studies in Shakespeare; British Academy Lectures,* ed. Peter Alexander (London: Oxford University Press, 1964), p. 216.

10. Kitto, *Form and Meaning*, p. 262.

11. Schlegel, *Lectures,* p. 404. It is doubtful, perhaps, how consistent Schlegel is being in calling *Hamlet* singular, in view of his definition of Romantic poetry in general.

12. Drama, Stoll says, is made of "contrasts and parallels, developments and climaxes, tempo and rhythm" ("The Dramatic Texture in Shakespeare," *Shakespeare and Other Masters* [Cambridge, Mass.: Harvard University Press, 1940], p. 25); see also *Art and Artifice in Shakespeare: A Study in Dramatic Contrast and Illusion* (Cambridge: Cambridge University Press, 1933), pp. 127–30 for a further discussion of Shakespeare's "musical method."

13. Knight, "Principles," p. 7.

14. Ibid., p. 8.

15. Ibid., p. 12.

16. Ibid., p. 3.

17. Kitto, *Form and Meaning*, p. 281.

18. Lewis, "Prince or Poem," p. 217.

19. To Knight, interpretation involves "the free use of a faculty that responds with ease, and yet with full consciousness of the separate elements involved" (*Wheel of Fire*, p. x).

20. See also Schlegel: "For Conception can only comprise each object separately, but nothing in truth can ever exist separately and by itself; Feeling perceives all in all at one and the same time" (*Lectures*, p. 343).

21. G. Wilson Knight, "The Embassy of Death: An Essay on *Hamlet*," in *The Wheel of Fire*, pp. 32–42; Roy Walker, *The Time Is Out of Joint* (London: Andrew Dakers, 1948).

22. Gilbert Murray, "Hamlet and Orestes: A Study in Traditional Types," The British Academy Annual Shakespeare Lecture, 1914 (New York: Oxford University Press, 1914), p. 18.

23. Ibid., p. 24.

24. Ibid., p. 26. Like Jones and Rank, Murray considers the Oedipus story to represent the basic myth from which both Hamlet and Orestes sprang. See also Maud Bodkin's Jungian treatment of the same comparative mythology in *Archetypal Patterns in Poetry* (London: Oxford University Press, 1934), esp. chap. 1.

25. Francis Fergusson, *The Idea of a Theater* (Princeton: Princeton University Press, 1949). All citations are from the Doubleday Anchor Books edition (Garden City, 1953).

26. Ibid., pp. 132–33.

27. Ibid., pp. 115–16.

28. Ibid., pp. 146–47.

29. An important recent study, along fairly similar structural lines, is Jan Kott, "Hamlet and Orestes," *Publications of the Modern Language Association* 82 (1967): 303–13. Using the Orestes-Hamlet archetype, Kott seeks to show how "the [tragic] situation is independent of the hero's character; it is given to him, as it were, from outside. . . . The situation precedes the tragedy; every

tragedy seems to be only one of its dramatic realizations" (p. 303), and, finally, "the dramatic model of Hamlet-Orestes contains all human situations in which choice is enforced by the past, but has to be made on one's own responsibility and on one's own account" (p. 313).

30. Caroline Spurgeon, *Shakespeare's Imagery and What It Tells Us* (Cambridge: Cambridge University Press, 1935), p. 309.

31. Caroline Spurgeon, "Shakespeare's Iterative Imagery," The British Academy Annual Shakespeare Lecture, 1931, in *British Academy Lectures,* ed. Alexander, p. 171.

32. Spurgeon, *Shakespeare's Imagery,* p. 316.

33. Ibid., pp. 318–19.

34. Spurgeon, "Shakespeare's Iterative Imagery," p. 173.

35. See Spurgeon, "Shakespeare's Iterative Imagery," pp. 197–200 and *Shakespeare's Imagery,* Part I. For a different view, see W. H. Clemen, *The Development of Shakespeare's Imagery* (Cambridge, Mass.: Harvard University Press, 1951), chap. 12. Although Clemen recognizes the disease motif, he insists that this imagery derives from the dramatic context.

36. See especially Kitto, *Form and Meaning,* pp. 255–56, for his treatment of "evils so great that Nature will not allow them to lie unpurged."

37. Harry Levin, *The Question of Hamlet* (New York: Oxford University Press, 1959), pp. 13, 74, 32, 105, 97.

38. Walker, *Time Is Out of Joint,* p. 110.

39. Maynard Mack, "The World of Hamlet" [1952], in *Discussions of Hamlet,* ed. J. C. Levenson (Boston: D. C. Heath & Co., 1960), p. 84.

40. Kitto, *Form and Meaning,* p. 333.

41. Ibid., pp. 269, 272.

42. Ibid., pp. 315–27.

43. Ibid., p. 252.

44. Ibid., p. 330.

45. The anagogist's concern with the entire cosmos of *Hamlet* need not preclude interest in the Prince himself, C. S. Lewis to the contrary notwithstanding. L. C. Knights suggests that "we are likely to see *Hamlet* more clearly if we see it as one of a series of studies of the mind's engagement with the world" (*An Approach to Hamlet* [Stanford: Stanford University Press, 1961], p. 90). The cosmos and Hamlet's mind thus being separate autonomous objects of interpretation, the anagogist can have his critical cake and eat it too.

46. Knight, "Embassy of Death," pp. 32–33. This argument is developed in the pages following the passage quoted and in "Rose of May" in *The Imperial Theme,* 3rd ed. (London: Methuen and Co., 1951).

47. Ibid., p. 34.

48. Ibid., p. 35.

49. Lewis, "Prince or Poem," p. 215.

50. Knight, "Hamlet Reconsidered," p. 300.

51. Kitto, *Form and Meaning,* p. 333.

52. Knight, "Embassy of Death," pp. 29–30, 35; Kitto, *Form and Meaning*, pp. 317, 325, 327.

53. See Kitto, *Form and Meaning*, chap. 9, part 2.

54. Knight, "Embassy of Death," p. 45.

55. Walker, *Time is Out of Joint,* p. xi.

56. Ibid., p. 102. For a similar treatment of Rosencrantz and Guildenstern, see ibid., pp. 81–82. See also Kitto, *Form and Meaning*, p. 252: "Denmark is rotten, Polonius is rotten; his death, and the death of seven others, are the natural outcome."

57. Knight, "Rose of May," p. 98.

58. Knight, "Principles," p. 10.

59. Jones, *Hamlet and Oedipus,* p. 31.

60. Bradley, *Tragedy,* p. 116.

61. Friedrich Nietzche, *The Birth of Tragedy*, sec. 7, trans. Clifton P. Fadiman, *The Philosophy of Nietzche* (New York: Modern Library, 1954), p. 984.

62. Ibid.

63. Knight, "Embassy of Death," pp. 19–20.

64. Knight, "Rose of May," p. 105.

65. Knights, *Approach to Hamlet,* p. 89.

66. Walker, *Time Is Out of Joint,* p. 58.

67. Fergusson, *Idea of a Theater,* p. 140.

68. Kitto, *Form and Meaning,* p. 290.

69. Mack, "World of Hamlet," p. 93.

70. Traversi, *Approach to Shakespeare,* pp. 83–84.

71. Lewis, *"Prince or Poem,"* p. 212.

72. Knight, "Hamlet Reconsidered," pp. 308–09.

73. Ibid., p. 322.

74. Maynard Mack gives a similar interpretation, though not against an explicitly Nietzschean background ("World of Hamlet," pp. 94–95).

75. Knight, "Embassy of Death," p. 45.

76. Knight, "Hamlet Reconsidered," pp. 322–23.

77. Lewis, "Prince or Poem," p. 215.

78. Walker, *Time Is Out of Joint,* p. 152. See also Geoffrey Bush, *Shakespeare and the Natural Condition* (Cambridge, Mass.: Harvard University Press, 1956), p. 127 (above, p. 74).

79. Knight, "Rose of May," p. 105.

80. Walker, *Time Is Out of Joint,* p. 18.

81. Knight, "Rose of May," p. 105.

82. Unless one takes him as a hypocrite; see Prosser's argument, above, chap. 4.

83. Knights, *Approach to Hamlet,* p. 89.

84. Fergusson, *Idea of a Theater,* p. 114.

85. See Kitto, *Form and Meaning*, pp. 264–67, 297, 334; Walker, *Time Is*

Out of Joint, pp. 41–42, 65, 121, 128. Anything may be carried too far: one hesitates before Walker's description of Ophelia's death "beside the glassy stream of appearance" (*Time Is Out of Joint,* p. 128).

86. See Walker, *Time Is Out of Joint,* chap. 10.

87. Ibid., p. 116.

88. Bernard Beckerman, *Shakespeare at the Globe* (New York: Macmillan Co., 1962), pp. 61–62.

89. Knight, "Embassy of Death," p. 23.

Chapter 7.   Conclusion

1. Clive Bell, for instance, describes the difficulties, both mimetic and interpretative, of an art scholar from Japan when first confronted with the Renaissance painters, in whom, "with their descriptive pre-occupations, their literary and anecdotic interests, he could see nothing but vulgarity and muddle" ("The Aesthetic Hypothesis," in *Art* [London: Chatto & Windus, 1924], p. 36, n. 1).

2. Mikel Dufrenne, *Phénoménologie de l'expérience esthètique* (Paris: Presses Universitaires de France, 1953), 1:395. In general I am indebted in this chapter to Dufrenne; see especially Part Two, chap. IV: "La structure de l'oeuvre d'art en général."

3. Robert H. West, "Night's Black Agents in *Macbeth,*" *Renaissance Papers,* 1956, p. 24.

4. I am using the term in a sense analogous to its use in Husserlian phenomenology. There, however, intersubjectivity ultimately reconstitutes the objective universe, while in aesthetics it cannot. In either case, nevertheless, the concept of intersubjectivity saves discourse from breaking down into a series of merely individual perspectives. See Edmond Husserl, *Méditations cartésiennes* (Paris: Armand Colin, 1931), Cinquième Méditation.

5. Samuel Johnson, "Preface to Shakespeare," in *Rasselas, Poems, and Selected Prose,* ed. Bertrand H. Bronson (New York: Rinehart & Co., 1958), pp. 241, 248–49. The crucial principle that art should represent a general nature underlying individual phenomena is found again in Imlac's discourse on poetry in chapter 10 of *Rasselas* and in Fielding's prefatory chapter to Book Three of *Joseph Andrews.* It is also an important tenet of Sir Joshua Reynolds's *Discourses on Art,* most notably the seventh, where he states with Newtonian certainty that the knowledge of good taste "is derived from the uniformity of sentiments among mankind, from whence proceeds the knowledge of what are the general habits of nature; the result of which is an idea of perfect beauty" (*Discourses on Art,* ed. Robert R. Wark [San Marino, California: Huntington Library, 1959], p. 141). Pope, to be sure, had praised the individuality of Shakespeare's characters, calling Shakespeare "not so much an Imitator, as an Instrument, of Nature" (Preface to his edition of Shakespeare's works [London, 1725], 1:ii–iii), but there is no indication that "Nature" here is any more mysterious or problematic than the Nature "methodiz'd" by the ancients, in the *Essay on Criticism* (I, l. 89).

6. Ibid., p. 249.

7. See Morris Weitz, *Hamlet and the Philosophy of Literary Criticism* (Chicago: The University of Chicago Press, 1964), chap. 10, and Dr. Johnson's comment on Homer, "that nation after nation, and century after century, has been able to do little more than transpose his incidents, new name his characters, and paraphrase his sentiments" ("Preface to Shakespeare," p. 240).

8. August Wilhelm von Schlegel, *A Course of Lectures on Dramatic Art and Literature*, trans. John Black, rev. A. J. W. Morrison (London: Henry G. Bohn, 1861), p. 404.

9. Johann Gottfried von Herder, *Literatur und Kunst*, cited by H. H. Furness in his New Variorum edition of *Hamlet*, 10th ed. (Philadelphia: J. B. Lippincott & Co., 1877), 2:277.

10. Dr. Johnson, "Preface to Shakespeare," p. 241.

11. "His characters are not modified by the customs of particular places, unpractised by the rest of the world; by the peculiarities of studies or professions, which can operate but upon small numbers; or by the accidents of transient fashions or temporary opinions: they are the genuine progeny of common humanity, such as the world will always supply, and observation will always find" (ibid., p. 241).

12. D. A. Traversi, *An Approach to Shakespeare*, 2nd ed. rev. (Garden City: Doubleday Anchor Books, 1956), p. 3.

13. Caroline Spurgeon, *Shakespeare's Imagery and What It Tells Us*, (Cambridge: Cambridge University Press, 1935), pp. 318–19.

14. Sir John Harington, "A Preface, or Rather a Brief Apologie of Poetrie, and of the Author," from his translation of *Orlando Furioso* (1591); in *Elizabethan Critical Essays*, ed. G. Gregory Smith (Oxford: Oxford University Press, 1904), pp. 202–03.

15. Ibid., p. 213.

16. Gilbert Murray, "Hamlet and Orestes: A Study in Traditional Types," The British Academy Annual Shakespeare Lecture, 1914 (New York: Oxford University Press, 1914), p. 24.

17. Ernest Jones, *Hamlet and Oedipus* (London: Victor Gollancz, 1949), p. 157.

18. Murray, *Hamlet and Orestes*, p. 24.

19. Weitz errs, I think, in insisting that Spencer invalidates his historical approach by calling attention to the universal significance of *Hamlet* (Weitz, *Philosophy of Literary Criticism*, pp. 73–76). That men grapple with different institutions does not mean that their problems in grappling are essentially different; on the other hand, it does not follow that we can always grasp the similarities without understanding the institutions. Hamlet's estrangement from God is emotionally not unlike Tennyson's, but without an idea of an anthropocentric universe we can understand neither.

20. Ernest Jones, it is true, dismisses Murray's myth of the death of the year-god, evidently because it directs attention away from what Jones considers central to the play—a psychological complex—and, perhaps, he rather

surprisingly fails to see the close relationship of this myth to his own psychological theories. The Summer-vs.-Winter myth can easily be taken as an analogue—or, the Freudian might say, a projection—of the oedipal myth of the conflict of generations. Indeed, at one point, Jones quotes a remark of Freud's that seems to be no more than a clinical expression of what Murray describes mythologically: "The detachment of the growing individual from the authority of the parents is one of the most necessary, but also one of the most painful, achievements of development. . . . Indeed, the progress of society depends in general on this opposition of the two generations" (Jones, *Hamlet and Oedipus*, p. 76). Francis Fergusson, meanwhile, relegates the Freudian interpretation to the second rank, Hamlet's psychological problems being but a "reflector" of the anagoge of the scapegoat myth. But the idea that the central subject of the play is Denmark and not Hamlet is itself an interpretative decision; the stress that each receives on stage *per se* is about equal. Fergusson's interpretation does allow him to treat the play as a unified whole, while the Romantic psychological critics could not; he wrote, however, before Jones had himself dealt with the mythological aspects of *Hamlet*, and Jones's study suggests that character is coordinate to myth, not subordinate to it, that myth may reflect character as well as character myth.

21. In addition to Hamlet's overt praise of his father, whom he likens to a god, we may note that Hamlet's account of his father's marriage closely parallels the account given by the Ghost:

> So excellent a king, that was to this
> Hyperion to a satyr; so loving to my mother
> That he might not beteem the winds of heaven
> Visit her face too roughly.
> (I.ii.139–42)

> O Hamlet, what a falling-off was there,
> From me, whose love was of that dignity
> That it went hand in hand even with the vow
> I made to her in marriage, and to decline
> Upon a wretch whose natural gifts were poor
> To those of mine!
> (I.v.47–52)

Hamlet has assimilated his father's attitudes.

22. In arbitrarily making the Ghost a symbol of death and evil, then, perhaps Knight is instinctively expressing in terms of poetic symbolism what Jones discusses clinically: the sudden awareness of evil.

23. T. S. Eliot, "Hamlet and His Problems," in *Selected Essays: 1917-1932* (New York: Harcourt, Brace and Co., 1932), p. 125.

24. William James, *The Varieties of Religious Experience* (New York: Modern Library, n.d.), p. 26.

25. Traversi, *Approach to Shakespeare*, p. 106.

Appendix A.   Doubt of the Ghost

1. Eleanor Prosser, *Hamlet and Revenge* (Stanford: Stanford University Press, 1967), pp. 102–03; see also Robert Hunter West, *The Invisible World; A Study of Pneumatology in Elizabethan Drama* (Athens, Georgia: University of Georgia Press, 1939), pp. 48–53. Indeed, as West observes, the Protestant disbelief in ghosts as the souls of the dead was bound up in Protestant opposition to the doctrine of purgatory.

2. See West, *Invisible World*, p. 48, and Lewes Lavater, *Of Ghostes and Spirites Walking by Nyght* (1572), ed. J. Dover Wilson and May Yardley (Oxford: Oxford University Press, 1929), pp. 127–33.

3. Lavater's chap. 12, which is a catalogue of ghost stories drawn from classical writers, is closely paralleled in accounts of seventeenth-century ghosts; see especially his report of a haunted house in Athens (pp. 58–59), taken from Pliny the Younger.

4. In Francis James Child, *English and Scottish Ballads* (Boston, 1864), 2:45 ff., ll. 13–16, 49–56. This theme is common: see also "Sweet William's Ghost," *Reliques of Ancient English Poetry,* ed. Thomas Percy (London, 1927), 3:130–33; "The Bonny Hind Squire," *Scottish Traditional Versions of Ancient Ballads,* ed. James Henry Dixon, Percy Society Publications, vol. 17 (London, 1846), p. 45; "The Unquiet Grave," *The Oxford Book of Ballads,* ed. Arthur Quiller-Couch (Oxford: Oxford University Press, 1910), pp. 140–41; and, for an English variation, "The Suffolk Miracle" (Child, 1:217 ff.; the ballad appears in a broadside in the Roxburghe collection):

> And unto him she thus did say:
> "Thou art as cold as any clay;
> When we come home a fire we'll have;"
> But little dreamed he went to grave.
> (ll. 57–60)

When the lover's grave is subsequently opened, the lover's body has decayed, but about its head is a fresh handkerchief that the girl had given the ghost. Devils, of course, could inhabit the corpses of the dead, but such is clearly not the case in these ballads.

5. See, for instance, "The Knight's Ghost" (Child, 1:210 ff.); "The Wife of Usher's Well" (Child, 1:214 ff.); "Clerk Saunders" (Child, 2:45 ff.); and the seventeenth-century English broadside "The Two Faithful Lovers' Tragedy" (in John Ashton, ed., *A Century of Ballads* [London, 1887], p. 106 ff.). Indeed, Marcellus himself simply observes that after the crowing of the cock "no spirit dare stir abroad": he does not necessarily exclude benign spirits, though Prosser paraphrases him as saying that "no evil spirits can remain abroad" (*Hamlet and Revenge,* p. 100).

6. "The dreadful day of doom draws near," in *The Shirburn Ballads,* ed. Andrew Clark (Oxford: Oxford University Press, 1907), pp. 75 ff.

7. "The Midwife's Ghost" [1680], in *The Pepys Ballads,* ed. Hyder Edward Rollins (Cambridge, Mass.: Harvard University Press, 1930), 3:30 ff., stanza 12.

8. Joseph Glanvill, *A Blow at Modern Sadducism* (London, 1668), pp. 86–88, and *Saducismus Triumphatus* (London, 1681), pp. 67–71. Henry More concurs in his prefatory letter to *Saducismus Triumphatus,* pp. 48–49. George Sinclair, in his *Satan's Invisible World Discovered* (Edinburgh, 1685), leans to the view that Samuel's apparition was demonic, but acknowledges the possibility that it could have been a bona fide ghost (p. xxi).

9. Glanvill, *Saducismus Triumphatus,* p. 71; More also denies that this interpretation is popish (Prefatory Letter, p. 53). In a facetious account of ca. 1590, the ghost of Richard Tarlton appears to a frightened interlocutor who expresses the standard Protestant suspicions, to which the ghost replies that there is indeed a purgatory: "and if any upstart Protestant deny, if thou hast no place of Scripture ready to confirme it, say as Pithagoras schollers did (*ipse dixit*) and to all bon companions it shall stand for a principle." At which the interlocutor observes, "I could not but smile at the madde merrye doctrine of my freend Richard" (*Tarlton's Newes Out of Purgatorie,* reprinted with *Tarlton's Jests,* ed. James Orchard Halliwell [London: Shakespeare Society, 1844], p. 57). The episode suggests that while the Catholic-Protestant dispute was a matter of common knowledge, it was not always taken very seriously.

10. Prefatory letter to *Saducismus Triumphatus,* p. 49.

11. John Aubrey, *Miscellanies upon Various Subjects* [1696], 4th ed. (London: J. R. Smith, 1857), p. 95.

12. See Hyder Rollins's introduction to "The Disturbed Ghost," in *The Pack of Autolycus* (Cambridge, Mass.: Harvard University Press, 1927), pp. 172 ff. Glanvill's account (repeated verbatim by Sinclair) appears in *Saducismus Triumphatus,* pp. 209 ff. The earliest account dates from 1674.

13. For a discussion of these criteria, see Prosser, *Hamlet and Revenge,* pp. 107–17.

14. Seeking to make a wholesale ad hoc distinction between the fairies and less benign spirits, Shakespeare conveniently makes Puck telescope the conflicting views of ghosts as demons or as risen spirits of the dead:

> . . . yonder shines Aurora's harbinger;
> At whose approach ghosts, wand'ring here and there,
> Troop home to churchyards; damned spirits all,
> That in crossways and floods have burial,
> Already to their wormy beds are gone.
> For fear lest day should look their shames upon,
> They wilfully themselves exile from light,
> And must for aye consort with black-brow'd night.
> (III.ii.380–87)

"But we are spirits of another sort," Oberon replies. Purgatory is left out: the ghosts are "damned spirits"; but like the ghosts of the ballads, they are semi-corporeal and return to their graves. The poetry is so fine that the anomaly passes unnoticed, or it may be a deliberate ploy to embrace as wide a range of audience preconception as possible. But see Prosser, *Hamlet and Revenge*, pp. 108–09, who argues that these are simply folklore ghosts.

15. See Robert H. West, "King Hamlet's Ambiguous Ghost," *Publications of the Modern Language Association* 70 (1955): 1107–17, who argues convincingly that Shakespeare is deliberately ambiguous in his presentation of the Ghost for the sake of dramatic impact. He bases his argument on standard theological views of the time.

16. H. B. Charlton, *Shakespearian Tragedy* (Cambridge: Cambridge University Press, 1948), p. 87. See also H. D. F. Kitto, *Form and Meaning in Drama* (London: Methuen & Co., 1956), pp. 286–88.

17. J. Dover Wilson, *What Happens in Hamlet* [1935] (Cambridge: Cambridge University Press, 1959), p. 142, n. 1.

Appendix B.   The Closet Scene

1. E. E. Stoll, *Hamlet: An Historical and Comparative Study*, Research Publications of the University of Minnesota, vol. 8, no. 5 (Minneapolis: University of Minnesota Press, 1919), p. 62. Draper offers a similar argument in *The "Hamlet" of Shakepeare's Audience* (Durham, N.C.: Duke University Press, 1938), pp. 157, 188.

2. Lily B. Campbell, *Shakespeare's Tragic Heroes: Slaves of Passion* [1930] (New York: Barnes & Noble, 1963), p. 144.

3. Ernest Jones, *Hamlet and Oedipus* (London: Victor Gollancz, 1949), p. 32.

4. Jones allows for this interpretation (ibid.). Nicol Williamson also seems to follow this interpretation in the recent film of *Hamlet* by Tony Richardson.

Selected Bibliography

Adams, Joseph Quincy. Commentary to his edition of *Hamlet*. Boston: Houghton Mifflin Co., 1929.

Alexander, Nigel. *Poison, Play, and Duel: A Study in Hamlet*. London: Routledge & Kegan Paul, 1971.

Alexander, Peter. *Hamlet, Father and Son*. Oxford: Clarendon Press, 1955.

————. *Shakespeare's Henry VI and Richard III*. Cambridge: Cambridge University Press, 1929.

Anderson, Ruth Leila. *Elizabethan Psychology and Shakespeare's Plays*. Iowa City: University of Iowa Press, 1927.

Ashton, John, ed. *A Century of Ballads*. London: E. Stock, 1887.

Aubrey, John. *Miscellanies upon Various Subjects*. 1696. 4th ed. London: J. R. Smith, 1857.

Babb, Lawrence. *The Elizabethan Malady: A Study of Melancholia in English Literature from 1580 to 1642*. East Lansing: Michigan State University Press, 1951.

————. "On the Nature of Elizabethan Psychological Literature," in *Joseph Quincy Adams Memorial Studies*, edited by James G. McManaway et al. Washington, D.C.: Folger Library Publications, 1948.

Bacon, Sir Francis. *The Great Instauration*, Proemium, in *Selected Writings of Francis Bacon*. Edited by Hugh G. Dick. New York: The Modern Library, 1955.

Baker, Joseph E. "The Philosophy of Hamlet," in *Essays in Dramatic Literature: The Parrott Presentation Volume*. Edited by Hardin Craig. Princeton: Princeton University Press, 1935.

Becker, Carl. *The Heavenly City of the Eighteenth-Century Philosophers*. New Haven: Yale University Press, 1932.

Beckerman, Bernard. *Shakespeare at the Globe*. New York: The Macmillan Company, 1962.

Bodkin, Maud. *Archetypal Patterns in Poetry*. London: Oxford University Press, 1934.

Boswell, James. *Boswell's London Journal*. Edited by Frederick A. Pottle. New Haven: Yale University Press, 1950.

Bowers, Fredson. *Elizabethan Revenge Tragedy.* Princeton: Princeton University Press, 1940.

––––. "Hamlet as Minister and Scourge," *Publications of the Modern Language Association* 70 (1955): 740–49.

Bradley, A. C. *Shakespearean Tragedy.* 2d ed. London: The Macmillan Company, 1906.

Bright, Timothy. *A Treatise of Melancholie.* London, 1586. Reprinted for the Facsimile Text Society. New York: Columbia University Press, 1940.

Bundy, Murray W. "Shakespeare and Elizabethan Psychology," *Journal of English and Germanic Philology* 23 (1924): 516–49.

Burton, Robert. *The Anatomy of Melancholy.* 1621. Boston: William Veazie, 1859.

Burtt, Edwin Arthur. *The Metaphysical Foundations of Modern Physical Science.* Garden City: Doubleday, 1954.

Bush, Geoffrey. *Shakespeare and the Natural Condition.* Cambridge, Mass.: Harvard University Press, 1956.

Campbell, Lily Bess. "Bradley Revisited: Forty Years After," *Studies in Philology* 44 (1947): 174–94. Reprinted as an appendix to *Shakespeare's Tragic Heroes: Slaves of Passion.* New York: Barnes and Noble, 1963.

––––. *Shakespeare's Tragic Heroes: Slaves of Passion.* Cambridge: Cambridge University Press, 1930. Reprinted, New York: Barnes and Noble, 1963.

Chambers, E. K. *Shakespeare: A Survey.* London: Sidgwick and Jackson, 1925.

––––. *The Elizabethan Stage.* 4 vols. Oxford: The Clarendon Press, 1923.

Charlton, H. B. *Shakespearian Tragedy.* Cambridge: Cambridge University Press, 1948.

Chesterton, G. K. "Hamlet and the Psycho-Analyst," *Fancies versus Fads.* New York: Dodd, Mead & Company, 1923.

Child, Francis James, ed. *English and Scottish Ballads.* 8 vols. Boston: Little, Brown and Company, 1864.

Clark, Andrew, ed. *The Shirburn Ballads.* Oxford: Oxford University Press, 1907.

Clemen, W. H. *The Development of Shakespeare's Imagery.* Cambridge, Mass.: Harvard University Press, 1951.

Clutton-Brock, Arthur. *Shakespeare's "Hamlet."* London: Methuen & Co., 1922.

Coleridge, Samuel Taylor. *Shakespearean Criticism.* Edited by Thomas Middleton Raysor. 2 vols. London: Constable and Co., 1930. Reprinted, London: Everyman Library, 1962.

Conklin, Paul S. *A History of Hamlet Criticism, 1601-1821.* New York: King's Crown Press, 1947.

Craig, Hardin. "A Cutpurse of the Empire," in *A Tribute to George Coffin Taylor.* Edited by Arnold Williams. Chapel Hill: University of North Carolina Press, 1952.

––––. *The Enchanted Glass: The Elizabethan Mind in Literature.* Oxford: Oxford University Press, 1936.

––––. "Hamlet's Book," *Huntington Library Bulletin* no. 6 (1934): 17–37.

––––. "Shakespeare's Depiction of Passions," *Philological Quarterly* 4 (1925): 289–301.

Curry, Walter Clyde. *Shakespeare's Philosophical Patterns.* Baton Rouge: Louisiana State University Press, 1959.

Dixon, James Henry, ed. *Scottish Traditional Versions of Ancient Ballads.* Percy Society publications, vol. 17. London: Percy Society, 1846.

Doran, Madeleine. *Endeavors of Art: A Study of Form in Elizabethan Drama.* Madison: University of Wisconsin Press, 1954.

Draper, John W. *The "Hamlet" of Shakespeare's Audience.* Durham, N.C.: Duke University Press, 1938.

––––. "Hamlet's Melancholy," *Annals of Medical History,* n.s. 9 (1937), 142–47.

Dufrenne, Mikel. *Phénoménologie de l'expérience esthétique.* 2 vols. Paris: Presses Universitaires de France, 1953.

Duthie, George Ian. *The 'Bad' Quarto of 'Hamlet'; A Critical Study.* Cambridge: Cambridge University Press, 1941.

Eckermann, Johann Peter. *Gespräche mit Goethe in den letzten Jahren seines Lebens.* 4th ed. Leipzig: Brockhaus, 1876.

Eissler, K[urt] R[obert]. *Discourse on Hamlet and "Hamlet"; A Psychoanalytic Inquiry.* New York: International Universities Press, 1971.

Eliot, T. S. *Selected Essays: 1917–1932.* New York: Harcourt, Brace & Co., 1932.

––––. Introduction to *The Wheel of Fire,* by G. Wilson Knight. 5th ed., rev. Cleveland: Meridian Books, 1963.

Fergusson, Francis. *The Idea of a Theater.* Princeton: Princeton University Press, 1949. Reprinted, Garden City, N.Y.: Anchor Books, 1953.

Forster, E. M. *Aspects of the Novel.* New York: Harcourt, Brace & Co., 1927.

Freud, Sigmund. *A General Introduction to Psychoanalysis; A Course of Twenty-Eight Lectures Delivered at the University of Vienna.* Translated by Joan Riviere. New York: Liveright, 1935.

––––. *The Interpretation of Dreams.* Translated by James Strachey. In the *Standard Edition of the Complete Psychological Works of Sigmund Freud.* Edited by James Strachey. Vols. 3–4. London: Hogarth Press, 1953.

––––. "Psychopathic Characters on the Stage." Translated by James Strachey. In the *Standard Edition of the Complete Psychological Works of Sigmund Freud.* Edited by James Strachey. Vol. 7. London: Hogarth Press, 1953.

––––. "A Religious Experience," *International Journal of Psycho-Analysis* 10 (1929): 1–4.

Frye, Northrup. *The Anatomy of Criticism: Four Essays.* Princeton: Princeton University Press, 1957.

––––. "The Archetypes of Literature," in *Fables of Identity: Studies in Poetic Mythology.* New York: Harcourt, Brace & World, 1963.

Furness, Horace Howard, ed. *A New Variorum Edition of Shakespeare.* Vols. III-IV: *Hamlet.* Philadelphia: J. B. Lippincott Company, 1877.

Glanvill, Joseph. *A Blow at Modern Sadducism.* London, 1668.

————. *Saducismus Triumphatus.* London, 1681.

Glaz, A. Andre. "*Hamlet,* Or the Tragedy of Shakespeare," *American Imago* 18 (1961): 129–58.

Goethe, Johann Wolfgang von. *Criticisms, Reflections, and Maxims of Goethe.* Translated by W. B. Rönnfeldt. London: Walter Scott Publishing Co., n.d.

Granville-Barker, Harley. "From 'Henry V' to 'Hamlet,'" British Academy Annual Shakespeare Lecture, 1925. Revised 1933 and reprinted in *Studies in Shakespeare: British Academy Lectures.* Edited by Peter Alexander. London: Oxford University Press, 1964.

————. *Prefaces to Shakespeare.* Princeton: Princeton University Press, 1946.

Harbage, Alfred. *Shakespeare's Audience.* New York: Columbia University Press, 1941.

Harington, Sir John. "A Preface, or Rather a Briefe Apologie of Poetrie, and of the Author" for his translation of *Orlando Furioso.* 1591. In *Elizabethan Critical Essays,* edited by G. Gregory Smith. 2 vols. Oxford: Oxford University Press, 1904.

Holland, Norman N. *Psychoanalysis and Shakespeare.* New York: McGraw-Hill, 1966.

Hooker, Richard. *Of the Laws of Ecclesiastical Polity.* Vols. 1–2 of *The Works of That Learned and Judicious Divine Doctor Richard Hooker.* Oxford: The Clarendon Press, 1890.

Husserl, Edmond. *Méditations cartésiennes; introduction à la phénoménologie.* Translated by Gabrielle Peiffer and Emmanuel Levinas. Paris: Armand Colin, 1931.

James, D. G. *The Dream of Learning: An Essay on the Advancement of Learning: Hamlet and King Lear.* Oxford: The Clarendon Press, 1951.

Johnson, Samuel. *Rasselas, Poems, and Selected Prose.* Edited by Bertrand H. Bronson. New York: Rinehart & Co., 1958.

Jones, Ernest. *Hamlet and Oedipus.* London: Victor Gollancz, 1949.

————. Introduction to *Hamlet.* London: Vision Press, 1947.

Joseph, Bertram. *Conscience and the King; A Study of Hamlet.* London: Chatto and Windus, 1953.

Kitto, H. D. F. *Form and Meaning in Drama.* London: Methuen and Co., 1956.

Knight, G. Wilson. *The Imperial Theme.* 3d ed. London: Methuen and Co., 1951.

————. *The Wheel of Fire.* London: Oxford University Press, 1930. 5th ed. rev. Cleveland: Meridian Books, 1963.

Knights, L. C. *An Approach to Hamlet.* Stanford: Stanford University Press, 1961.

Kott, Jan. "Hamlet and Orestes." *Publications of the Modern Language Association* 82 (1967): 303–13.

Kris, Ernst. *Psychoanalytic Explorations in Art.* New York: International Universities Press, 1952. Reprinted, New York: Schocken Books, 1964.

Lavater, Lewes. *Of Ghostes and Spirites Walking by Nyght.* 1572. Edited by J. Dover Wilson and May Yardley. Oxford: Oxford University Press, 1929.

Lewis, C. S. "Hamlet: The Prince or the Poem?" British Academy Annual Shakespeare Lecture, 1942. Reprinted in *Studies in Shakespeare: British Academy Lectures.* Edited by Peter Alexander. London: Oxford University Press, 1964.

Lewis, Charleton M. *The Genesis of Hamlet.* New York: Henry Holt, 1907.

Levin, Harry. *The Question of Hamlet.* New York: Oxford University Press, 1959.

Loening, Richard. *Die Hamlet-Tragödie Shakespeares.* Stuttgart: J. G. Cotta, 1893.

Lucas, F. L. *Literature and Psychology.* London: Cassell, 1951. 1st American ed. revised. Ann Arbor: University of Michigan Press, 1962.

Mack, Maynard. "The World of Hamlet," *The Yale Review* 41 (1952): 502–23. Reprinted in *Discussions of Hamlet.* Edited by J. C. Levenson. Boston: D. C. Heath and Co., 1960.

Montaigne, Michel Eyquem de. *Essais.* Paris: Bibliothèque de la Pléiade, 1958.

Muir, Kenneth. "Some Freudian Interpretations of Shakespeare," *Proceedings of the Leeds Philosophical and Literary Society* (Literary and Historical Section). 7 (1952): 43–52.

Murray, Gilbert. "Hamlet and Orestes; A Study in Traditional Types." The British Academy Annual Shakespeare Lecture, 1914. New York: Oxford University Press, 1914.

Nashe, Thomas. *The Vnfortvnate Traveller.* In Ronald B. McKerrow, ed. *The Works of Thomas Nashe.* 5 vols. London: A. H. Bullen, 1904.

Nietzsche, Friedrich. *The Birth of Tragedy.* Translated by Clifton P. Fadiman. In *The Philosophy of Nietzsche.* New York: The Modern Library, 1954.

Odell, George C. D. *Shakespeare from Betterton to Irving.* New York: Charles Scribner's Sons, 1920.

Olson, Elder. "Hamlet and the Hermeneutics of Drama," *Modern Philology* 41 (1964): 225–37.

O'Sullivan, Mary Isabelle. "Hamlet and Dr. Timothy Bright," *Publications of the Modern Language Association of America* 41 (1926): 667–79.

Overbury, Sir Thomas. *The Overburian Characters.* Edited by W. J. Paylor. Oxford: B. Blackwell, 1936.

Percy, Thomas. *Reliques of Ancient English Poetry.* 3 vols. London: G. Allen & Unwin, 1927.

Poe, Edgar Allen. Review of Hazlitt's *Characters of Shakespeare's Plays,* in *The Complete Works of Edgar Allan Poe.* Vol. 12. Edited by James A. Harrison. New York: T. Y. Crowell and Co., 1902.

Pope, Alexander, ed. *The Works of Shakespeare in Six Volumes.* London, 1725.

Prosser, Eleanor. *Hamlet and Revenge.* Stanford: Stanford University Press, 1967.

Quiller-Couch, Arthur, ed. *The Oxford Book of Ballads*. Oxford: Oxford University Press, 1910.

Reik, Theodor. "In My Mind's Eye, Horatio," *Complex* 7 (1952): 15–31.

Ringler, William A., Jr. "Hamlet's Defense of the Players," in *Essays on Shakespeare and Elizabethan Drama in Honor of Hardin Craig*. Edited by Richard Hosley. Columbia, Mo.: University of Missouri Press, 1962.

Robertson, J. M. *"Hamlet" Once More*. London: Richard Cobden-Sanderson, 1923.

————. *The Problem of "Hamlet."* London: George Allen and Unwin, 1919.

Rollins, Hyder Edward, ed. *The Pack of Autolycus; Or, Strange and Terrible News of Ghosts, Apparitions, Monstrous Birds, Showers of Wheat, Judgments of God, and Other Prodigious and Fearful Happenings As Told in Broadside Ballads of the Years 1624–1693*. Cambridge, Mass.: Harvard University Press, 1927.

————, ed. *The Pepys Ballads*. 8 vols. Cambridge, Mass.: Harvard University Press, 1929–32.

Schlegel, August Wilhelm von. *A Course of Lectures on Dramatic Art and Literature*. Translated by John Black and revised by A. J. W. Morrison. London: Henry G. Bohn, 1861.

Schücking, L. L. *Character Problems in Shakespeare's Plays*. New York: Henry Holt and Co., 1922.

————. *The Meaning of Hamlet*. Translated by Graham Rawson. London: Oxford University Press, 1937.

Shakespeare, William. *The Tragedy of Hamlet Prince of Denmark: As it is Now Acted by Her Majesties Servants*. London, 1703.

————. *Hamlet, Prince of Denmark, A Tragedy, As it is now Acted by his Majesty's Servants*. London, 1718.

Sharpe, Ella. "The Impatience of Hamlet," *International Journal of Psycho-Analysis*, 10 (1929): 270–79.

————. "An Unfinished Paper on Hamlet," *International Journal of Psycho-Analysis*, 29 (1948): 98–109.

Sidney, Sir Philip. "An Apology for Poetry," in *Criticism: The Major Texts*, edited by Walter Jackson Bate. New York: Harcourt, Brace & Co., 1952.

Siegel, Paul N. *Shakespearean Tragedy and the Elizabethan Compromise*. New York: New York University Press, 1957.

Sinclair, George. *Satan's Invisible World Discovered*. Edinburgh, 1685. Reprint. Gainesville, Fla.: Scholar's Facsimiles and Reprints, 1969.

Slochower, Harry. "Shakespeare's Hamlet: The Myth of Modern Sensibility," *American Imago* 7 (1950): 197–238.

Spencer, Theodore. *Shakespeare and the Nature of Man*. 2d ed. rev. New York: The Macmillan Co., 1949.

Spurgeon, Caroline. *Shakespeare's Imagery and What It Tells Us*. Cambridge: Cambridge University Press, 1935.

————. "Shakespeare's Iterative Imagery," British Academy Annual Shakespeare Lecture, 1931. Reprinted in *Studies in Shakespeare; British Academy Lectures*. Edited by Peter Alexander. London: Oxford University Press, 1964.

Stoll, E. E. *Art and Artifice in Shakespeare*. Cambridge: Cambridge University Press, 1933.

————. *Hamlet: An Historical and Comparative Study*. Research Publications of the University of Minnesota, vol. 8, no. 5. Minneapolis: University of Minnesota Press, 1919.

————. *Shakespeare and Other Masters*. Cambridge, Mass.: Harvard University Press, 1940.

————. *Shakespeare Studies*. New York: The Macmillan Co., 1927.

Tillyard, E. M. W. *The Elizabethan World Picture*. London: Chatto and Windus, 1943. Reprinted. New York: Modern Library, n.d.

————. *Shakespeare's Problem Plays*. London and Toronto: Chatto and Windus, 1950.

Traversi, D. A. *An Approach to Shakespeare*. 2d ed. revised and enlarged. New York: Anchor Books, 1956.

Trench, W. F. *Shakespeare's Hamlet; A New Commentary*. London: Smith, Elder and Co., 1913.

Waldock, A. J. A. *Hamlet; A Study in Critical Method*. Cambridge: Cambridge University Press, 1931.

Walker, Roy. *The Time Is Out of Joint*. London: Andrew Dakers, 1948.

Walkley, A. B. *Drama and Life*. London: Methuen & Co., 1907.

Weiner, Albert B., ed. *Hamlet: The First Quarto*. New York: Barnes & Noble, 1962.

Weitz, Morris. *Hamlet and the Philosophy of Literary Criticism*. Chicago: University of Chicago Press, 1964.

West, Robert Hunter. *The Invisible World: A Study of Pneumatology in Elizabethan Drama*. Athens, Georgia: University of Georgia Press, 1939.

————. "King Hamlet's Ambiguous Ghost." *Publications of the Modern Language Association* 70 (1955): 1107–17.

————. "Night's Black Agents in *Macbeth*." *Renaissance Papers*. A selection of papers presented at the Renaissance Meeting in the Southeastern States. 1956, pp. 17–24.

Whitaker, Virgil. *Shakespeare's Use of Learning*. San Marino: Huntington Library, 1953.

Wilson, John Dover, ed. *Hamlet*. The New Cambridge Shakespeare. Cambridge: Cambridge University Press, 1934.

————. *What Happens in Hamlet*. Cambridge: Cambridge University Press, 1935. 1st paperback ed. Cambridge: Cambridge University Press, 1962.

Windelband, Wilhelm. *A History of Philosophy*. Trans. James H. Tufts. New York: Macmillan, 1926.

Wulf, Maurice de. *Histoire de la philosophie médiévale*. 5th ed. 2 vols. Paris and Louvain: Institut Supérieur de Philosophie, 1925.

Index

Major discussions of individual critics are listed in boldface type. Except for *Hamlet,* works are listed under author.

PR
2807
.G63   The meanings of Hamlet

Gottschalk, Paul, 1939-